Dick

The Changing of Kings

Leslie Glass

The Changing of Kings
Memories of Burma 1934–1949

With a Foreword by Jan Morris

PETER OWEN · LONDON

ISBN 0 7206 0641 1

All Rights Reserved. No part of this publication
may be reproduced in any form or by any means without
the prior permission of the publishers.

PETER OWEN PUBLISHERS
73 Kenway Road London SW5 0RE

First published 1985
© Sir Leslie Glass 1985

Photoset by Grainger Photosetting Southend-on-Sea Essex
Printed in Great Britain by
St Edmundsbury Press Bury St Edmunds Suffolk

FOR JULIA

Foreword

History is perhaps not bunk, but it is certainly not absolute. Since it is a matter of ideas, reactions, motives and emotions, just as much as mere facts, its truth is of a prismatic kind, presenting itself in an infinity of flashes. It never dies, either, but goes on generating new interpretations, new aspects, renewing itself year after year, century after century and turning itself sometimes into other matter altogether, like Art, or Influence.

One of the historical memories least likely to wear itself out is that of the British Empire, a great and ambiguous adventure which is, as the wine merchants say of a certain vintage, ageing well. So endlessly varied was this astonishing affair, so intense in character, so puzzling of morality, so rich in events and personalities, that it seems to get more interesting every year, and we need not doubt that there will be scholars debating it and archaeologists digging up its remains until the end of time. There is one imperial genre, though, which by the nature of things must presently go out of production – the personal memoir, the first-hand report of how things were in the British Empire by the person who experienced them. Of such an historical kind, this book, about the life of a British official in Burma, is an invaluable and vastly entertaining example.

Imagine if we were to find, say, the recollections of a centurion in the dying days of the Roman Empire, telling us not how the Empire worked in his province, or the ratio of tax to tribute, but how it all seemed, in uninhibited personal detail, to one functionary on the spot. It would revolutionize Roman studies! *The Changing of Kings* is exactly such a work, about a hardly less significant empire. It is not the only one, of course – British colonizers were great memorialists – but it is one of the few written about the very last years of the imperial enterprise, and is thus of true historical importance.

We may not learn much from it about the mechanics or the ideology of the British Empire in the East. What it does give us is an insight into the mind of a young and very lively imperial official in Burma in the last decades before Independence – how he felt, what he thought he was doing, how he viewed his subject people, and how he imagined they viewed him. It is history of an exuberantly subjective kind, but none the less revealing for that. How enthralling it will be for scholars a thousand years hence to read for example about a young British official who, having lost his temper with a Burmese and thrown a law-book at him, hitting him on the chest, became overcome with remorse and invited the Burmese to throw one back! Which the Burmese duly did: but in what frame of mind, with how much forgiveness or amusement, we do not know.

Leslie Glass was evidently a most genial kind of imperialist, the very image of Santayana's 'sweet and boyish master', full of fun, not without a streak of mischief, sympathetic and unstuffy. He liked people as a rule, they seem generally to have liked him, and his natural instinct was to assume that on the whole the empire which he represented was as benevolent and as popular as he was. He tells us that even at the start of his career he never supposed the empire to be eternal; he recognizes that bad self-government is often preferable to good government by aliens, and that anyway there is an insuperable moral objection to the principle of one nation ruling another. But in his heart, I suspect, he believes that the Burmese in general, rightly or wrongly, welcomed the authority of the British in their country.

Did they? Who can say? Sir Leslie Glass, as he was to become in the fullness of his career, does not discuss this inner riddle or the imperial idea – the general willingness of the subjected to be subdued. The ruler can seldom judge the emotions of his subjects, and doubtless the Burmese were as tactful towards Glass as he was towards them. What this book does tell us, though, for a certainty, is that this one young British official performed his imperial tasks in a spirit of genuine goodwill: he thought he was acting honourably, and being useful. He wished the Burmese well – nothing less. There is not a trace of racial superiority in his attitudes, certainly no hint of vulgar exploitation or brutality.

If you happened to live in his part of the British Empire, you were lucky to have Mr Glass as your master. On the other hand, if you happened to be Mr Glass, you were lucky to live in such a place. What a marvellous time he had out there, until in the later chapters of this book the Japanese murderously enter the scene and so many delights and illusions collapse in tragedy! No memoirs could be more full of enjoyment, and imperial historians of the future, closing their dusty pages, may well look back with bitter envy upon an age so unenlightened, but evidently so merry.

Jan Morris

Contents

Illustrations		xii
Acknowledgements		xiii
Prologue		1
1	Training	13
2	The Frontier	40
3	In Charge	53
4	The Oilfields	83
5	Home Leave	96
6	Settlement	104
7	The Japanese Invasion	134
8	India 1	154
9	India 2	175
10	Return to Burma	191
11	British Embassy, Rangoon	210
Epilogue		231
Index		237

Illustrations

PLATES

1 Burmese Minthami or dancing girl
2 Outer wall and moat of Mandalay Palace
3 Timber elephants
4 Traditional Burmese shallow-well oil worker
5 Winnowing paddy
6 Japanese generals march into Government House to sign surrender documents, 1945
7 Return to Rangoon by Sir Reginald Dorman-Smith, 1945
8 General Aung San with party on his successful trip to Britain, January 1947
9 Lord Mountbatten with U Thant and the author at the UN, March 1948

MAP

Burma (pages 234-5)

The illustrations have been reproduced with kind permission of the following:
The British Library, Plate 8; Centre of South East Asian Studies, Cambridge, Plates 4 and 5; Imperial War Museum, London, Plates 1, 6 and 7, and also the line illustrations on pages 165 and 167, Arnold Lawson, Plate 3; Noel Singer, Plate 2; United Nations, Plate 9. The map was drawn by Malcolm Porter.

Acknowledgements

I am grateful to Frank George and Richard Usborne for reading my manuscript and making helpful suggestions, to Joyce Gilbert for typing it and to Michael Levien for his sympathetic editing. I am also indebted to George Allen & Unwin Publishers Ltd for permission to quote from Arthur Waley, and to A. & C. Black Publishers Ltd, Ernest Benn Ltd and Vernon Donnison for permission to quote from the latter's book, *Burma* (1980).

My thanks are due for information on the Irrawaddy Flotilla Company to Alistair MacCrae; on the Bombay Burma Trading Corporation to 'Jonah' Jones; and on the Burma Oil Company to Tony Gowan; to Dr Robert Taylor of the School of Oriental and African Studies for insights into Burma politics; to Anna Allott, also of SOAS, for help with Burmese script; and to my wife for much help with correspondence.

L.G.

မင်းပြောင်းမင်းလွှဲ ကာလကျပ်ကြီး

Prologue

The Second World War was a watershed between the last days of the British Empire and the era of rapid decolonization and readjustment. I had the good fortune to enjoy two separate careers in these two eras. The second, from 1947 to 1971, was in the Diplomatic Service. This took me to Rangoon, Budapest, Beirut, Nicosia, Washington, DC, Whitehall, Bucharest, the UN in New York, and Lagos. In my first career, from 1934 to 1947, I served (with an interruption in India during the war) in the distant country of Burma as a young officer of that élite instrument of Empire, the Indian Civil Service. Those very different imperial periods are now far enough off to be fading from many memories, so I thought it might be fun to jot down some fairly light-hearted recollections in an attempt to recapture a little of their flavour.

While from 1934 to 1941 things were on the whole relatively peaceful in Burma, during the period 1941 to 1947 control of the country passed from the British to the Japanese, back to the British again, and finally in 1948 to the Burmese themselves – so those years were, as the Burmese saying has it, 'The very difficult Time of the Changing of Kings'. I had kept no diaries, taken few snapshots, and my letters home were not worth preserving. All my pre-war papers were lost to the Japanese. Writing now in the depths of the Herefordshire countryside I have few books of reference. So this is in no sense an attempt to write a history of those years. It is just time remembered; mainly a string of personal anecdotes of far away and long ago and impressions of memorable personalities – an album of 'verbal snapshots' of events as they seemed to me when I experienced them.

Perhaps a brief description of my origins and education may

help to show what sort of young man it was through whose eyes those years were seen. In the average middle-class English family before the Second World War it was natural to work overseas. On my mother's side one uncle, after being a mining engineer in South Africa, became a missionary and penetrated further up the Amazon in his day than anyone except the doomed Colonel Fawcett. Another uncle, after serving in liaison with the Portuguese Army in the First World War, eventually became captain of a steamer on the Canadian Great Lakes. One of my mother's sisters was principal of a ladies' college in Cairo (and married the principal of a men's college there). On my father's side I had one uncle who was Head of the Survey Department of the Government of Siam; and one who was Agent (Managing Director) of the Indian North-West Frontier Railway. My grandfather worked in India most of his life; my father was born in India and worked in India throughout his career as an irrigation engineer; and I, too, was born in India (peering through a porthole of a P & O steamer I had glided by the sand dunes, the camels and the palm trees of the Suez Canal five times before I was eight years old) and later worked in Burma and India. My daughter was born in Simla during the Second World War.

This was an era when many British homes showed evidence of the Indian connection. Indeed, in Budleigh Salterton, where as children my sister and I spent a seaside summer holiday when our parents returned to England on leave, there were so many retired officials from India that different areas were popularly known by the names of the respective provinces whence their particular cluster of pensioners had largely come. We would go to 'the Punjab' for tea or play tennis in 'Madras'. And there can have been few homes in the British Isles without some brass Benares trays, carved elephants, little silver place-card holders for the table, as well as numnah and kalim rugs and more valuable carpets. Many a floor had a tiger- or leopard-skin rug, and many a wall had the horns and heads of the antelope and deer which were so plentiful in India in our fathers' days. An elephant's foot umbrella-stand was by no means uncommon. Britain and India seemed as interwoven as parts of the same country; the British were almost honorary Indians, linked with native Indians by a complicated love-hate relationship which

Americans, in particular, found it difficult to comprehend.

My earliest memory is of a Christmas camp by an Indian river (as my father was an irrigation engineer I have many memories of great rivers, as of dams and weirs and canals) where we found crocodiles' eggs and my father shot jungle fowl and green pigeon. I remember the bliss of my main Christmas present, a box of lead soldiers, scarlet-coated heroes of the King's Own Shropshire Light Infantry.

My earliest friends were the numerous Indian servants who attended my father and mother: the syce (groom) who led the little pony on which I was held by a saddle with a leather rail round it; the mali (gardener) with whose children I made mud pies decorated with marigold flowers in the garden; the bearer (servant) who played ball with me. Just before my father died, at the age of eight-four, in his tiny house at Burnham-on-Sea, I talked to him of my memories of this bearer. My father fell silent. Then, 'Marakhan – dear fellow,' he said tenderly. 'When I was a young bachelor, sick in the jungle, Marakhan defied his caste rules to look after me night and day, and do the most menial functions for me. I never had a truer friend.'

Naturally as a child I spoke fluent Hindustani. Indian visitors were charmed by my eloquence, if occasionally shocked by below-stairs obscenities I innocently used in my chatter.

No memories of my childhood are more vivid than certain scents – the strong metallic scent of marigolds in ceremonial garlands, the scent of spices in cooking curry, the beautiful smell the parched earth gave out when first hit by the monsoon rains, the exciting smell of hot tent canvas.

Not long before the end of the First World War I remember being taken over an Australian cruiser, HMAS *Sydney*, moored in the Hooghly river at Calcutta before she set out to chase a German raider, the *Emden*. And just after the war I recall, on the great Maidan at Calcutta, holding my father's hand amidst the enormous crowd welcoming, with bands playing, the first big Handley Page aircraft to fly into Calcutta. It hit a tree coming in, and had to stay for several days, but it was headlined in the newspapers as 'a new link of Empire', drawing us closer to England.

After the war I returned to England with my mother in a ship full of troops, and listened entranced one moonlit night when they had a singsong on deck. I can still hear the rough men's voices as they sang 'If You Were the Only Girl in the World' and 'Let the Great Big World Keep Turning'.

At the age of seven I was sent to a prep school in Worthing. From then on my sister, Kathleen (two years my junior) and I saw our mother intermittently and our father rarely. To start with we spent our school holidays with the family (two boys and two girls of their own) of an Army colonel in Southsea. I remember being driven to church parade in a horse and trap; and each Sunday the soldiers, as a gesture to their brothers in the Navy, singing

> Eternal Father strong to save,
> Whose arm doth bind the restless wave,
> O hear us when we cry to Thee
> For those in peril on the sea.

As we grew a bit older my sister and I were sent for the holidays to live with the family of the Rector of Presteigne, in Radnor, Wales. He had two boys a little older than I was, and two girls a little younger than my sister. The Rector ran a strict but kindly household. All the summer we played tennis in the large Rectory garden, or we fished, bicycled or took picnics up into the hills. I have now retired within sight of those 'blue remembered hills'. One day the boys dared me to walk across a glass roof. I tried, and fell through. It took weeks to patch me up enough for me to return to school. Twenty years later I stopped in Presteigne to have my hair cut. When I talked to the barber about the Reverend Kewley he said, repeating what was by now obviously unshakeable local history, 'You must have been here, sir, about that time that foreign boy at the Rectory tried to commit suicide!'

My sister and I thus had the unusual experience of being brought up by three different families; our own, the Stewarts of Southsea, and the Kewleys of Presteigne. When you are one of six children, as we were in the two latter families, you learn to look after yourself. I suppose the separation from our parents toughened us and made us more independent than we might otherwise have been. Yet, though I was a cheerful and pragmatic child who took the ups and downs of life more or less for granted, I know that Kathleen missed our parents a great deal.

Generations of young English children bore this family separation more or less stoically. Saki's story, 'The Lumber-Room', tells of the trials of children who had the bad luck to be left with unsympathetic foster-parents – and of course Kipling's early childhood in England was horrendous. My sister and I were among the lucky ones. When our parents were in England home was 'where father hung his hat'. We lived in hotels, rented houses, flats, wherever. A life of change seemed the natural one. The longest consecutive connection I had anywhere was with my public school, Bradfield College in Berkshire, where I spent five happy years. It was towards the end of the 'tough' era of public schools – cold showers each morning, long runs in the rain and snow, frequent canings and rough punishment from the senior tearaways of the houseroom. But I supposed that was how life was elsewhere. Happily a gentler regime took over after a few terms. I was a clever little boy, good at examinations and reasonably good at games. As a prefect I learned early the responsibilities (and the pleasures) of the exercise of authority. I was taught to write Latin prose in the style of Cicero, and learnt the history of the Roman Empire. Kipling's implied analogy of the centurion on Hadrian's Wall and the British officer on the North-West Frontier of India seemed to me obvious and natural enough. One master used to make his form learn four lines of Greek or Latin poetry or eight of English every night. 'One day,' he said, 'you may be shipwrecked on a desert island, or you may be shut up in a prison cell. Then you will thank me for your glorious inbuilt library!'

Bradfield, with its open-air Greek theatre, was a great school for acting, and I begun to have dreams of becoming an actor or writer – idle dreams, for I really didn't know what I wanted to do, and I had no thoughts of India. In fact, I was enjoying life so much that I failed to get the expected scholarship, which meant extra sacrifice by my parents to send me to Oxford, where I entered Trinity College.

Trinity was at that time an unashamedly lowbrow college, full of blues. Almost everyone drank too much. For a time I kept to my more intellectual friends, many in other colleges, such as neighbouring Balliol. I joined the OUDS with the intention of acting. I wrote little pieces and drew cartoons for the *Isis* magazine. I started out determined to get a good degree, but in this small friendly, cheerful, high-spirited college I fell an easy prey to *la dolce vita*. I played a variety of games with much enjoyment, including football sometimes for the OU Centaurs.

Before my second summer vacation my father suggested I should come out to India for a visit. He added gently that my mother had been much distressed at being shown, by another wife in the station, a letter from her son at Oxford in which he said, 'As I look from my window I see Glass being carried back to Trinity from a dinner at the Gordouli Club', and he hoped that I was taking my studies seriously.

The journey by P & O revived old memories. I made the traditional visit to Simon Arzt's store at Port Said; took part in the traditional ship's fancy-dress ball; and took young ladies to the bows of the ship to observe the traditional (and legendary) green flash at sunset. From the first sight of the marbled 'Gate of India' on Bombay's waterfront, all the old scents and sounds were on me, familiar but exciting.

In Ranchi, the summer capital of Bihar and Orissa, for a couple of months I lived the Kipling life – pony gymkhanas, amateur dramatics, dancing in the Club to the erratic thump of the police band. I was even presented to the Viceroy, Lord Willingdon, a tall dandy of a man with sweeping moustaches and a grey top hat, on one of his regal visits. With him was the powerful figure of Lady Willingdon, in her favourite mauve. Her unpunctuality was so notorious that Calcutta memsahibs called it 'Lilac Time'.

Touring with my father I learnt how entrenched in history was the British hold on India. It was also strangely Victorian. The dak bungalows scattered around the province were furnished with the heaviest and most ornate mahogany furniture. The great dams and canals seemed to have been constructed a long time ago. And I had hints of stresses to come. By one river I accompanied my father when he was making a private adjudication (for a peppercorn fee) between two rich landowners who both claimed certain areas of the shifting river. One of the zamindars who lagged behind me said, 'If all Englishmen were like your father, we should never want you to leave.' I accepted this tribute to my father, who was one of the gentlest and most honourable of men, but took in the further implication of the remark. One evening in the Club the burly, sandy-haired Deputy Inspector-General of Police reappeared, looking tired and drawn after a rather long and mysterious absence. 'Where have you been?' someone asked. 'Making the province a little safer' was his sombre reply.

I talked to him later. 'What do you think of the Indian Civil Service as a career?'

'All right, I suppose, if you've nothing better in mind,' he said morosely. 'And it won't last through your time, you know.'

Meanwhile my mother was glad to see me bright-eyed and tanned, far from the dissolute layabout she feared I was becoming. I was well back in the family's good books when a telegram arrived from my Balliol friend (today a successful and respected headmaster). 'Hank' was a tennis blue and a talented song-writer, and as an engaging, self-taught light pianist was an automatic invitee to any party. He and I particularly enjoyed asking hearties from the Philistine Club, and aesthetes from the OUDS, to dine in the rival clubs, to both of which we exceptionally belonged. The telegram read: REGRET I HAVE FAILED ALL FINAL COLONIAL OFFICE EXAMS STOP COLONIAL OFFICE HAVE REQUESTED RETURN OF £300 ADVANCED FOR PROBATIONARY YEAR STOP PLEASE SEND BY RETURN £200 REPRESENTING THE AMOUNT OF MY TIME I RECKON YOU WASTED LAST YEAR. Very funny – though my father was not particularly amused.

He was, of course, right to worry. I was to come down in the middle of the great slump of the thirties, when jobs were very hard to get. I had begun to see the writing on the wall before I sailed for India. Somehow I managed a creditable second-class honours in modern history.

What to do for a job? My mother had always had ambitious plans for her son. 'The Diplomatic Service?'

I laughed heartily at the idea. 'You have to be brilliant, Ma, fluent in two European languages and have a decent private income!'

The manager of the Balliol Players in my year had been Paul Gore-Booth, distinguished and urbane even as an undergraduate. He was destined for the Diplomatic Service and in fact became head of it and eventually Lord Gore-Booth. I did not feel I was in his class.

'Home Civil Service?' My mother would have liked that, as I could stay in England.

'Only those top in the examination can choose that.'

'Will you try the Indian Civil Service?' This was for my mother as high an aim as the others – she had spent her life in the shadow of the Heaven-born. It seemed natural enough for me to try, immediately after my Schools.

As a saver I went to be interviewed by Major Furse, the famous Colonial Service one-man selection board. At the end of the interview he asked me what my hobbies were.

'A bit of drawing and a bit of writing, I suppose,' I said.

Furse looked depressed. 'I suppose the writing might come in useful if you had to write reports,' he commented doubtfully. He had a wonderful nose for exactly what he wanted in his Colonial Service, and my scent wasn't quite right.

Would-be mandarins of the ICS had, as in historic China, to sit long written examinations. At my first shot, soon after my Schools, I failed, but did well enough to have another try. So I crammed at Davies's, the famous tutorial establishment in London. We were a mixed bag. Some of those aiming for the Diplomatic Service had the eccentricities of the well-born and rich. One elegant young man kept a chimpanzee in his flat and took it for walks in the Park. I never saw him reading any book except Duff Cooper's *Talleyrand*, which he must have known by heart. I think in the end he decided not to sit the exam. Most of us tried hard enough, but when the list of successful candidates appeared in *The Times* my name was not on it. I hoped that perhaps there was still a chance when the top candidates had opted for their selected service.

Meanwhile I relaxed from my efforts. Late one evening, after a night out with the boys, I let myself quietly into our flat at Coleherne Court. There, on a hard chair in the middle of the hall, under a bright ceiling light, sat my mother, determined to stay awake until I came in. She had an official letter in her hand, which was for her the culmination of years of loving economy and planning. I was in! Fairly far down, though.

When we got the full book of everyone's marks my father studied it with interest. 'Have you noticed', he remarked drily, 'that at the end of the first five compulsory papers you were top of all the Services, Diplomatic and all? And that you dropped fifty places when it came to the subjects you were supposed to have studied at Oxford?'

I couldn't have cared less. I was in, and had an exciting new life to look forward to.

In order to spend some time with my parents in London after our many and long separations, I did my probationary year at the School of Oriental Studies, then in Finsbury Circus. My friend Peter Knight from Cambridge and I took our studies lightly. This seemed to us a bonus prolongation of undergraduate life, paid for by HMG. We were taught Indian history by our course supervisor, a Welsh ex-officer of the Indian Army, who shook his head at our insouciance but came and played snooker with us round the corner.

I learnt the Burmese language from the first Indian civilian from the province of Burma whom I had yet met, Dr Stewart. He was a short, plump, sun-browned Scot of about sixty, who looked like a Buddha. He had a Burmese wife and was a great scholar in the Burmese language. Besides being an authority on Jane Austen, he was engaged on a history-making, definitive Burmese dictionary. He held a pencil in his mouth when talking Burmese to us, as he said Burmans always had a cheroot in their mouths, and we must get used to understanding the language so spoken.

One exam we all had to pass was in riding. The final test was in an Army riding school, and taken by a supercilious cavalry captain. One exercise had us riding round the school bareback, with our arms crossed on our chests. The horses were fairly docile, but mine was a trifle eccentric. It wandered over to the officer to take a nip at his ear. No amount of desperate steering by knee pressure, which the exercise demanded, would divert him. Which would lose most marks? I wondered. Disobeying orders and seizing the reins, or keeping my arms crossed and being unable to stop the disaster? I kept my arms crossed. I got poor marks for the exercise. I suspect I should have, whatever I had done. It was an early lesson in the facts of life – sometimes there is *no* good solution to a problem.

Two of us probationers were posted to Burma, then a province of the Indian Empire, and so under the Viceroy. The other, Dugald McCallum, very high in the final markings, was the son of an ICS Commissioner just retired from Burma, and was returning from choice to the scenes of his childhood. I had made Burma my first choice because it sounded romantic, and because my father had worked for and liked the then Governor, when the latter had been Governor of Bihar and Orissa. Although I was low on the list, I got my choice. Burma was not favoured by ambitious candidates: it was considered too remote and backward, the 'Cinderella' province. I was never to regret my choice for a moment.

Like all my colleagues, I enjoyed the country and its people. It was essentially a different country from India, to which it was attached only for administrative convenience. When in 1937 it was formally separated from India, all the 'Indian civilians' in Burma were given the option of transfer to India or of remaining permanently seconded to the Government of Burma. None of us had the slightest difficulty about the choice: we were Burmese.

The three ICS fellow-probationers I saw most of during my time at the School of Oriental Studies all died in their early thirties. Peter Knight was a victim of typhoid in Baluchistan in 1943; Seth Drucquer was killed in a plane crash in Bengal in 1944; and Dugald McCallum killed himself in despair in 1942 when the Japanese overran Burma.

The short history above will suggest what sort of person I was when I arrived in Burma – an extrovert, fun-loving, pragmatic, somewhat superficial young man, but brought up in a tradition of service and used to change, easy to transplant. I took the British Empire very much for granted and was proud that so much of the map was pink. I believed British rule in India was broadly benevolent. I knew my mother and father had worked hard, often in disagreeable conditions (no electric fans or lights or refrigerators in their day), and that they had seved India well and loved it. When we talked about Partition soon after the event, my father could scarcely restrain his tears: abandonment of the unity of India seemed to him a tragic betrayal of British work in that vast country. I know too he had retired on a modest pension, with hardly any savings. Years later he said to me when discussing diplomacy (in which eventually and unexpectedly I had found myself occupied), 'I could take you back to areas which when I first saw them were dusty deserts, and now there would be green crops as far as the eye can see. In not many jobs can a man look back and see the practical results of his labours.'

I was untroubled by Marxist analyses of imperialism. It seemed to me that the history of the world had largely been the history of strong tribes driving out or dominating weak ones, of wars between countries in which those that won the battles took the prizes. In India we were the conquerors who had succeeded the Moguls. The Viceroy, one more in an historical series of alien rulers, sat in natural succession on the throne of Akbar and Aurangzeb. By whatever methods, morally admirable or not, we had acquired India, the plain historical fact was that we did have it, and held current responsibility for it. The idea of a sudden and wholesale withdrawal from India on idealistic grounds, without our having trained enough Indians to run a modern state, or having organized a viable successor government, would have seemed to me irresponsible and itself immoral. It was drummed into me in my probationary year that the transfer of responsibility into Indian hands was accepted British policy. I never expected to complete a full career in India, and I doubt if many of my young colleagues did so either. Gandhi's historic Salt March and the start of satyagraha was in 1930, before I first sat the ICS exams, and we did not ignore the portents.

I remember in 1947 having an argument with Kingsley Martin. I had criticized one of his articles in the *New Statesman*, of which the theme was that the average British official in India was determined to hang on to power and privilege as long as possible, was politically conservative and reactionary, and obstructed moves to Independence. I protested that of my generation nearly all were acquainted with volumes of Gollancz's Left Book Club, had many sympathies with Labour, and that we had carried out devolution willingly and responsibly and to the best of our ability. We were certainly not opposed to Independence. He seemed unconvinced.

Yet the fact remains that when I first arrived in Burma I did not worry much about why we were there. I believed we were doing a good practical job with the broad consent of most of the subject peoples. Rightly or wrongly, I took life in Burma for granted, in a cheerful and rather unquestioning spirit, and this is reflected in the somewhat light-hearted tone of my memories. From 1934 to 1941 anyway I was mostly up-country, unconnected with high policy, engaged on day-to-day administration in the field. (For anyone interested in the history of Burma, the best concise book is F.S.V. Donnison's *Burma* [Ernest Benn, 1980], which takes the story from earliest times almost up to the present day.)

Just before I sailed for Burma, my mother, gazing anxiously at me, said, 'There is some special advice I want to give you about living in the East.' I braced myself for a homily on drink, money-lenders and native women. 'Never try to save money on food,' said the dear woman. 'Always insist on the best and freshest there is. And make sure all your vegetables are properly washed in permanganate.'

1 Training

The Burmese Scene

When the Paddy Henderson boat docked at Rangoon, I was met by a tall, elegant young Under-Secretary from the Home Department. 'You are to stay with the Lloyds,' he said, 'the Financial Commissioner and his wife.'

'Sorry,' I replied, 'I long ago accepted an invitation to stay with Ebden, the Accountant-General and an old friend of my father's from India.'

My new colleague seemed put out. Further argument was cut short by the appearance of Ebden himself, an amiable eccentric with cropped grey hair, wearing crumpled khaki shorts. 'Go round the other side of the ship and sniff the breeze' was his welcome. 'It's the last you'll sniff for some time!' He bore me off to his house, which he was sharing with the Bishop Elect of Rangoon, George West, a famous missionary from the hills, with an MM from the First World War. It was only later that I learnt that Idwal Lloyd's household still contained two of his three red-headed daughters, reckoned amongst the prettiest girls in Burma. Not long ago, watching television, I saw for the first time a stunningly attractive young actress. I did not know her name, or anything about her, but I was not in the slightest doubt of who she must be. Gabrielle Drake is the image of her beautiful mother, née Lloyd.

In my rounds in Rangoon I lunched with the Governor, Sir Hugh Stephenson, and his wife. A portly, shrewd and vastly experienced man, he rumbled kindly to me about my parents and wished me well. It was a long time before I glimpsed His Excellency again.

Lady Lloyd forgave my spurning of her invitation and took a kindly interest in my future. 'You're going up-country tomorrow, aren't you, Mr Glass? Well, if there's anything I can do for you from here, write and let me know.' What she saw in my eye I don't know, but it alarmed her. 'As long as it's nothing very much!' she added hastily.

My friend Ebden took me to a charity fancy-dress dance at the Victoria Jubilee Hall with some lady missionaries. Later in the evening I was hailed by a strange apparition in a sort of Viennese shako, a kilt made of towels, and a naval tunic covered with medals, which on close inspection turned out to be religious. I recognized an ebullient contemporary of mine from Corpus, Oxford – John Brownrigg, then with the Burma Oil Company. John was a man of imagination. He wrote a regular gossip column for the *Rangoon Gazette*, and, bored with the same old cast, gradually invented a new character. For some time the fictitious name of this character appeared amongst those unfortunately unable to attend some function or another; then he merited a mention as also present; then he began to take a brief but active part in events. Mothers began to suggest to their daughters that the new young bachelor should be asked to dances. His very elusiveness seemed to make him more attractive. By the time John was transferred from Rangoon several people claimed to have met the character personally. John joined a tank regiment early in the war and was killed in action.

Rangoon, with its large European, Indian and Chinese population, and its ugly Victorian buildings, was not Burma. Only the Shwedagon, the huge golden pagoda which floated over the town, gave promise of a more mysterious and beautiful interior. The country of Burma is more than three times the size of England, Scotland and Wales. Its main features are the two great river valleys of the Irrawaddy and the Salween, running north and south. In the north there is a great horseshoe of hills and forests, inhabited largely by non-Burman tribes, cutting off the country from its giant neighbours, India and China, and coming down on the east to the beautiful and temperate Shan plateau. The central area of Upper Burma is the dry zone, hot in summer and cool in winter. Lower Burma consists of the wet zone, the great flat paddy-plain of the Irrawaddy delta, featureless and humid. The long south-eastern tail of Tenasserim is a land of tropical beaches and archipelagos. I was lucky enough to spend most of my service in the dry zone of Upper Burma. My first posting was to Monywa, headquarters of the Lower Chindwin district, west of Mandalay and situated on the Chindwin river, the Irrawaddy's mightiest tributary, which joins the Irrawaddy near Mandalay.

Here at last I met the Burma of which Dr Stewart had told us. The Civil Station was strung along the bank of the broad Chindwin river, separated from the river by a bund or earthwork, shaded by tamarind trees and decorated by a few clumps of purple bougainvillaea. Down the river floated at the appropriate season huge rafts of teak logs, each with its little hut of navigators, bound for the far-away sawmills of Rangoon, or rice-carrying tonkins, their huge, clumsy sails filling the wind. Some of the logs took years to reach their journey's end. The railway from Mandalay ended at Monywa. From there on north-west communications were mainly by the Irrawaddy Flotilla Company's big stern-wheelers, up the Chindwin river.

I found myself lodging with the Executive Engineer, a neat, thin, middle-aged grass widower, whose bungalow and life were run by strict routine. He was a kindly and courteous host. He conversed with his Burmese servant in what I assumed to be some special Burmese dialect, as I couldn't understand a word. Afterwards I discovered that this was a language of its own. The two had been together for many years, and the servant could understand the curious words his master used when he thought he was talking Burmese. No one else could.

My host made a simple suggestion for household finances. 'Shall we cut all expenses straight down the middle?' he asked. 'Food, servants, lighting, the lot?' This seemed to me sensible enough. One snag slowly began to appear. Drink expenses were cut down the middle too. My host, whom I never saw the worse for drink, had nevertheless an established drinking routine far in advance of anything I was used to – beer and pink gins in the morning, followed by whisky, pink gins and whisky again in the evenings. No orders were necessary. At prescribed moments in the day the proper drink for the hour was pressed into his outstretched hand, which automatically assumed the shape adapted for holding the glass appropriate to the time of day. After thinking things over, I told my Burmese servant to bring me a drink whenever the other Thakin (Sahib) was given one.

This divided the household expenses more equitably, even if at a high level, and initiated me into the customs of my fairly hard-drinking compatriots. Not as bad as it sounds, since spirits were always well diluted and soon sweated out.

My Burmese servant, the first Burman I got to know, was an old gentleman with long hair twisted into a bun on the top of his head, and with one very long hair dropping from a mole on his chin. Always immaculately clean and neat, with coloured skirt, white tunic and pink Burmese head-dress, he was courteous, diligent and cheerful. I trusted him entirely. I had been told his name was Maung Mo. Later when on tour with my other Burmese friend and mentor, the local Superintendent of Land Records, the latter chided me gently when I called for 'Maung Mo'. 'I don't like to hear you calling him that,' he said. 'He is an old man, and in Burma we like to honour the old by special honorifics. "Maung" means brother, and is suitable for younger or more junior men. For senior men and older men we say "U", which means Uncle.' I got a tiny smile of acknowledgement from U Mo when I addressed him properly for the first time.

The SLR, U Pe Maung, took me specially under his wing, as by chance the Deputy Commissioner had suddenly been transferred, and there was a long gap before his successor arrived. Under Pe Maung's tutelage I tramped about with chains and theodolite and learnt how to survey. He took me on my first tours through the countryside and began to teach me about his native land. I grew to admire his honesty and integrity, and to love the gentle decency of his character. When at work he did not wear Burmese clothes, but dressed in khaki shorts, shirt and stockings and heavy boots, and topped this off with one of the largest sola topis I have ever seen. I wore a smaller topi myself. Later experience in the Second World War showed that a topi was in fact an unnecessary burden, and that what for years had been regarded as 'sunstroke' was in fact 'heatstroke'. But over many years the topi had become a European symbol, and a sign of Westernization and superior status. This mystic symbolism still hangs on in remote parts of our ex-Empire. And the Emperor Haile Selassie, the Lion of Judah, used to wear one as a sort of crown.

Pe Maung, sitting on the verandas of creaking old wooden dak bungalows, taught me how to tie the Burmese skirt, the longyi, which I took to wearing on tour in the evenings. He brought in the local headman's daughters who, sitting demurely and elegantly coiffured at my feet, helped me practise conversational Burmese, much more agreeable tuition than I had with the aged hsaya (teacher) in Monywa. He taught me to appreciate Burmese food – somewhere between the Indian and Chinese cuisine, but nearer to the Chinese. There were lots of little relishes, such as sesame seed, dried shrimps, pickled tea-leaves, fried garlic, roasted peas and salted ginger. Then there was a sort of light consommé, hingyo, and mounds of white rice, and the various curries, the hins of fish, meat, chicken and vegetables. Rice was of course the basic dish, and for the poorer peasants curries and other relishes were in small quantities, just to give savour to the rice. Hence the popularity of ngapi, an evil-smelling paste of dried fish and chillies which gives the maximum flavour for the minimum amount. I was initiated too into smoking the Burmese 'whacking white cheroot'. Everyone smoked cheroots in Burma, from small children to grandmas. The small green cheroots and the light black ones I did not fancy, but the medium-sized brown ones were so good that I abandoned cigarettes for them for ever. To this day cigarettes have no savour for me, and a Scott's No. 1 or 2 Burma cheroot is as good to me as a cigar. But the 'whacking white cheroot' was a different matter. Up to a foot long, with an outer wrapping of maize-leaf, it contained tobacco-leaves and chopped tobacco-stalks, and constantly sent out showers of sparks. It was usually smoked with a little tin tray underneath. I smoked my first in a highly respectable Burmese household. The inevitable happened: sparks showered on my trousers and set them on fire. I had to retreat, to the delighted laughter of my host's daughters, who had known perfectly well what was likely to happen.

The Burmans I met in Monywa were delightful people. Dressed in their best, which they frequently liked to be, they had style and colour. Even the poor ones had some silk garments, and their skirts, wide and full, were a tasteful mixture of bright colours. Spotless white jackets were for the ladies decorated with crystal buttons. Men wore on their heads a pink silk gaung baung, rather like the kerchief traditionally worn by pirates of old. Women dressed their hair with false buns and artificial flowers. A natural tolerance and courtesy, allied to an egalitarian tradition and a love of laughter and fun, made them the pleasantest of companions and the most hospitable of hosts.

With Pe Maung I talked to the village elders about their crops and their cattle – traditional farmers' talk about the cost of every item and the poorness of the harvest. With him I shot my first green pigeon, partridge and jungle fowl. I proudly showed him my first snipe, and was crestfallen when he broke the news that it was not a snipe but a snippet – a bird I learnt later was sometimes called 'the subaltern's snipe'. With him I lay all night in ambush by ripe crops, hoping to shoot a saing, one of the great wild cattle that came to raid the fields. We shot and missed. But I remember the comradeship of that night, the stars above and the roasting and eating of fresh corn-cobs from the fields in the company of farmers, and the tension before dawn as the great shapes of the saing could dimly be seen in the mist.

My first impression of the country was of the vast number of small pagodas. Buddhism was so much a part of an average Burman's life that, when asked his nationality for any official or judicial purpose, he answered 'Burman-Buddhist'. The ordinary Burman had no ambition to be a rich man in Western terms. If he got money he spent it (liberality was one of the Ten Great Virtues) on parties or pious works such as feeding hypongyis (monks) or building a pagoda. By so doing he could accumulate kutho or merit, which would help him toward Nirvana, or Oblivion. There was little kutho in repair, so many pagodas were crumbling. Pagodas ordinarily have no chambers. They are solid structures of sun-dried brick, often plastered and whitewashed, standing on a round brick platform, and topped with a gilded metal umbrella. Besides a well-kept shrine by each village, one found pagodas on bluffs overlooking the great rivers, half-way up hillsides and in forest clearings. They were usually guarded by two statues of mythical lion-type beasts called chinthes. It was after these beasts that Wingate intended to name his men, and was mortified that by a slip of memory at a press conference he had announced that they were to be called Chindits. This name stuck and became an honoured one.

Each village of any size had a monastery nearby, and first thing every morning the monks with shaven plates and saffron robes, accompanied by their young acolytes, proceeded silently round the village carrying their black lacquer begging-bowls. They looked neither to right nor to left, and accepted the gifts of food without a word. Pe Maung taught me to remove my shoes on entering a monastery compound, and what honorifics to use when speaking to a monk. I visited the schoolchildren as they howled out their lessons at the top of their voices. There were very few illiterate Burmese. At eight or nine years old, all went to a monastery school and learnt to read and write. As the culmination of this traditional shinbyu (growing up ceremony) each Burmese had spent a period with shaven head in the saffron robes of a monk. Accompanying Pe Maung, I sat at the feet of one venerable sayadaw, while Pe Maung translated his exposition of the Four Noble Truths, and the Eightfold Path. The message that all is suffering, all is impermanent, there is no soul or self and that the secret of ending suffering is to crush all desire and to break all bonds of attachment, was too austere for me. I was, anyway, a dilettante dabbler in a novel faith, not a genuine seeker after truth.

Many of the abbots were good and holy men. But in the big cities of Rangoon and Mandalay large, sprawling monasteries housed colonies of undisciplined layabouts, more interested in football, politics and crime than in keeping the strict standards laid down for them. It was estimated that there were some 100,000 monks in the country. Some blamed the relaxation of monastic discipline on British short-sightedness in abolishing the ancient office of Thathanabaing, the Buddhist Archbishop, who had had powers of enforcing religious law. In later years I met and talked with Archbishop Makarios, the Ethnarch of the Orthodox Church in Cyprus, the most powerful of nationalist leaders, an experience which has led me to think that, from our point of view, we were perhaps sensible to let the post of Thathanabaing lapse.

However ascetic was the message of Buddhism, it never inhibited the Burmese love of fun, of dressing up, or festivals, and of theatrical performances. One evening different coloured paper lanterns appeared in all the Burmese houses. And then down the wide, dark Chindwin came a procession of flickering lights, floating in tiny cockleshell boats. It was the Burmese festival of Thadingyut, the Festival of Lights at the end of the Buddhist Lent. There is a heart-tugging symbolism about lots of little individual lights in a vast black night; and I thought back to my first Thadingyut when years later I stood at the bottom of the slope leading up to the Patriarch's Church in Bucharest, soon after midnight in the first minutes of Easter Day. There, in Communist, officially atheist, Romania I watched the crowded congregation coming out, each of them carefully carrying a lighted candle, so that a cascade of glowworms seemed to flow down the steps to the heart of the dark city.

In addition to the traditional New Year, Light and Water Festivals, there were hosts of pagoda feasts, weddings and funerals. All these meant dressing up in fine silk clothes of varying colours, bringing out the brightest parasols and the presentation to the monks of offerings of flowers and food, to the sound of music. Everyone seemed decorous and happy.

I went with Pe Maung to my first pwe. Pwes, or public stage performances, are the most Burmese of occasions. There are four main types of performance: the historical drama (zat pwe), the marionette version of the former (yok thay pwe), the song-and-dance show with solo dancers and comedians (anyein pwe), and the dancing ensemble (yein pwe). All are held in the open air and are free to the public, the expenses being met as an act of charity by some local rich man. They start in the cool of the evening and continue to sunrise.

My first pwe was of even then a rare type, a puppet show. A bamboo and matting stage was set up in the fields, with various attendants pumping up pressure lamps as darkness fell. Families from far and wide arrived in their bullock-carts, set down their mats, huddled the children in blankets and set out their picnics. The play was set in the days of the Burmese kings, with princes and princesses, courtiers, wizards, dragons and ogres (beeloos). The speeches were long and involved, covering some complicated medieval story, but the puppets took on an almost human life of their own. Members of the audience watched raptly for a bit, got up and strolled about, had a cheroot and a snack to eat, and often rolled up in their blankets and had a bit of a snooze. As a huge yellow moon rose above (full-moon time was pwe time), and as the puppets, lit by the petrol lamps, bowed and gesticulated in their ancient and tinselly finery, I caught a glimpse of what life must have been like in the court of the Burmese kings, who had ruled in Mandalay such a comparatively short time ago – fifty-one years, to be exact. The British took Mandalay in 1886. Until then the Upper Burma kings had lived in seclusion in their teak palaces, surrounded by shimmering silks, proud to be 'Guardians of the White Elephant'. At his accession in 1878, the last king, Thibaw, goaded on by his young queen, had not less than seventy-nine of his close relatives – men, women and children – put to death in 'The Massacre of the Kinsmen', allowed by custom to a new king uncertain of his throne. One story has it that, in order to conceal from onlookers the sight of royal blood being spilt, the victims were trampled to death under carpets by palace elephants. This world, and indeed the world of spirits and demons, was still vividly alive in the minds of the simple Upper Burma villagers.

Zat pwes had real actors and actresses, and anyein pwes had actress-dancers, called Minthamis – or princesses – who danced and sang and exchanged repartee with two comedians who could extemporize bawdily, topically and locally all night. The Minthamis, their faces smeared with a white paste made from the bark of the thanaka tree, their black hair lacquered and adorned with flowers, wore white tunics with flower-like epaulettes of stiff gauze, and bright silk, floor-length skirts. Exquisite-looking little dolls, they danced rather like marionettes themselves. Their dancing involved short steps, kicking back their long skirts, strange gyrations, and the most graceful of arm and hand movements – a style of dancing to be found across South-East Asia to Indonesia. Their singing was loud, nasal and strident, and their throat muscles were taut from effort. They made up in every corner of the stage in full view without the slightest trace of self-consciousness. In a moment of rest, one of these flower-like creatures would roll back the matting and expectorate noisily through the bamboo flooring of the stage.

Most haunting and most Burmese of all was the music, which brayed and clashed and thudded all night. The orchestra was based on a carved and gilded circular frame, on which were numerous gongs, cymbals, drums and a xylophone. The braying came from a shrill flute with a horn, called a hnay. There were signature tunes for characters in the plays, and other traditional airs, but a lot of the music in anyein pwes seemed to be made up as the band went along. An unattractive modern addition to the instruments was often a police whistle. At the climax of the dance, or after a particularly witty and ribald exchange between the clowns, the orchestra indulged in a short burst of frenzy. Drums, gongs, flutes and cymbals went at it double time, as loudly as they could – an exciting noise.

In the evenings in Monywa I often used to sit and watch the village families coming down for their end-of-day bath in the Chindwin – the little naked children gambolling in the water, and the maidens, slim and graceful, dipping and swimming in short skirts tucked up underneath their arms. When they were finished, they put a dry garment over the wet one and deftly kicked the wet one away. All was cheerful and decorous. Years later, in an existence I never dreamt of in my Burmese days, I found myself Head of Chancery in the British Legation at Budapest. The year was 1950, when communism in Hungary under Comrade Rakosi (remembered for his 'salami' method of destroying his opponents slice by slice) was harsh and Stalinist. At a farewell cocktail party for the head of my mission, an unexpected guest was a female Communist Minister of the government. She was aggressively unattractive, with a sacklike dress, black hair cut in a straight fringe, and a dour, doughy face. She was accompanied by a pale wraith of a female translator, as few foreigners mastered Hungarian.

When I went across to chat the Minister up, she spoke curtly and disdainfully. 'The Minister says', said the translator, 'that she does not like cocktail parties. She does not drink or smoke. And she cannot make small talk on trivial matters.'

I decided that attack was the best form of defence. 'Let us talk about important and fundamental matters, then. Ask the Minister what she considers are the proper objectives of mankind.'

This produced a suspicious silence.

'Would the Minister agree that it is to achieve the greatest happiness of the greatest number?'

Reluctantly, 'Yes.'

'Would the Minister say that, after providing basic shelter, food, clothing, warmth and medical attention, the more people were provided with the material comforts of life, the happier they would be? For example, the more sewing-machines, bicycles and radios, the better?'

The Minister supposed so.

'Would the Minister then not agree that Communist and American systems agree on the necessity of industrialization, and that the major difference between them is that the Communist system aims to control the *means of production* and organize *distribution* of the fruits of industrialization more equally?'

'Yes.'

'Has the Minister every really analysed what "happiness" is? As a young man I saw Burmese villagers, with virtually no cash and hardly any mechanical aids, growing enough crops for their own food, calmed by Buddhism, and happier than any two-car steel worker in Pittsburgh. Was perhaps Gandhi right in thinking "happiness" did not depend on material possessions and on heavy industry?'

The Minister's reply was vague. The conversation was getting *too* serious. She excused herself and moved off.

I certainly believe that the average villager in a prosperous village in Upper Burma was, if at a low level of sophistication, a contented and happy human being.

The English Thakins

Against this charming, picturesque and in many ways primitive background the British (called in Burma Thakins, the equivalent of Sahibs) lived their separate lives in the enclave of the Civil Station. Here were the classic cast of the Kipling stories: the Deputy Commissioner (Head of the District), the District Superintendent of Police, the District Forest Officer, the Executive Engineer, the Civil Surgeon and the Sessions Judge, and so on. And here were the government offices, the law courts, the hospital, the schools and the gaol.

No administrator from an Indian province could have had difficulty in slipping into an equivalent slot in Burma. In fact, a group photograph of the British community in Monywa looked very much as a similar photograph of an Indian station would have looked fifty years before. It would be comprised of much the same lean, brown Sahibs, often with military moustaches, in their khaki shirts, shorts and stockings, glasses in their hands, with the same fox-terriers and labrador dogs at their feet. Only the hats and clothes of the Memsahibs had changed. Much of our slang and many of our conventions and superstitions were Anglo-Indian. The tall, turbaned and bearded sowars of the Governor's Bodyguard in Rangoon, pennants fluttering from their lances, were Indian, and the Viceroy in far-away Delhi was our ultimate chief in the East. The ICS, the Police, the Forest Service, the Medical Service and so on were all in origin local branches of Indian Imperial Services. There were Sikh taxi-drivers in Rangoon, Chittagonian crews on the river steamers, Bengali money-lenders and coolies in the docks and mills, and a host of minor clerks and technicians who had come in with the British, capitalizing on their knowledge of English and of imperial bureaucratic procedures. The Indians, of whom there were perhaps a million in Burma, were not very popular with the local Burman population. But the connection with India was fortuitous. Burma was an essentially different country, and to most of the British there it was 'a cleaner, greener land', less complicated than India, less burdened with poverty and caste, more old-fashioned and easy-going, more tolerant of eccentrics.

Here too in Monywa were local managers of the Bombay Burma Trading Corporation, the famous British teak firm involved in the dispute which had led to the annexation of Upper Burma in 1886. The Corporation was popularly referred to as the Bombaing, which is an approximation of a Burmese effort to pronounce Bombay. The Bombaing in Monywa had offices and bungalows and a chummery (bachelors' quarters) for its young assistants.

The domestic lives of the Thakins and Thakinmas were partly shaped by their adaptation to the climate and the country, and partly by this determination to hang on to Western habits and associations. Wide, cool verandas, with hanging orchids in moss, and long, cane-bottomed chairs built to hold a glass and provide for lolling with one's feet up, gave on to drawing-rooms with chintzes and water-colours and photographs in silver frames.

In the evenings the British forgathered in the Club. There was no colour bar, but there were few Burmese officials in the station then, and they came rarely, mostly to play tennis. Apart from the tennis-courts there was a rather scruffy little library, a billiard-table stained with blood from late-night revels, and a refrigerator which, as well as providing the luxury of ice for drinks, contained from time to time such delicacies as cold-store butter, sardines and kippers. Here at the Club we met the few Englishwomen, wives of officials and Forest firm staff, and played bridge under the swaying punkahs.

Life is full of the truth that values are relative. When I and my young friends from the Forest firms, after long, dusty tours in the jungle, saw the lights of the little one-horse town of Monywa twinkling in the distance, and thought of ice in our drinks, mixed doubles on the tennis-court, and some cheery station polo with good companions, our hearts beat with excitement. The lights of Monywa twinkled to us with all the allure of Paris to a sophisticated European.

My own training went on apace, in all the fields in which an administrative officer was expected to operate. In 1934 Burma was ruled over by a British Governor in Rangoon, who had special responsibility for defence, foreign affairs, frontier areas, finance and justice, law and order, excise, and so on. Most domestic departments, such as education, health, public works, forests and agriculture, were under elected Burmese ministers, drawn from the Prime Minister's party in the largely elected Legislative Assembly. The actual administration of the country was directed by the Secretariat in Rangoon, where civil servants strove to turn policy into action. The Administration was separated into five Divisions, under commissioners. Each division contained six or more Districts (the basic unit of administration) under Deputy Commissioners. Each district was about the size of an English county. The DC, who had considerable powers, was 'the father of his district'. Responsible for law and order, he was also the District Magistrate, in charge of a number of magistrates; and as Collector he was generally responsible for the welfare of his district in all aspects. In 1934 the backbone of the Administration was still comprised of the comparatively few officers of the ICS in the Secretariat and the Divisions. But not all DCs were Europeans. At my first post I served under a Burmese DC, who was under a Shan commissioner. (Nearly all the officers below the DC were Burmese.) Below the DC came two or three Subdivisional Officers, each controlling a number of Township Officers.

Below these permanent officials came the Village Headman, to whom a system of popular election was being applied. There were about 300 village tracts in each district. It would have been impossible for a handful of Britons to have governed the millions of Indians and Burmese without the close co-operation of local nationals in all aspects of administration, and without the broad consent of the masses. Both these conditions still prevailed in Burma in 1934.

As a trainee I was learning to become a Subdivisional Officer and, after some years' experience, a DC. I studied Criminal Law, the Law of Evidence, the Code of Criminal Procedure (all English law brilliantly codified by Macaulay), the Village Act, the *Land Revenue Manual*. With the kindly help of my Burmese Bench clerk I tried my first petty cases. At this low level the pleaders, as local lawyers were called, were not very high-grade. They tried me out like a new boy. Lolling about the court they chewed and spat scarlet streams of betel-juice. After a brief consultation with my Bench clerk I ruled that there should be no betel chewing in court. They stopped at once and cheerfully, and henceforth were as good as gold.

Polo was naturally part of my education. It was comparatively cheap to buy and keep a pony, and we could often borrow ponies from the Mounted Police, whose steeds were in fact often too good as polo ponies to risk pushing them over rough ground in pursuit of dacoits. On station polo we sometimes played half-speed chukkas in which ladies joined and beginners began.

Full-speed polo is a tense, exciting and dangerous game. A bad infringement of the rules, such as crossing another pony's path, could lead to fearful injuries, so tempers were often high and language lurid. On small stations the standard was low but almost always redeemed by some Indian mounted policeman who rode like a centaur and hit the ball with the graceful accuracy of a Duleepsinghi. Beginners like me were taught initially to play without a stick. The beginner was posted at number one, and told to concentrate on riding the opposing number four (the back) off the ball. This, if one were faced with a good horseman, was a full-time and exhausting job.

My particular friends in Monywa, on and off the polo field, were the young assistants from the Forest staff at the Bombay

Burma Trading Corporation. The BBTC had been on good terms with King Thibaw's predecessor, the mild King Mindon. William Wallace, one of the founders of the firm, was clearly on His Majesty's wavelength, as he is on record as presenting him with a golden telescope set with 524 small diamonds. But the greedy Thibaw had placed huge and unjustified fines on the Corporation, eventually giving the British Government, which was anxious to pre-empt a feared French thrust from Indo-China, the excuse for the Third Burmese War and the annexation of Upper Burma. So the Bombaing had a special place in Anglo-Burmese history.

The young assistants in Monywa were a cheerful bunch. Teetotal while in the jungle, they made up for it in Monywa. Only my alcoholic training at Trinity enabled me to keep pace with them. These forest men led a tough life. In the rains (roughly from June to September) the assistants from the Bombaing, Steel Brothers, and Macgregor's, lived in the jungle in constant damp and mud, working the felled teak logs down to the creeks and rivers. They suffered from malaria, dysentery, tropical ulcers and numerous other diseases. They were persecuted by hungry leeches whose blood-bloated bodies had to be shrivelled off with lighted cigarette-ends or handfuls of salt. They were not particularly well paid, especially during the years of the slump from 1929 onwards. Some of them had Burmese mistresses who saved their money, and in sickness in the jungle often saved their lives. These liaisons were well understood by the Burmese villagers and did not mar the girls' prospects of eventual marriage to one of their own countrymen. In the hot season (February to May), the Forest Assistants were usually given a few weeks' holiday in the cool and civilized surroundings of Maymyo, the Government's summer headquarters, on the Shan plateau.

Once I was invited up by a friend to spend a week-end in one of the Maymyo chummeries. 'Candacraig', modelled on a Scottish hunting-lodge, had roof pinnacles, galleries, a wide teak staircase, and a huge log fire in the grate in the evenings. No one was in and I took to bed early. About two in the morning there was a great commotion. I leant over the landing rails and saw my friend, in a wrinkled linen suit and with a drooping flower in his buttonhole, inquiring loudly where I was. 'Here I am,' I said. 'Where have *you* been?' Came the answer: 'Out to lunch, old boy'. The next morning one of the young Forest bachelors passed me on the landing, dressed in immaculate riding-clothes. Out in the drive I could see a party of friends, the girls slim, blonde Missahibs, elegantly attired, waiting with the ponies and the syces for an early-morning ride. The cavalier paused for a moment beside his open bedroom door, and spoke sternly but kindly to his Burmese girl therein. 'How many times have I told you I don't like your hair that way! Put it back the old way!' I wondered idly what the colonel's daughter outside would have thought of this. Perhaps if she could have seen the young man's normal working life in the rains, she would have understood. The brief social whirl of Polo Week was not his real world.

In the cold season (October to January), again spent in the jungle, life was better. They enjoyed an outdoor life as a sportsman enjoyed it – life in tents, by big camp-fires, and a chance after work to shoot. One of the most exciting beasts to stalk and shoot was the Burmese saing, which the Bombaing sportsmen called bison and which stood nearly six feet at its withers. In some of the Bombaing forests rides were cut and beaters trained and jungle fowl shot in passable imitation of a pheasant shoot in England. One manager, an excellent shot, arranged his big shoot to coincide with the arrival of the Flotilla paddle-steamer, which was equipped with a 'cold room'. He would send a hundred brace of jungle fowl down to the cold store in Rangoon, and at Christmas time his friends in the city would receive a docket of vouchers entitling them to draw so many birds from the store – a very popular gift. But all in all, it was a lonely and arduous life.

There was a strong feeling of comradeship amongst the young men of the Bombaing. They believed themselves to be the élite of their kind, and they had high standards of courage and responsibility. With these qualities it is not surprising that many of them slipped naturally into daring exploits against the Japanese in the war which was soon to come. Famous among the Bombaing heroes was John Hedley, who lay concealed behind the Japanese lines radioing information of such meticulous detail that the Headquarters Intelligence officers were reluctant to believe him; also 'Red' Parker, Jonah Jones and Robin

Stewart of Z Force; and others in the Chindits. In the war in Burma the comparatively small staff of the Bombaing won the astonishing total of four DSOs and thirteen MCs (two with bars). The other Forest firms in Burma, such as Steel Brothers and Macgregor's, also contributed brave young officers. Men who spoke Burmese and knew the jungle not as an enemy but as a friend, were worth their weight in gold.

When I arrived in Monywa the 'senior subaltern', so to speak, at the Bombaing chummery was a large, laconic, red-faced man with bright blue eyes called Edward Bailey. All his colleagues loved him and would follow him anywhere, and the jungle Burmese adored and revered him. He spoke good Burmese and was the banker and family adviser of most of his oozies (elephant drivers). He knew every detail about them and their children. He used to stride through the jungle, twirling a knobkerrie, and followed by his two Great Danes, Duster and Sweep, like some hero of old.

The handling of elephants was one of the major responsibilities of Forest officers of the timber firms. The Bombaing alone had getting on for 2,000 elephants in their herd. A Forest manager had about a hundred elephants in his charge, in an area bigger than an English county. 'Elephant Bill' (J.H. Williams of the Bombaing) has written classic books about life with these animals, but there must have been another twenty men in Burma who knew as much as he did about elephants and their management. I found elephants slow movers and very uncomfortable to ride. I was surprised to find that baby elephants were covered with gingery hair and full of childish mischief. Once, for a bit of fun, one of these pocket mastodons butted me down a river bank into the water. At the other end of the scale nothing was more alarming than to see a bull elephant in 'musth'. When a bull elephant came into season, and liquid began to trickle from a small hole in his temple, it required fetters of superlative strength to keep him from going on a rampage and spreading death and destruction.

Timber elephants were relatively delicate creatures and required a lot of doctoring. One way to administer an inoculation to the huge animal was to manoeuvre it into a stout teak pen, into which it only just fitted. An enormous needle was then smacked into its hide and an equally enormous syringe screwed on to it for the inoculation. No one who has travelled with elephants will forget the hollow 'klonk' of the wooden clappers round the necks of hobbled elephants put out in the evening to forage for themselves in bamboo thickets.

In the war Elephant Bill in dangerous and arduous conditions rescued some hundreds of elephants from the Japanese, and built invaluable roads and bridges for the 14th Army. But by the end of the war, mechanical technology was ready to push the great beasts on one side. Bulldozers, earth-moving machinery, tractors and trucks did much faster and more cheaply what elephants had done for centuries. Burma in the thirties saw the last real age of the 'elephants' a'piling teak in the slushy squdgy creek'.

I became a friend of Edward Bailey of the Bombaing, and when he went on leave he asked me to look after Duster and Sweep for six months. 'In the mornings,' he instructed me, 'the dogs have a wash-basin of milk and biscuits each. In the evening they each have a basin of rice and meat and bones. If they go off their feed, I sometimes give them a tonic.'

'What tonic, Edward?'

'Well, I starve them for a couple of days. Then I tie them to a tree while I shoot a small cow in front of them and then I let them loose. This seems to pep them up.'

I looked after the dogs, but never adminstered the tonic. The dogs took me over in good part. Once when, after a riotous evening I did not quite reach my bed, they slept each side of me on the floor all night, and would not let the servants approach me in the morning until I had woken up and reassured them. Then one day Duster, the big 'harlequin' dog (Sweep was, of course, black), who had seemed a bit out of sorts for days, suddenly began to blunder round the room, blindly knocking over the furniture, and then fled upstairs with a howl. The ever-present and terrible fear of dog-owners in the East is rabies. I nerved myself to creep upstairs. Duster was lying on the floor and I was ready to run. But I caught his eye, which was intelligent and lucid, and he essayed a feeble wag of his tail. He was very ill and grew weaker each day. I could not have faced Edward if Duster had died.

Friends told me of a wonderful Japanese lady vet up in Maymyo. As there was no DC in Monywa then, and no one in the station who could formally grant me leave, I took matters into my own hands and loaded Duster (and Sweep) on to the train and set off on the long journey to Maymyo. There the Japanese lady (perhaps – who knows – an agent of Japanese Intelligence and a colleague of the famous Colonel 'Minami' Suzuki) examined the dog. 'Velly bad distemper,' she pronounced. And true to her reputation, she fed the dog every few hours for days with spoonfuls of egg, milk and brandy, and saved his life.

Meanwhile, I had to put my position straight. I called formally on the Government's Chief Secretary, Sir Walter Booth-Graveley, Knight Commander of the Indian Empire. Sir Walter, who had the head and profile of a Roman emperor, passed a weary hand over his distinguished brow and looked stern when I presented myself. 'What are you doing here? Who gave you leave?' he asked coldly.

I went into my sad story. At one stage I whistled in the enormous Sweep to give verisimilitude to my claim.

'Get him out of here!' said Sir Walter, still looking grave. 'You should not have left your station without permission. It is, furthermore, very odd that you should have chosen to arrive here on the first day of Polo Week.'

I stammered that I knew nothing about Polo Week (the main annual week of social festivities).

The Chief Secretary's expression did not change. 'But you might as well stay and enjoy it,' he said. 'Take a week's leave. Good morning.'

Going up to the Maymyo Club the next day, I was introduced to a large, red-faced, middle-aged major, one of Burma's greatest horse-masters, and, looking much too heavy for his pony, a redoubtable polo player. He made a kindly gesture to the young newcomer. 'Care for some tiffin?' he remarked. I assented and we moved to the dining-room, where we ate and drank our way through a large lunch without any tiresome conversation. He knew that I knew who he was and what he did, and he knew who I was and what I did. We were both members of the same Club, and presumably had much the same views on things. What was there to talk about? After lunch we sat and dozed quietly on the veranda. About four o'clock his eyes opened. His moustache flickered. At last he was going to say something. 'Wonder what's for "char"?' said my host slowly.

I still remember the benign and utterly companionable silence of that sunlit afternoon.

Edward Bailey was duly gratified to receive the great dogs safe and sound on his return from leave. On his next tour of duty he contracted blackwater fever and died. He couldn't have been much more than thirty years old.

The companionship of dogs meant much to lonely Europeans. My friend Dick Richards, DC of Tharrawaddy District, once heard three Burmese girls talking at the village well. They were speaking of reincarnation, in which all Buddhists believe.

'When I am reincarnate,' said one of them, 'I'd like to be a Thakin's dog.'

'Whatever for?' asked one of the others.

'Because they are always such happy creatures,' she replied. 'Always well fed, sleep in blankets at night, and if they are ill the Thakins call the dog doctor. The Thakins love them so much they might be human beings.'

Soon a new DC arrived, a Burman called Oo Kyaw Khine, from the district of Arakan, where many of the cleverest Burmese came from. Unlike most Burmans, he liked riding and played an adventurous game of polo. Already by 1935 it was quite normal for an English officer to serve under a Burman DC. There were only some 145 ICS officers in Burma (then a country of some 15 million), of which thirty were Burmese. Since 1923 half the recruits each year had been Burmese.

We were all sad when this kind and cheerful man moved on rather quickly to another district. The new DC, Bernard Binns, was a stocky man, prematurely white-haired, who had seen service in the Great War. He was a somewhat touchy Midlander, with a brusque, no-nonsense manner. He had a pungent turn of phrase. Once when a number of somewhat meaningless 'political gestures' were recommended, he commented that he was 'against Government by gesticulation'. The Burmans liked and trusted him more than most. He rose to high office in Burma on the basis of his integrity, hard work and deep knowledge of land revenue, land reform and the rice trade. He eventually died (as Sir Bernard Binns) in Rome some years after Burma's independence, as a specialist in land tenure in the

Food and Agricultural Organization of the United Nations. Indeed, he had been on the UK delegation to the Hot Springs Conference where FAO was founded. He suffered from asthma, and got through the night smoking menthol cigarettes and sipping gin. During bouts of insomnia he liked to have companions. 'It is impertinent for a junior officer to go to sleep while his DC is awake,' he ruled at one late-night session. And in a loud, somewhat tuneless vibrato, he liked to sing. I was often required to sing with him into the early hours. One of his favourites was an old Irish rebel song, 'And Boney's on the sea, said the Shan Van Vaugh!'

After one all-night musical session, he called in the early hours of the morning for our ponies. 'Let's go and spot check a sub-treasury out in the district,' he decided. 'Good for your training.'

Half-dead from lack of sleep, I clung to my pony, and found the counting of money in the sub-treasury an almost impossible task. But somehow I survived.

While he was down in Monywa his wife in Maymyo Hospital gave birth to a longed-for son, but he died because no doctor was at hand to assist. His wife took a dislike to Burma and made for home, rarely appearing in Burma again. Bernard Binns was thereafter a lonely man. He remained a good friend to me throughout my service, and I was glad to serve under him again later.

Most of our concerts took place after evening swims in the Chindwin in the months of March, April and May, when heat in the dry zone could be intense – about 110 degrees at midday. One Bombaing manager, tired of lying awake at night in pools of sweat, arranged two camp-beds in the open with a tin bath full of water between them. Behind the beds he set up a large fan, like a windmill, run on a kerosene engine. When he felt too hot he rolled over half-asleep into the water, and up again on to the other bed, where the fan playing on his damp body set up cooling evaporation. He maintained that his system was a great success.

One of the best-known characters on the Chindwin was the riverine chaplain, the Reverend Caldecott. A short, tubby, middle-aged bachelor, with a bun of a face split by the widest of grins, he lived on the paddle-steamers and dropped off along the river for a spasmodic 'cure of souls'. He claimed he had the longest parish in the world, as he also covered stations far down the Irrawaddy. He had a meagre salary, and while the Burmese monks got their tribute in the daily oblations of rice, curry and fruit, he was happy to accept beer and black Burmese cheroots, as well as bed and board.

Although few Europeans in the station could remotely be described as religious, a good contingent, washed and brushed, turned up for the occasional services in the little church – which seemed to have less to do with religion than with the reassuring reaffirmation of certain home-grown values. The services were rattled through at top speed: 'Onward Christian Soldiers' cut to three verses, a few greetings bawled at the very few Burmese present, and we were off to the Club, where the padre dived for his favourite billiard-cue. He had extraordinary short stubby fingers. I never knew if he had been born with them, or lost the tips in some accident or by frost-bite, but he was nevertheless an excellent snooker player. We knew he could beat most of us young fellows, and we put up little stakes which we knew would be welcome to him. He lived a strange nomadic life, but he seemed a happy man. Christenings and the occasional wedding brightened his days. Funerals could not wait for him: in that climate the dead were usually buried within twenty-four hours. I have heard the carpenters hammering a coffin before the dying man had drawn his last breath.

One Sunday morning we went to church in a rather chastened mood. Dawn had surprised a marauding leopard under one of the forest firms' bungalows on the edge of the town. In the excited hunt which ensued the cook had killed the night-watchman with a wild shot from a small .22 rifle. But on the whole life was peaceful and uneventful enough.

As in any small and confined community, the Club members of Monywa sometimes fell into feuds over trivial matters. The wife of our tough District Superintendent of Police, who had just had a letter from her husband on tour, played golf that afternoon with the District Forest Officer, to whom she innocently remarked that her husband had shot a brace of partridge the day before. The DFO, a florid, sandy Scotsman, who favoured a large double terai hat in place of a topi, went a shade even more pink with rage. 'The close season started a week ago,' he snorted. There was a furious row when the DSP returned. The friends of the two opponents took sides. 'Was the information in a letter to his wife privileged?' 'Did the odd partridge a few days into the close season matter anyway?' 'If the chief policeman did not keep strictly to the rules, who would?' The two groups would hardly speak to each other for days. Then the subject just evaporated and everyone forgot about it.

When people who have lived and worked together in a small station in countries like Burma meet years later, they find that, even if they did not particularly like each other at the time, the load of memories is so similar and shared by so few, that in an odd way they are friends willy-nilly. Now, even forty years later, if I meet a survivor from the old days, we pick up as if we had met yesterday.

George Orwell's *Burmese Days* morbidly describes life in a small station in Upper Burma. It was a strange fate which pitchforked a young man of such personal and political sensitivity as Eric Blair into the job of a colonial policeman. He grew to hate it. But his bitter pen was catholic in its targets; the most unpleasant character in this book was a Burman, Oo Po Kyin – just as in later work he lashed into the Left as well as the Right. His descriptions of the sights and sounds and scents of Burma were exceptionally perceptive and accurate. People he saw almost uniformly with a jaundiced eye. I suppose if you selected the more unpleasant characters from the thirty-odd districts of Burma over a period of thirty years, you could in one place at one time assemble an Orwellian cast.

Not many people realize that Eric Blair was an imperial policeman for as long as five years. I have talked to an officer who served with him. Blair was a loner who did not much care for his fellow-Europeans. But in spite of learning Burmese well, he did not particularly like or feel at ease with the Burmese either. The Burmese have a very keen nose for those who genuinely like them, and their reaction to his prickly character may have been one reason why he was unhappy amongst them. I was told too that he was first posted to the dismal and gloomy swamps of the Irrawaddy delta (enough to drive anyone to melancholia), and that he had the bad luck to start his career under a harsh and unsympathetic Superintendent of Police. Perhaps if he had been posted at the start to a better climate, under a more charming chief (and there were such), we might have lost a major writer and political thinker. But I think his daemon of brutal honesty would have driven him on anyway. The fact that he did not really fit in anywhere gave him a precious independence.

One amiable DSP I knew would certainly have treated him kindly, but I fear would have proved an unstimulating companion intellectually. One night I had to share a bedroom in a dak bungalow with this officer. Stroking his bushy moustache, he inquired politely if I would mind if he kept the light on for a bit, as it was his habit to read in bed before going to sleep. I readily agreed, but kept one eye open out of curiosity to see what sort of book my companion would choose. He sat up in bed under his mosquito-net, his face solemn and concentrated, adjusted his horn-rimmed spectacles, and slowly turned the leaves of a large flat volume. This proved to be *Art Prints in Glossy Form*, featuring lovingly photographed studies of the female nude.

Eric Blair found the role he had to play very distasteful. But in his five years in Burma he must have been aware that there was a fairly easy-going and well-meaning side to British rule. Many years later he conceded that the British were not 'oppressors' in Burma. The evil he felt was in the situation itself, the wrongness of any one country arrogating to itself the role of ruling another, and as with Burma that of a different people with a different culture.

Somerset Maugham, in the introduction to one of his volumes of short stories containing his vignettes of murder and adultery and other nefarious goings-on in colonial Malaya, carefully disclaimed any pretence of presenting an objective overall picture; as a writer he had selected and embroidered the unusual. 'Most Government officials', he said, 'were ordinary people, ordinarily satisfied with their station in life. They did the job they were paid to do more or less competently.'

The idea that tropical stations were hotbeds of sexual intrigue is, of course, a fiction. To start with, there was no privacy at all. Old-fashioned bungalows (built to attract breezes) were as open as possible, and there were always a couple of servants lurking around. And everyone in a small station knew the details of each other's lives and of their daily routines. Maugham-type situations might, of course, occasionally be found in the city of Rangoon, and amongst the grass widows in the hill station of Maymyo. There was, I recall, one suicide over a lady in Maymyo. I had earlier described her to another woman as 'a nice, quiet girl'. 'Pussy-quiet' was the guarded reply. And one afternoon in Rangoon I sat beside an attractive woman watching her husband play tennis with another man. They both played a weary game and served an unusual number of double faults. I asked the woman what was behind her Giaconda smile. She was an old friend and trusted me. 'Because I am in a special position to know why they are both so tired today,' she said, looking demurely ahead.

On the whole, people in Rangoon led respectable or at least discreet lives. But when I first arrived in Burma there was in Rangoon a suave and dapper officer to whom in later years in England a divorce judge, on his bench gave a little bow of recognition: 'Ah yes, Colonel X! A *veteran* of these courts!' And once when I inquired about the history of a pleasant and educated Anglo-Burman who was trying to sell me life insurance, I was told that he was a convicted murderer. He was accused of shooting dead the husband of a woman with whom he was in love. At the trial his lawyer argued that he had been deranged by a bout of cerebral malaria and had thought his friend was a tiger. He was committed to a criminal lunatic asylum, but after some years of playing bridge with the warders was released as cured.

In another old and yellowing group photograph, from before the First World War, I was shown a blurred face said to be that of H.H. Munro, a young Burma policeman who had left the service after only eighteen months, his health shattered by malaria. He had been born in Burma, where his father was Inspector-General of Police, and he had, like Kipling, spent a lonely childhood in England in the care of strict and unsympathetic aunts. Again an unlikely background for one who became a witty and sophisticated writer – modern readers finding 'Saki's' throwaway style and black humour much to their taste. Underneath it all he had something of Eric Blair's independence and integrity. In the First World War he refused a commission and was a sergeant when he was killed in the trenches by a sniper's bullet one night in 1916.

George Orwell and Saki – what an improbable pair to have started their lives as imperial policemen in Burma, rounding up dacoits and raiding gambling parties and opium dens! Fortuitously they became two of my favourite writers.

Before I left Monywa we were inspected by our Divisional Commissioner, C.F. Grant. The senior officers who held the posts of Divisional Commissioners when I first came out were perhaps the last of the muscular Christians in the traditional ICS image. They were old-fashioned gentlemen of high standards. Grant (always meticulously dressed with collar and tie in the hottest weather), with his grey military moustache and monocle; C.R.P. Cooper, with his actor's profile and trained light tenor voice; Bernard Swithinbank, the classical scholar – these were the men who had come out in the first decade of the century, and were perhaps the last generation to believe in their task in the way the Victorians believed in it, before we began to lose confidence in the considerable merits of our civilization. They were men of intellect, intelligence and devotion to duty, and at least some of their standards rubbed off to the lesser mortals who succeeded them. And some of their confidence rubbed off too. We dealt effectively with difficult and dangerous situations because we believed we were well capable of dealing with them.

Instinctively we believed in the superiority of the Western way of life, and that we were bringing the Burmese higher standards of efficiency, honesty, hygiene, communication, democracy, rule of law, and so on. We had the same feeling of superiority about our cultural heritage – the Bible, Shakespeare and Goethe, Mozart and Beethoven, Newton and Darwin, Locke and Mill – and that it had something of value to pass on to less fortunate peoples. The educational system we devised for Burma was a Western one, teaching Western cultural values. Perhaps the first crack in our self-satisfaction came from the realization that Buddhism could hold its own moral grounds with Christianity. Later, we began to have doubts about the applicability of British institutions to Burmese society and in our grounds for telling people how to run their lives. And, finally, there came the pressures from below, from the Burmese people themselves, wanting to be free and run their affairs as they liked. But in 1935, in the more remote Upper Burma districts like the Lower Chindwin, there was little nationalist unrest, and British rule looked as if it would last for a long time yet.

2 The Frontier

Out of the blue came an order to cut short my Monywa training and take over a post at Sinlumkaba, 6,000 feet up in the Kachin hills, far in the north-east of Burma, on the frontier with China. The Frontier Service officer holding the post had fallen ill suddenly, and since, owing to a number of accidents, there was no immediate replacement available from his own Service, an ICS trainee was sent up as an unusual and temporary stopgap.

It was the end of the hot weather, and after a dusty and sweaty train journey I arrived at Katha and boarded one of the Irrawaddy Flotilla Company's paddle-steamers. The top deck, under a roof, stretched right to the bows, and one could sit in a deck-chair, with one's feet on the rails, and watch the river scenery unfolding ahead without interruption. The cabins had solid mahogany bunks, as in ocean-going steamers, and cool white sheets. A smartly dressed Indian butler served drinks and meals on deck. I felt as if I were going on holiday. And, indeed, the journey up to Bhamo, 1,000 miles north of Rangoon, was a holiday trip. Almost immediately the river breezes and the spray made the temperature degrees cooler, and gave me a tremendous appetite for bacon and eggs. River terns flew ahead, and lapwings called 'Ti-ti-du' from the banks. On the lower decks squatted all the deck passengers, mostly Burmese, with their belongings in bundles, live chickens in baskets, and all manner of merchandise. When we pulled into a village there was a fearful commotion as passengers got on and off. For long stretches there were no villages, and the forests came down from the hills almost to the water's edge. Looking ahead with binoculars, I could see deer drinking on the little beaches. Strange birds flew over. I suddenly realized how horribly hot and uncomfortable Monywa had been when I left.

A bit nearer to Bhamo than Katha the river makes a dramatic passage through the famous Second Defile. The steamer seems to be advancing on a wall of rock, then a small cleft 300 yards wide suddenly appears, and for the next few winding miles sheer cliffs drop down from a great height straight to the water, as the Irrawaddy splits a mountain. This is the awe-inspiring entrance to the wilder parts of Burma.

Bhamo was a frontier town (the Chinese border was only 50 miles away) visited by many tribesmen other than Burmans and hence full of strange faces and costumes. From and to Bhamo Chinese traders drove their caravans by immemorial trade routes, and smugglers probed the less-known passes. Salt, cotton and jade went into China, and silks and (illicit) opium came back. Augustus Margary, the explorer who had journeyed through China from Hankow to Bhamo in 1874–5 (and who was murdered on his way back), had written optimistically of this trade route: '... a perfect flood of British goods could be swallowed up at once for Kweechow and Szechwan markets'. But somehow this had never happened.

A battalion of the Frontier Force was stationed here, and the office buildings seemed to have more of an air of authority about them. Its very remoteness from Rangoon gave the Deputy Commissioner more freedom of action, and with a reasonable climate, rugged and wild country close by, good shooting and mahseer fishing accessible, it was for a certain type of officer one of the plum postings in the country. Some of the Service's best officers served as DCs in Bhamo and in Myitkyina, the station still further north. One of the best known of these was J.K. Stanford, the naturalist, sportsman and writer, whose books and articles became even better known in Great Britain when he returned home and wrote of shooting grouse instead of jungle fowl. The DC when I arrived in Bhamo was Robin McGuire, a short, tough, dark Irishman. He loved Bhamo with its shooting and polo and its generally independent air. He must often have thought of it nostalgically when struggling with jobs as Governor's Secretary, and Chief Secretary, which he later became.

I was soon equipped and sent on my way – a two-day steep climb up the mountainside. A train of mules with Chinese muleteers met me at the caravanserai village of Kyipondap, some 20 miles from Bhamo. My kit was strapped on to the wooden baggage frames of the mules, and off we went.

U Mo's nephew, whom the old man had provided as a replacement to serve me in my new posting, took one look at the mist-shrouded heights of the Sinlum hills and retreated rapidly to Monywa. The Burmans hated and feared the hills and the hill tribes. The hill peoples – Kachins, Chins, Nagas, Karens, together with the Shans (a civilized plateau people of kindred stock to the Siamese and not quite in the same category) – numbered then, with other minor tribes, about $3\frac{1}{2}$ million and occupied nearly 40 per cent of the total area of Burma. The Burmans had never conquered these peoples (though the Shan Sawbwas were technically subordinate to the Burmese kings), and like minorities throughout the Empire they relied on the British to see that they got fair play. Like other such minorities, we had to abandon them when we finally left, in the pious hope that the Independent Union of Burma would in time accommodate them all happily.

Recruiting desperately in the Bhamo bazaar for a cook, I took on a strange black-faced, grey-haired apparition who claimed he could fill the bill. 'Can you make bread?' I asked. 'Certainly,' replied Wadi Maroo. He was an unlikely person to find in Bhamo, as he was a native of Abyssinia. The story as I heard it was that in 1868, during the Abyssinian war, a British officer had found a black piccaninny crying on the battlefield at Magdala and had rescued, adopted and educated the little boy, who eventually fetched up in India as a Government civil surgeon. On a trip back to his own country the doctor had picked up a local servant and brought him to Burma, where he left him (now with a Burmese wife) when he left the country. The doctor, with his unusual knowledge of English, became Ethiopian Ambassador at the Court of St James's. My new cook marched sturdily ahead of the mule train up the mountainside. Doubts arose in me as he served his first meal, which proved to be the contents of a tin of salmon, heated up and served, without any accompaniments, in the uncompromising shape of the tin.

The climb up to Sinlumkaba took two days. The slopes were steep, and so the temperature, as well as the flora and fauna, changed rapidly. After many parched months in the plains of the Lower Chindwin in the hot weather, it was exhilarating to pass through green forests, decorated with little orchids, and hear and see clear mountain rills (the water exquisitely cold) trickling through moss and ferns, and to feel cool and energetic again. From here onwards the hills were great hunting-grounds for botanists. It was from the highlands of Yunnan just across the border that the seeds of several flowers now in English gardens first came, including many azaleas and rhododendrons. Kingdon Ward, the explorer and botanist, has written of his adventures seeking seeds across this frontier in the Chinese uplands.

Many of his best finds came from farther north. The last district headquarters in Burma was Myitkyina on the river above Bhamo, and twenty-one days' march north from there was the last British post, Fort Herz. This lay in the Golden Plain, ringed by the snow-capped mountains of India, Tibet and China, and it was a botanist's paradise. Stories were told too of two legendary and dramatic places: the 'Confluence', where from the mountains the Mali Hka river crashed into a deep basin and joined the N'mai Hka (both rivers had their sources in the Himalayas) to start the Irrawaddy; and the 'Triangle', an unadministered segment of territory between two rivers in the extreme north-west, where tribes still practised head-hunting. These areas were very many days' travel from Rangoon, but the names of these remote places hung romantically over our heads from the mists of the north.

As we approached the tiny frontier outpost of Sinlumkaba, we entered thick monsoon clouds, which remained on the mountain tops for many weeks, during which I had no idea what my surroundings looked like more than a few yards from my bungalow. This was a small stone house with an open fireplace. In its little hillside garden turkeys gobbled amongst rose bushes lovingly planted by some Frontier Service officer's wife. Across a narrow gully was a small office and court-house.

No one in Sinlumkaba spoke English. My colleagues consisted of a tall, bearded Punjabi Mussulman subedar of the Frontier Force detachment, a little Chinese sub-assistant surgeon, three Kachin clerks, and a Kachin interpreter whose only other language was Burmese. My Burmese was still pretty rudimentary, but when a foreign language is one's sole means of local communication it certainly speeds up the learning process. Always attending on me I had a Kachin orderly, a policeman with a smart white Kachin turban and a hillsman's sword, adorned with scarlet cords.

Sitting in the clouds it was not possible to tour, and there was little work to do. I riffled through past files, read the history of the Kachin hills, studied Kachin customary law, and even tried an occasional case, usually on opium smuggling. The courthouse smelt strongly of the sweet cloying odour of raw opium, from the black sticky parcels seized from the smugglers. By the time the illicit opium reached Rangoon, a piece the size of a fingernail was worth almost as much as a sizeable lump on the frontier. Later on, in the plains, I was to see the emaciated and apathetic victims of opium addiction, living only for their pipes. But for some jungle peoples small pellets of opium, swallowed like pills, were an important medicine. In the most rugged parts of the hills porters used to consuming opium regularly are reported to have outmarched, with bigger loads, their brethren not so accustomed. I have myself, when attacked by dysentery in the jungle, been persuaded to try a pellet or two, and found they gave great relief. We had, of course, as children been innocently dosed with opium derivatives through Owbridge's Lung Tonic and Dr Collis Browne's Chlorodyne. The blurb accompanying the little blue bottle of the latter contained a tribute from a young ensign in the British Army, to the effect that he could never have survived the Crimean War without it.

One of the most impudent bits of smuggling on record was the occasion when smugglers hid opium in the Governor's private railway carriage, and had it transported under His Excellency's protection all the way to Rangoon.

Above all, I gloried in my local title, and wrote home proudly to my mother that I was now 'Bumdukaba of Sinlumkaba'. Bum is Kachin for mountain, and the Bumdukaba was the mountain chief.

Before long we ran out of the bread we had brought with us from Bhamo, and Wadi Maroo's test as a baker began. Full of confidence and jollity he brought in misshapen and inedible lumps. Finally, I issued an ultimatum: edible bread must be produced in one week or he must return to Bhamo. Smoke billowed from the cookhouse. One day, with the help of a bottle of Guinness, he produced a not bad-looking brown loaf. It tasted terrible. The cook's Burmese wife and my Kachin orderly took a hand, and finally, with the help of some potato, an edible loaf emerged.

Sometimes storms raged through the forest fleece of the Sinlum hills. The rainfall was prodigious. Large sections of the road down to Bhamo were swept away. Huge rocks dislodged by the heavy rain bounced down the hillside flattening trees, and looking, when the clouds finally lifted, like the footsteps of some enormous giant.

I read voraciously, every word of the crate of books I had brought up the mountain, returning again and again to old favourites like Boswell and Montaigne and Samuel Butler's notebooks. I practised my Burmese with the Kachin interpreter and cook's wife in front of my crackling fire. I grew sloppy and eccentric with my clothing, and haphazard with my mealtimes. I called for food when the fancy took me, and in the perpetual mist hardly knew what time of day it was.

I had always been a gregarious young man, fond of company and conversation. Now for the first time in my life I was more or less alone for a longish period. I was lonely to start with, but gradually, to my own surprise, I began to succumb to the real charms of solitude. I found I enjoyed my own company, that the simplest happenings of the day were interesting and amusing, and that plenty of time to read and think, even to fantasize, was a sort of luxury.

Eventually the clouds lifted. One morning I awoke to see great wooded hills close round me, and to the east the hills falling away to a valley along which ran the Chinese frontier. For 1,500 miles Burma and China are immediate neighbours. On the first day of sunshine I accompanied the subedar to a signal-point to the west, and felt right in the Frontier tradition as we heliographed the military headquarters in Bhamo to say that we were all all right, and to list the supplies we needed when the track had been repaired. I asked for a crate of Guinness. Except for Maymyo, Sinlum was the only place in my service where I found it cool enough to drink Guinness.

Before long, Robin McGuire came up on tour, accompanied by the Inspector-General of the Frontier Force, and a young English Frontier Force captain. I was delighted to see them. At the first meal after their arrival I hardly stopped talking for a second. Within twenty-four hours I had an acute nostalgia for the untroubled independence of my solitude, and wished they were all gone. My addiction to solitude has never left me. I don't know for sure, but I believe I could survive in prison for a reasonable time.

The Indian soldiers took their exercise by playing football on a small plateau. Robin McGuire and I joined them. Determined to show my prowess, I shoulder-charged my Deputy Commissioner with great vigour. He was unyielding and knobbly and my respect for him increased. The Indians did not really care for football. Every now and then one would take a wild kick and send the ball down 'the khud'. This provided at least a ten-minute respite, as the ball was fetched back, during which the stalwart jawans (young soldiers) wandered happily hand-in-hand round the field.

My visitors soon left, except for the young captain, who took up temporary residence not far from me. We were friendly enough, but he was also a solitary, and we did not spend much time together except for the odd shooting expedition. He had a large Alsatian which he trained to chase and catch wounded game, and which would mark shot birds and stand with his paw on them until his master came up. I had no dog then, but I was visited daily by a young Chow bitch from the village. She was the most beautiful dog I have ever seen: she had a thick tawny coat, golden eyes, bushy, curling tail, and was both sturdy and graceful in movement. Chows, traditional guard dogs for Chinese caravans, are notoriously savage, but this one was gentle and well-mannered, and I looked forward to her regular visits and the friendly wagging of her tail. I missed her when I left the hills. She would have wilted in the hot plains.

Before long I was left alone again, and able to start my own touring. The hills were dotted, at a day's march interval on the main track, with little two-roomed stone dak bungalows, each with an iron stove in the living-room. One in particular I remember as possessing an idyllic outdoor loo. It was festooned with honeysuckle, and sitting there with the sun shining through the open half-door shutters one could gaze over the forest to the mysterious tableland of Yunnan, just across the way. I discovered that, in days gone by, there had been a clearing out of old periodicals from the Bhamo Club, and that some of them had been distributed haphazardly through the rest bungalows in the hills. Once again I smelt the musty Victorian air of the old Empire. There were magazines from well before the First World War, with a beguiling period charm. I became intrigued with a serial about the love of a young lady for an ambitious curate, and tried to plan my tour to new places in the hope of coming across missing chapters. I still regret being transferred before I reached the dénouement.

I took my tours very much for granted. What I was doing seemed all in the day's work for a young Englishman in the Indian Empire, with nothing special about it. But in fact I was having a unique experience which I only wish I had enjoyed more consciously and more greedily.

Our tour cavalcade, which I led on a handsome black riding mule, consisted of four Kachin policemen (confident and cheerful hillmen), my cook, my clerk, my interpreter, and half a dozen Chinese muleteers, together with all my touring baggage, personal and official. My mule was tall and immensely strong and made light of the steepest and most dangerous slopes. On the level he could be persuaded into a skittish canter.

On one tour I left my razor behind and grew a reddish beard. I wore a straw coolie hat over a black oilskin cape, and more than once, riding ahead of my troop, I was mistaken for a priest by Catholic villagers and presented with infants to be blessed. I thought I might cheer them up and do no harm if I blessed them, so I did. Later, deep in the hills, I came across a genuine Catholic priest, a fine-looking young French Canadian Jesuit, with his habit tucked up over his bare legs and sandals. He astonished me by producing good coffee and a passable bottle of wine to go with our simple meal. He was a highly educated and sophisticated man, and I wondered at him burying himself in such a remote and sparsely populated area. It was, of course, true that Christian missionaries made almost no converts in the plains of Burma. The moral truths of Christianity and Buddhism are much the same. Buddhism well satisfied the moral and spiritual needs of the Burman. It was only amongst the animists of the hills, the Karens, Kachins and Chins with their primitive and fear-ridden religions, that Christianity made any real appeal. Outside many Kachin villages I still came across shrines fluttering with coloured rags and adorned with the forlorn skulls and feathers of animals sacrificed to the unpredictable spirits of Nature, often with the offering of a pot of zu, the local liquor, at their base.

The Kachins (there were getting on for half a million of them) had never been conquered by the Burmans, and the Frontier Service jealously protected their rights and customs. Much of the law was customary, and for many offences there was a traditional scale of fines, in terms of livestock or gongs. The latter – strange bronze objects, sometimes the size of a stool – were short drums with pinched-in waists. They were valued according to the number of 'frogs' modelled on them. To be fined a 'six-frog gong' or drum was a serious business. Many of the Frontier Service officers studied anthropology, and they strove to maintain the roots and customs and balances of Kachin society, and to maintain it uncorrupted and unexploited by the plains.

Some years later, during the war, I shared a bedroom for some weeks with an old bachelor artist, E.G.N. Kinch, who had devoted years of his life to teaching the Kachins. He knew both Burmans and Kachins so well that he could draw at a moment's notice, with accuracy and sympathy, any scene or activity in their lives. We used his art for illustrating the leaflets and newspapers we dropped by air over Japanese-occupied Burma. He had a cropped and grizzled head, and didn't care what clothes he wore. A man of the utmost integrity, uninterested in money or worldly success, he was perfectly happy to live like a villager.

I found him something of a trial as a room-mate. He was a chain-smoker of short black Burma cheroots, which he suspended in a small tray round his neck when he was working. His last action before going to sleep at night was to stub out his cheroot on the lid of an empty cigarette-tin by his bed; and his first action on waking was to stretch out from beneath his mosquito-net, fumble for the discarded soggy and noisome stub, and light it up to start the day.

One morning after a long silence, he burst out: 'We've got it all wrong about the hill peoples! All this concern to protect their tribal structures, and their traditional way of life, all this fancy anthropological nonsense! I believed in it for years, but I now see we were doing those peoples a disservice. When we go they must fend for themselves, and unless they can compete in the tough modern world, they will be outwitted and exploited by the Burmans! We should have pushed ahead on a much bigger scale with modern primary and secondary education all over the hills, taught them more Burmese and English and tried to make, in one generation, modern university material out of the brighter hill boys – sad to see a traditional society broken up, but it's unreal and sentimental to try to preserve it. You can't turn the clock back!'

Certainly it was a primitive society I travelled through on my tours. The many small sub-tribes had lived in mutual suspicion and in a state of war, such that villages were often built on inaccessible but easily defensible ridges. The women (many suffering from goitre through lack of iodine in the mountain water) had to struggle down the steep hillsides each day with hollow bamboo tubes to fetch water. This isolation meant that quite small groups developed their own customs and their own distinctive clothing. When under the *Pax Britannica* they gained confidence to meet in large markets, such as the famous one at Namkham, the variety of colours and costumes and headdresses, together with silver, amber and jade ornaments, was wonderfully exciting. Kachin women favoured red-and-black striped skirts, and wore lots of silver trinkets.

I wish now I had overdrawn my meagre pay and bought more in the hill markets. Amongst the cheap Western ironmongery and china, and the local vegetables and chickens and spices, were the boldly patterned, locally woven clothes and the primitive silver ornaments – such as necklace beauty sets, which included tweezers for pulling out hair, pins for piercing ears, and little spoons for removing wax from the ears. Above all, since we were not far from the main world source of jade, there were carved jade ornaments and even large uncut lumps of jade, all for sums which years later would have seemed a trifle. At the time it seemed more desirable to spend my pay on whisky, shotgun cartridges and books from England.

I came across one market rather late in the evening. Everyone involved, including the old headman, was happily tipsy on local spirit. The headman seemed rather ancient for his post; indeed, when I asked him his age he laughed uproariously, showing his blackened teeth, and said that he was one hundred and twenty-five years old! Eating breakfast in the morning, I became aware of a dejected old figure, clearly nursing a monumental hangover, squatting below the veranda. I called the interpreter to find out what he had to say. 'The headman says', explained the interpreter, 'that he is afraid he may have misled the Duwa [Chief] last night. He is told that he gave his age to the Duwa as one hundred and twenty-five. This was not true. He is, of course, only forty-nine.' His amended age seemed almost equally unbelievable, but he was clearly nervous of being asked to retire. I reassured the old man (who was very popular with his villagers and still perfectly able to fulfil his function) that his job was safe, and invited him to include me in his next party.

There were few birds and animals, except the odd troop of howling gibbon monkeys, on the eastern slopes of the hills (the Kachins with their crossbows and aconite-tipped arrows had been too busy), though on the western side towards Bhamo I once leant over a cliff-edge to watch two tigers sunning themselves, as lazy and gentle as domestic cats, on a ledge below.

The valley along which the Chinese border ran in these parts was lush after the bleak hills. I shot partridge and the larger variety of green pigeon, and bathed in a clear, fast little river. In the evening I went out with some Kachin villagers to try to catch fish with a net. The fisherman stood waist-deep in the fairly shallow stream and cast out a round net with little weights around it. He then paddled after it and felt with his toes to see if the falling net had trapped a fish on the way down. I made many clumsy and unsuccessful casts, to the great delight of the local children, but every evening I dined off delicious fresh fish. I was not yet properly kitted out as a sporting fisherman, and so missed the wonderful opportunity in this region of some of the finest mahseer fishing in Burma. The little Government resthouses had visitors' registers, and in many of these the occupants had recorded their fishing experiences and successes, with advice for those who followed.

Down in the valley markets still more varieties of tribal dresses were to be seen. I remember particularly the dark and light blue ensembles of the Shan-Tayokes (Shan Chinese) and the erect stature and handsome pale faces of the women. I imagined the pleasures and comforts of persuading one of these girls back to my lonely house in Sinlum, and exchanged long and lingering glances with one especially beautiful creature – but all sorts of righteous inhibitions stopped me. At night, over the border, we could see the glow of a burning village, the work of Chinese bandits. I was confident that the villains would not dare to cross the border to challenge the might of the British Raj. At least there was peace and order in our hills.

I was sorry that my brief stay in the post did not coincide with one of the famous Frontier meetings. Every three or four years British Frontier officers met in the valley with their Chinese opposite members to sort out trans-frontier disputes and cases. It was quite an event. The British team took with them a smart detachment of the Frontier Force, and a pipe band. They regaled the Chinese with whisky and champagne. The Chinese also had an escort of soldiers, and a cacophonous brass band, and regaled the British with, amongst other delights, tankards full of *crème de menthe*. Frontier officers with the hardest heads were chosen for this meeting. One ex-Marine officer with a head like teak was reported never to have failed to make his side of the case prevail. The Chinese magistrates just could not keep up with him.

The Frontier Service was not like the ICS recruited in London by open competition exam, but by personal interviews, and it contained a wide variety of eccentrics, mostly passionately devoted to their tribesmen. One officer entranced me with his description of accompanying a military column on a punitive expedition into the Wa States, to try to stop the local head-hunting. The head-hunting tribes were known as the Wild Was, as opposed to the more pacific Tame Was. Always interested in medical matters, he had been nervous of suffering deficiency diseases from living solely on dry rations in the long trek through the barren hills, so he arranged to take along with him a mule with a 'window-box' slung on each side, which was carefully watered daily. In these boxes he grew rotating crops of mustard and cress, and each night cut himself a regular ration of fresh green stuff. He afterwards became a successful homeopathic practitioner in Dublin, and an expert in interpreting the magic Black Box.

Frontier Service officers were to serve with great courage and determination in their hills during the Second World War against the Japanese probing up from the plains. Noel

Stevenson and John Leyden (the real Bumdukaba of Sinlumkaba) with the Kachins; Norman Kelly, with his massive brass-bound 'staff of office'; and Philip Barton with the Chins, and many others endured great hardships in their stout defence against the Japanese, and everywhere kept the loyalty of their tribesmen.

Camping in the open one evening on the heights, I lay in rough Army blankets, smelling the comforting smell of woodsmoke, listening to the tinkling of mule-bells in the dark, and looking at the brilliant stars above. My father had told me that whenever he was worried and depressed by life he would go out for a good long look at the stars. He would think of some of the distances involved, and of the whole pattern of the universe. Pretty soon, he said, the things which were worrying him seemed unimportant; before long *anything* which could happen to him, an infinitesimal speck on one small planet, seemed to matter not at all. The Victorian B.L. Taylor got it right in his verse:

> When men are calling names and making faces,
> And all the world's a-jangle and ajar,
> I meditate on interstellar spaces,
> And smoke a mild seegar.

As I gazed at the eastern galaxy wheeling above me I could see what my father meant about bringing things into proportion. But what happened to me still seemed of importance, at least to me! I thought of the prospect of war, and wondered where in the world it might be possible for people to avoid the conflict. I supposed that life would go on undisturbed in the islands of the Pacific; perhaps in the fjords of Norway; certainly up here in the North-East Frontier of Burma battles would never reach. By the end of the Second World War fearful struggles had been waged in all these places. I was seeing these hills in conditions which would never be quite the same again.

3 In Charge

Headquarters

My next post was at Pyinmana, a small town half-way up Burma, in the Yamethin district, and as officer in charge of a Sub-Division life began in earnest for me. My bungalow was a dark, unfurnished, wooden building on stilts. Upstairs there was a living-room, a veranda, two bedrooms and two bathrooms. No vehicles could approach the front door, as a culvert on the path had collapsed. When I asked the then DC, Colonel Batten, for funds to repair it, he was incredulous. 'When I was your age,' he exploded, 'I lived all the year round in a tent. Now you have a watertight teak bungalow of your own, and you ask for money to primp up your bloody drive!'

In this accommodation, as in all houses officials lived in during their service, I was in fact 'camping' for what I knew would be a limited period. The other day I reckoned up that, apart from the cottage in Herefordshire to which I have now retired, I had not lived more than three years in any one house since I was born. It never worried me, but this sort of gipsy life saddened many wives and even some men. It was no new sensation for Government officials. Arthur Waley's translation of a poem by Po Chü-i, written in AD 825 when the poet was Governor of Soochow, starts wistfully:

> A Government building, not my own home,
> A Government garden, not my own trees.

Unlike many officers, he looked ahead:

> But at Lo-yang I have a small house,
> And on the Wei river I have built a thatched hut....

If I retire, I have somewhere to end my days.

When I first moved in, all I inherited in the way of furniture was a vast double bed with a cross-webbing base. Otherwise I imported one of everything – one chair, one table, one tin tub, one 'thunderbox', even one table-knife, -fork and -spoon, and the necessary bedding. The bathroom had a large Ali Baba type pottery jar, called a Pegu jar, for holding cold bathing water, and a tin scoop. Later I added a few more things, but not many. If I invited people back to eat, somehow my servants on their own produced the crockery and cutlery and food for as many people as appeared at whatever hour.

As a solitary bachelor I was served by a Burmese bearer, my friend and companion Maung Shway Ba, a cook, a cook's boy, a jamadar for sanitary duties and carrying the kerosene tins of hot water for my bath, an Indian syce for my two ponies, and later, when I sank to the decadence of running a car, a driver. Also at my disposal when their services were needed, were a washerman, a tailor, a 'grass-cut' for the ponies' fodder, and a gardener for my largely non-existent garden. Such large staffs of servants, on comparatively low rates of pay, were the local form of social security, with custom providing the 'job separation' imposed by trade-union regulations in England. Each servant maintained a family and other relations, so the compound was a pretty busy area. I moved nowhere in Burma without Shway Ba, who always saw that I had clean clothes of the right sort, never let me travel without my bedding roll and mosquito-net, and who advised me as a brother on all aspects of life. When I came back from India to Burma after the years of Japanese occupation, I found Shway Ba waiting to resume his duties. He told me that on one occasion he had heard of a British plane which had crashed in his district, carrying four officers in uniform and one man in a dinner-jacket. Fearful that the one in the dinner-jacket might be me, he had walked 50 miles to check.

As SDO Pyinmana Sub-Division, I was in charge of a large area, and in my way responsible for everything that happened in it. An ICS officer was never really off duty – a ride through the fields meant keeping an eye open for the state of the crops, a drink on the veranda in the evening could be interrupted by some Burmese visitor with troubles to unload. 'Always be accessible', we were instructed, in the Mogul tradition. I was ex-officio Chairman of the Pyinmana Municipality and of the Pyinmana Hospital Committee. I was Sub-Divisional Magistrate, and Sub-Divisional Officer (responsible for administration and revenue matters). I also captained the team at the bottom of the Pyinmana football league. Rather proud of myself as a footballer, I thought I could help this failure of a team out of the basement. My Anglo-Burmese friend, 'Bull' Kiernander, a well-known all-round sportsman, if getting a little old for football, joined me. All the other members of the team were young Burmans. We fought some valiant battles – but by the end of the season were exactly where we started, at the bottom of the league.

The next year I played for Pyinmana's representative team in the great Upper Burma football trophy, the Ruby Merchants' Shield. The other Englishman in the team, Leo Edgerley, an assistant in the Government Forest Service, had been brought up in India and Burma by his father, who had been an NCO in the British Army. He was a natural athlete and ball-game player; if he had been given an opportunity in England he could have represented his university at three or four sports. Older than I, he was one of the best men I have known and the gentlest of critical glances from him would pull me up short if I seemed to be going off the rails.

Our team, otherwise all Burmans, with Edinburgh-trained Dr Ba Than as dodgy inside left, battled through to the Finals in Mandalay. A good deal of the travelling expenses and entertainment costs were borne by two jovial Chinese shopkeepers, who always accompanied us on away matches, and lay laughing with us on the floor of our railway carriage as the train pulled out, to showers of bottles from disgruntled supporters of defeated teams. We lost our Mandalay match, but I remember that season with great pleasure.

The Burmese for 'glass' is 'hman', and from my early footballing days in Pyinmana I was known to the Burmans as 'U Hman'. Fortunately for me this also meant 'Mr True'.

Burmans knew how to handle life. While I was at Pyinmana, King George V died. A solemn-faced Burmese gentleman in silks and pink gaung baung came to condole with me in my capacity as the King-Emperor's local representative. 'Don't you think, sir,' he said, 'we should do something to show our respect for the late King-Emperor?'

'What had you in mind, U Pay Tun?'

'Well, sir, what about an open-air lunch for 200 leading citizens – chicken curry and beer?'

'Splendid idea.'

Of all the mourning ceremonies throughout the Empire I dare say Pyinmana had the jolliest. Eulogies were pronounced, toasts drunk, and the King-Emperor affectionately remembered in the most respectful spirit. Those were the days when many 'subject peoples' were proud of belonging to a world Empire of such apparent stability, prosperity, power and glamour. It gave them some extra dimension and status in the world. The symbolism of the Crown attracted a much deeper loyalty from many of the King's Eastern subjects than it is now fashionable to admit.

The next year, Jim Lindop, the Deputy Commissioner, invited all the senior officials of Yamethin, the District Headquarters, to come to his bungalow to hear King Edward VIII's abdication speech. This was a station where almost all the officials were Burmans, Anglo-Burmans or Indians. They sat round the wireless set in silence, and as the speech ended there were tears running down several cheeks. Partly I suppose the Burmese, with their monarchist and romantic traditions, were moved by the drama of a king giving up his throne for love. Partly there was in their sorrow some of the emptiness felt worldwide when Jack Kennedy was killed. In each case a young, bright and hopeful leader was lost to us.

If I had any doubt as to whether I was on my own and really responsible, I had this soon put at rest. Pyinmana Sub-Division was the constituency of Dr Ba Maw, the Burmese Prime Minister and the leading politician of his day. Soon after I arrived, rival political party meetings generated into open clashes, and violence looked as if it would get worse. Being new and inexperienced, and aware that there might be repercussions if things went wrong in the Prime Minister's home territory, I thought I had better telephone my DC, Jim Lindop, in Yamethin. After I had described the crisis I expected the DC to say that he would collect the District Superintendent of Police and be with me as soon as he could. Instead, 'What's the matter?' said a cold voice. 'Can't you manage?'

'Oh yes, sir, I can manage,' I hurried to reply, and put down the phone with a feeling of exhilaration. This was what the ICS meant. I really was in charge, and expected to manage on my own. I managed, without disaster, and gained a confidence that a lesser boss would not have let me gain.

Jim Lindop, with an MC and bar from the First World War, was the beau idéal of a Deputy Commissioner. A slight, lean, brown man with a close-cropped moustache, and eyes which squinted in the sunlight, he was a sportsman and naturalist. He was one of those whose observations and records made possible the beautiful book, *The Birds of Burma*, compiled by two British Forest Officers. The coloured plates of this book, painted by Lt-Commander Hughes of the Burma Navy, are said to have been lost in the Japanese invasion, making the book a collector's item. Jim Lindop delighted in touring and making contact with the most remote parts of his charge. Efficient, even a bit hard, he set exacting standards. When I was given a large farewell party by many Burmese friends on my eventual departure from Pyinmana, he was not particularly impressed. In his book popularity had in it a somewhat suspect element. He would have agreed with Confucius. When Tuan-Mu Tz'u inquired, 'What do you say of a man who is liked by all his townsfolk?' the Master replied, 'It is better that the good people of the town like him, and the bad dislike him.' He carried out conscientiously the instructions of the Government, but could not conceal his distaste for the inefficiencies, the hypocrisy and the corruption of the sort of 'parliamentary democracy' through which we were gradually devolving authority to the Burmese. Jim and his staunch and attractive Scots wife, Janet, both in their second marriage, were a wonderfully well-suited couple. Their mutual understanding extended to making them by local standards a devastating pair of bridge partners. They were both unfailingly kind to me.

I met Dr Ba Maw before long, on a visit to his constituents. Like other passionate nationalists, such as de Valera, he was reputed to have the blood of another nationality in him, perhaps Armenian. With a pale, long elegant face, he was not typically Burmese. Something of a dandy, he wore a velvet cap of his own design pulled down over one eye. He was a PhD of the University of Bordeaux, had been called to the Bar in England, and spoke excellent English. He first came into prominence as a lawyer defending Saya San, the leader of the 1930 Burma Rebellion in the Tharrawaddy district. The dignity of my official call on him at the Pyinmana dak bungalow was somewhat spoiled by the appearance from his bedroom of my mongrel puppy carrying one of his gold slippers. But with his good manners the Prime Minister ignored the incident and we talked of district affairs.

A few years later he was to become Adipadi, or Leader of the Burmese people in the Japanese occupation. To British eyes he was a Quisling, or at least a Pétain. Whatever his motives, when the Japanese were defeated his political career was finished. I do not think he was in serious touch with the Japanese before the war; I believe he was working for Burmese Independence on the same lines as Indian politicians. It may have been his vanity and opportunism which led him to become Adipadi, but he had brains and ingenuity and maybe the Burmese could have done much worse at that critical time than have a puppet leader of his ability.

'Galone' U Saw (the galone is a mythical dragon-bird used as a symbol by the rebels in 1931), the other leading politician who used to pass through Pyinmana, and another future Prime Minister, was much less civilized and a more buccaneering type, who came himself from the notoriously tough district of Tharrawaddy. He was in appearance much more obviously a true Burman – thickset, jovial and confident. When I called on him in his official carriage on the train, he greeted me cheerfully.

'Hullo, Glass. Have a drink!'

'What can I have, sir?'

'Well, I am drinking my own special drink – rum and monkey's blood. I had the monkeys killed down the line for me. Excellent potency qualities!'

'May I have a whisky, sir?'

Unlike Ba Maw, and some other political leaders, U Saw was not one of the Western-educated and travelled élite but an indigenous product, son of a provincial Burman landowner and of limited educational qualifications. Hedging his bets, or rather willing to use anyone to achieve nationalist objectives, he was eventually shut up by the British in the war for corresponding with the Japanese.

Burma was a country virtually without class. The Prime Minister's brother might be a simple cultivator. There was little 'colour' feeling. The Burman did not suffer from an inferiority complex – he quite naturally thought himself as good a man as anyone, which made for relaxed and easy relationships. It is true that Burmese self-confidence was not always justified. I remember taking on a lugale, a second servant. He was an engaging young man with a carefree air.

'Can you drive a car?' I asked him.

'Yes, Thakin.'

'Well, here are the keys. Move my car round to the back, will you?'

Moments later I heard an ominous noise, and ran out to find my car half-way up a tree.

'I thought you said you could drive a car, Maung Tin. Have you ever driven a car before?'

'No, Thakin.'

'Then what made you say you could drive a car?'

'Thakin' (with a beaming smile) '*anyone* can drive a car!'

Any ICS officer had to work hard and there was little time to spare. An early arrival at the court-house, a long, two-storeyed teak building with verandas at both levels, signalled to the Bench clerk to go outside to the waiting petitioners and shout 'Shaukhlwa! Shaukhlwa!', which means 'Petitions'. I then heard a variety of requests and complaints. In response to some I could advise legal remedies, to others I promised to initiate inquiries; but in many cases – long, rambling stories of obscure injustices and family quarrels – there was nothing I could do. However, I suppose it did the petitioners good to get their grievances off their chests.

I remember one petition, written in English. 'Your Honour, Maung Maung has threatened to kill me, to beat me, and to slap my cheek whenever I am out from my house. I beg to inform Your Honour that I am not a man who can stay at home always.' I recall too a charming First Information Report from a young Burman police officer: 'Sir, I beg to report that last night, whilst the moon was wearing her silver shoon, six buggers attacked the police station.'

After the 'Petitions' I mounted the Bench as Magistrate (Class 1) and tried cases of cattle theft, assault, fraud, rape, affray (even committal cases for murder) – country crimes throughout the ages.

The more violent and important crimes like murder and dacoity had to be submitted to the Sessions Court. It was a strange thing that in Buddhist Burma, where theoretically all life was sacred, there was a high incidence of murder. In a population of 15 million, there were some 900 murders a year. Every Burmese peasant carried a sort of machete called a dah. This had a keen enough edge to sharpen a pencil, and was heavy enough to chop down a sapling. It was primarily an all-purpose tool and agricultural implement. When, particularly at the torrid end of the hot weather, tempers were high, quarrels broke out very quickly amongst the excitable Burmese, sometimes over gambling and cock-fights, and sometimes over the most trivial matters. A quick whack over the head with a dah would bring the bickering to tragedy. In fact, we hardly regarded these unpremeditated killings as important crimes.

The peaks of crime in Burma, naturally enough, were between harvest and ploughing, and again between transplanting and harvest. The most serious crimes were dacoities, armed robberies by gangs of four or more men, which were endemic in Burma and carried out with savage cruelty. It was as if in an era of peace young bucks needed some excitement to reaffirm their 'machismo'. Sometimes dacoit bands were led by a chief or boh, who acquired the legendary notoriety of Ned Kelly or Billy the Kid.

One legal device, available to magistrates, would no doubt offend the English Council of Civil Liberties. This was the application of Section 110 of the Penal Code. According to this section, if a magistrate were satisfied by evidence that a man was widely regarded as a bad and criminal character, he could bind the man over for a period of time to be of good behaviour and could require him to produce two sureties for a suitable sum. These sums were usually small, and when there was difficulty in finding anyone to risk a few rupees on the accused, the magistrate could feel reasonably sure the man was indeed a luzo, a rascal.

Talking to a Burmese headman after the war, a friend of mine asked him how he had found the Japanese. 'First class', was the surprising answer. 'They came into my village, asked me to point out the worst rogues and trouble-makers, lined them up and cut their heads off. The Japs understood the Burman much better than the British, with their court cases and laws of evidence.'

Hearing the same story, with roughly the same main vocabulary, told in court in many different ways by different witnesses, did wonders for my Burmese language study. And I learnt one unexpected lesson: catching a witness out in a lie did not necessarily mean that the main tenor of his story was false; the temptation to embellish the truth was often too much. But it was hot and muggy in the court-room, and the cases were often long and dreary.

One morning I was so infuriated by the inefficiency and ignorance of the law of the young Burmese police prosecuting officer that I literally 'threw the book at him', the book being *The Laws of Evidence*, and knocked him back into his chair. That night I lay awake, ashamed of my behaviour. The next morning before the case started I told the young man I was sorry and that the best way I could make amends was to let him throw the book at *me*. He hesitated at assaulting the Magistrate, but finally let me have it full in the chest. We then shook hands, I mounted the Bench, and we proceeded amicably with the case.

Bench work over, I had an early 'brunch', and then struggled with files, many of them revenue cases. After tea was the hour of exercise, sacred throughout the Indian empire, which consisted of riding, polo practice or tennis. The small Pyinmana Club was much the same as that in Monywa. It had two tennis-courts, tables with the *Illustrated London News*, the *Sporting and Dramatic*, *The Bystander* and *Punch*, a little library with a small consignment of new books received each month from 'home', several bridge-tables, a battered billiard-table, a bar and a moth-eaten Indian butler. There the European community met every afternoon or evening. Most of us came from the same middle-class English background (though there were throughout the services a big contingent of Scots and Irish, and a few Welsh), and nearly all our jobs were interwoven. Within the limits of individual human prickliness we were comfortable with each other.

The European community in the East was permanently unbalanced. We rarely saw children between the ages of seven and seventeen, and equally rarely men or women over fifty-five.

But one cold weather Tim Healy, our Sessions Judge, had his mother and father out to stay from Ireland. Tim's father was a retired barrister, with a dignified white moustache, while his mother was a dominating and ample lady, whose skill at bridge soon showed us up as mere tyros. One evening this elderly couple were taken out for a drive beside the river. Both were delightfully old-fashioned and set off in full semi-Victorian fig. Mrs Healy was wearing a large picture hat and carrying a parasol. By chance at that time Aspinall, a local Bombaing manager, was returning to Pyinmana from a long tour. When he reached the river, hot and dusty, he decided to swim across it, wearing only his topi, and then walk along the shore to collect his clothes at the bridge. Rounding a bluff an unexpected meeting took place. The nude Aspinall, by nature a punctilious man with a strict regard for the conventional, raised his topi and murmured 'Good evening' in a polite tone. Mrs Healy graciously inclined her head. Aspinall walked on.

That evening at the Club Mrs Healy commented, 'We met a charming man with a fair moustache by the river this evening.' Only later did we hear the full story.

Most of the young Forest men were a tough bunch. One of the Steel Brothers' Forest Assistants in Pyinmana was Verney Lovatt-Campbell. He had the pale, taut look of an overtrained athlete, and his hobby was riding unridable horses. Consequently, he had over the years broken a great many bones. He had also managed to be mauled by a tiger. Later he was involved in a fracas with Burmese armed with dahs, badly slashed and left for dead. In the war, fighting with the Chinese, he was blown up by a booby-trapped mine. After the war, in Kenya, he broke some more bones riding, and, almost inevitably it would seem, he was badly mauled by a lion. I doubt if any living man had a greater variety of scars, and none of his friends was surprised when he finally became the subject of a special article in *The Lancet* on the theme of what the human body can survive.

The contingent from the Bombaing chummery owned an ancient Rolls-Royce limousine, once the property of some long-dead governor, in which they creaked their way down to the Club. Theirs was a comradeship which had something regimental about it. All of us took illness in a pretty matter-of-fact way. Anti-typhoid inoculation was, of course, compulsory, and there were special and unpleasant shots for cholera and plague if these threatened. When dead rats warned of bubonic plague in Pyinmana a mass-inoculation campaign was launched, and I went down to the middle of the bazaar to have my own inoculation in public, to encourage the townspeople to follow. But malaria, dengué fever, sand-fly fever, prickly heat, dysentery, both amoebic and bacillary (all of which I suffered at one stage or another), we took more or less as a matter of course. I was playing bridge once with three friends in the Bombaing chummery, when my partner suddenly started to shake with the icy ague that was the onset of malaria. 'Sorry', he chattered, withdrawing to his bedroom to prepare with quinine and blankets for the temperature of 104 or 105 degrees which might follow. Rather irritated, we went off to search for another player.

Our pets were at risk, too. My first dog, a large, ungainly, brindled mixture of Labrador and Pegu hound, died of hookworm. A later Springer bitch died of suspected rabies, and I was subjected to the interminable series of Pasteur injections. My first polo pony died of anthrax and its corpse had to be burnt. But many such animals lived to a ripe old age without mishap, and to many a lonely man his horses and dogs were a lifeline.

Close understanding often developed. Old Ebden had had a little fox-terrier bitch in India which astonished me. One day when he was playing golf with my sister, who owned an undisciplined Airedale, her dog ran ahead and her approach shot hit him, and then bounced off into the hole. Ebden's face did not change. He murmured something to his little dog, Bint, whereupon she picked up his ball, trotted forward, and demurely dropped it into the hole. All square.

At the headquarters of the district, Yamethin in the north, there resided a District Superintendent of Police who was perhaps the most famous policeman in Burma. Mr Xavier was an Anglo-Burman with some Goanese connections. Large, brown and fat, he talked Burmese perfectly and thought like a Burman – so he could outthink and outguess the Burmese criminals in a way no English officer could. At the time of the Burma rebellion he had understood the mentality of the rebels better than anyone, and it was to him that many surrendered in 1931. It was rumoured that some of his methods of interrogation had a Burmese flavour, and he was greatly feared by all luzos or bad men. He had a flair for detective work and prided himself on knowing everything that went on in his district.

One of his very rare errors was when he reported to Jim Lindop that I was in danger of being trapped into marriage by an Anglo-Indian girl with a somewhat chequered past and with whom I had been involved in a car accident. I admired the lady's bold good looks, and her courage and good sense over the accident, but Xavier's informers had for once misled him. We had had very little to do with each other. She afterwards married an English businessman with an almost equally colourful record, and I last saw her in Calcutta, waiting cheerfully and loyally for her man to come out of prison, where he had temporarily landed.

Two of my Burmese friends in Pyinmana were local lawyers. One, very tall and heavily built for a Burman, was a senior and respected citizen. Once when I was taking evidence in a village in a case in which he represented the defendant, he towered over me as I sat at a camp-table in so dominating a manner that I was greatly relieved to get back to Pyinmana. There, on the raised dais of my Magistrate's Bench, I could psychologically reaasert my authority as 'the man on the horse'. He was always warning me against my other friend, a younger lawyer called U Pe Khin, who was of much lower grade and accepted unreliability. But the latter was the most amusing and volatile of companions. Together we organized football competitions, schoolboys' boxing-matches and tennis tournaments and had a great deal of useful fun. Through him I got to know some of the more prominent of the rather exclusive Chinese community and first developed my liking for Chinese food – one of the world's great cuisines.

Alas, in the end my pompous mentor was right. My pal decamped, leaving a Burmese tennis-club with considerable debts, which I as President of the club had somehow to settle. I can still see his rakish, humorous face, with his gaung baung tilted on one side of his head as he enthusiastically proposed some new venture.

Pyinmana housed not only the Burma Forest Department's

main depot and museum (Burma had the biggest Forest Department in the world) but an important Agricultural Department Research Centre, and a big experimental vegetable farm run by 'Boh' Case, the famous American Baptist missionary. Little did 'Boh' Case imagine, in those peaceful days, that his vegetables would be used to feed the Chinese Army defending Toungoo against the Japanese in 1942.

When years later I worked in the UK Delegation at the United Nations, and became familiar with the work of the UN Development Agency, with its highly paid experts staying on overseas assignment for comparatively short periods, advising the Third World in agriculture and technology, I thought of the dedicated lifetimes of work put into such development by my colleagues in Burma. Angus Maclean, of the Agricultural Department, whose kind and motherly wife mourned infants buried in Pyinmana cemetery, had spent years perfecting a new strain of sugar-cane especially suited for Burmese farmers. Mitchell and Pfaff of the Veterinary Service evolved the first anti-anthrax vaccine for elephants. The Foresters were amongst the world's leading authorities on conservation and re-afforestation of tropical forests. In so many fields, education, roads and railways, medical services, irrigation and agriculture, the British administration improved life for many Burmese. There was something in Kipling's view of the British Empire as a giant 'technical consultancy'.

The Pyinmana court-house was guarded by a small Burmese section of Burma Military Police. One day as I passed their guard post, I saw the Naik and his three soldiers far off down the steps, watching a passing wedding procession. For some reason Burmese music 'on the move' became more Westernized. Brass-band instruments were often used, and the most popular tune was a curious oriental version of 'The Belle of New York', closely followed by a rhythmic rendering of 'Nick, Nack Paddywhack, Give a Dog a Bone'. Western culture has left some odd footprints round the world. After my friend John Russell had presented his credentials as British Ambassador to the Emperor Haile Selassie in Addis Ababa, the imperial band struck up an Ethiopian version of a rousing and strangely familiar tune.

'What's the name of that tune?' the Ambassador asked the resplendent bandmaster.

'"Bollocks", Your Excellency, "and the Same to You"!' said the bandmaster, saluting respectfully, and giving the British troops' version of 'Colonel Bogey'.

To return to Pyinmana, enjoying the fun and smoking cheroots, the four Military Policemen had left their four rifles in a heap outside their hut. Shocked at this unmilitary behaviour, I scooped up the rifles and took them to my office. Their CO, a Sandhurst-trained Burman officer, Captain Tun Hla Oung, who arrived that evening, was an excellent professional soldier who spoke the English of his fellow-professionals and he was very cross with his men. But he hinted delicately that I had gone too far in retaining their rifles. This had been such a great blow to their pride that I had perhaps put myself in some danger.

The Burmese temperament is not ideally suited to regular peacetime soldiering. The Burmans can be as brave as lions, and they are intelligent, quick and adaptable, and good mechanics – but the grind of daily discipline bores them. The Military Policemen's defence had been a simple one. Times were peaceful, and they knew that no one was going to attack the court-house.

In New Delhi in wartime an over-zealous security officer dressed up in Nazi uniform, complete with Hitler moustache, to test the security of Indian sentries round GHQ. He gained easy admission without a pass. The Indian sentry brought to book for this, said simply, 'But I knew it was a British officer-sahib!' Unanswerable.

Years later, wondering what the British had left behind in India, I was reassured to read of an Indian general who had been put in charge of the North Korean prisoners in the Korean War. 'General,' asked an American journalist, 'what would you do if all the prisoners linked arms, sat on the ground, and refused to move?'

The general stroked his moustache. His answer was sensible, pragmatic, and genuinely British. 'Search me, old boy!' he said.

Touring

It was a great joy to get out of the Headquarters town into the countryside for a day's shooting, or on fairly lengthy tours of inspection.

Not infrequently in Pyinmana I had to battle with files after dinner in the evening. If the mounds of files became too menacing, I went off for a couple of days to a little bungalow in the foothills, and really tore into the paper from dawn till dusk. Neat piles of files on my left were dealt with and flung higgledy-piggledy on the floor on my right, whence my clerks packed them back into office boxes. Exhausted at the day's end, I would climb up the nearest foothill to clear my brain and try to bag a jungle fowl before dusk fell.

Shooting was indeed one of the great relaxations and pleasures of life in those days. Hardly anyone had the time to organize big-game shooting, though occasionally a Forest officer, in response to villagers' appeals, sat up for a tiger. Mostly it was a bunch of friends having a day in the fresh air with a picnic and some sport after jungle fowl, partridge, snipe, duck or the little barking deer called gyi.

It would still be dark when we assembled and the early morning air sharp. The village beaters, ragged blankets round their heads and shoulders, would be squatting by the embers of a fire, sharing puffs on a large white cheroot and clearing their throats. As we started in single file through the jungle, the sky would begin to lighten and the village cocks crow behind us. In front was the morning mist, drops of moisture decorating the cobwebs which everywhere covered the grasses. We would talk little and quietly. Occasional rustles on either side of the narrow track marked birds or animals scurrying off. We would think with excitement of what sport the day might bring.

So began a typical day's shooting. A whiff of gunpowder from an empty shotgun cartridge still brings back to me good memories, of the 'squark' of a startled snipe, of the explosive 'whirr' of a rising partridge, and of the clatter of wings of a jungle cock bursting, a blaze of colour, from the trees.

Colonel Batten, who was briefly DC Yamethin, was the hero of a real *Blackwood's* shooting story. At a shoot up in Myitkyina, in the far north, he had been loaded with No. 6, but slipped some heavy slugs into one barrel when he heard a commotion among the beaters that he thought might mean a pig. The next bird to fly out was an unexpected woodsnipe, which he shot. Then something heavy burst through the undergrowth, not a pig but a full-grown young tiger. As it raced by, he rather rashly let go with his second barrel, though successfully. When he met the others at the end of the beat to discuss their bag, he confessed modestly to 'rather an unusual right and left'.

I do not think that, throughout my time in Pyinmana, I had more than a couple of days off inside the district, except on Sunday. But one of the days is still clear in my memory. Some Burmese friends invited me to go down the little river on our eastern boundary on a raft. The sun was bright, the air cool and soft, we paddled slowly under the trees, landing occasionally for a shot at green pigeon or jungle fowl, drinking cold beer and talking and joking. Flights of bright emerald-green parakeets flashed through the orange-red blossom of the 'flame of the forest'. Towards evening we came to a remote village where we were made cheerfully welcome. Near the village the river seemed to slope down in a glassy green glissade, and in this stretch it was the local practice to fish, standing up to one's waist in the water, with a long bamboo pole and a comparatively short line, from which dangled a barbless hook baited with a live grasshopper. When the insect was dropped on the water, from time to time this lured a short, powerful fish with a large head. The trick was then to jerk the pole over one's head, and the fish flew through the air and landed yards away on the grass. We spent a successful hour at this sport. Our catch, grilled on an open fire, provided one of the courses of our dinner. The stars came out, the villagers sat round the fire with us, and we talked of crops and ghosts. We seemed miles away from the urban worries and corruptions of Pyinmana. More and more bottles of beer were opened. I felt an enormous affection for everyone sitting in the firelight. I recall thinking, what a wonderful day! I wonder if I shall remember it when I am old? Shall I be able to recapture the happiness of this day?

Touring was, of course, the great way to get to know the country and the people. When I could get away from the office I would set off on my pony, with my Bench clerk on a smaller Burmese pony, and we would ride in leisurely fashion across the country, looking at crops and stopping at the villages. There we would confer with the headman, look at his registers to check births, deaths and vaccinations, and serious diseases of men and cattle, to see what strangers had passed through, and listen to his pleas for Government help with a road or a bridge, or river-training. When, for example, a riverside village was being eroded by a loop in the river, George Cheyne, the River Training officer, a man with the biggest calf muscles I have ever seen, would come striding in. With the willing help of the villagers the river would be realigned by the simplest of methods. A series of bamboo-mat screens by the threatened bank would induce the corner to silt up, while his practised eye saw the spot to make a small cutting early on the curve, where the force of the river seemed straightest and strongest. At first flood the water would sweep down this cutting and plough through a new course for the river away from the village. The total cost was negligible.

We did not have much money, but what we had we used very economically. For a village needing a bridge I would wheedle free timber from the Forest Department, on condition that the villagers supplied the labour to build the bridge, under expert supervision. They did this willingly, and proudly referred to the bridge as 'Our Bridge'. This sort of co-operation would be transformed by politicians in speeches in Rangoon into 'iniquitous imposition of the corvée'.

Headmen often had land revenue problems to discuss. A regular duty of a District Officer at harvest time was to deal with applications for remission of land revenue. This required riding through the fields, and consultation with local elders about the extent of damage to crops by flood, insects or diseases, and assessment of the percentage by which the harvest would fall short of the average yield for that class of soil. Sometimes the application was obviously a try-on. Sometimes the forlorn fields clearly merited full remission. Like many aspects of British administration, it was a fair system, humanely and impartially applied.

I became a less and less self-conscious horseman as riding became the natural means of locomotion. Swimming the pony across a stream, scrambling her down steep banks, I was not trying to master an art, or to prove anything; I was just trying to get somewhere. I am not a romantic about horses, but the combined smell of the sweat of a healthy horse and leather saddlery is almost as ancient and evocative a scent as woodsmoke. Occasionally I rode a Burmese tat. These tough little horses, not more than twelve hands high, were trained to a strange flowing gait called the athagya, or amble. Sitting on a stiff, decorated Burmese saddle, one stuck one's legs straight out each side in primitive stirrups, clung firmly to ornamental, rope-like reins and whirled along.

It was often the custom in Upper Burma for a headman to accompany a touring officer to the boundaries of his charge, where the next headman took over. Pattering along the baked kazins (the raised paddy-field boundaries) with a mounted escort of brightly clothed Burmans, all going hell for leather, gave one a great feeling of excitement and importance. At some villages it was the practice of the villagers, glad of an excuse for a bit of fun, to come out to welcome senior touring officers with their local band and dancers.

If it could not be avoided, I travelled on a bullock-cart. Passengers were provided with a mat, perched on a deep bed of straw, which acted as primitive springs. With one wheel often much higher than the other, on the high-baked sides of deep ruts, it was a vilely uncomfortable way to travel. Bullock-cart drivers like their wheels to squeak and squeal, as they believed when travelling at night these noises kept away 'ghoulies and ghosties'. The driver guided his bullocks by twisting their tails or prodding them with a small stick with constant cries of 'Hey nwa!' ('Hey, bullock!'). Once I had a ride in a racing bullock-cart drawn by two magnificent white racing bulls. Their owner cherished them as a motorist cherishes his Rolls-Royce. At intervals we stopped, he dismounted, filled his mouth with water from a pot by his side, and blew a fine moist spray into the nostrils of his darlings to clear them of dust.

We were always hospitably received by the villagers, and offered tea or fresh coconut milk. The most hygienic way to drink the latter was from a hole in the nut, sucked through the hollow of a freshly cut papaya stem. Sometimes I tried a simple case under the trees, and everywhere I talked with the village elders on whatever concerned them at the time.

In the evening we would catch up with the bullock-carts carrying our baggage, which had left very early in the morning. A tent would be ready, or cloths strung round the side of a zayat, a sort of rest platform for travellers. Then a bath in a tin tub, with a couple of dozen entranced children watching this comic interlude; a solitary dinner under an Aladdin lamp; more talks with local villagers; and an early bed.

Once in a village I came across a ramshackle travelling cinema show. The showman was screening a streaky and tattered version of one of the great films of all time, *King Kong*. The epic of the great ape did not require translation or explanation. The villagers squatted spellbound. To their magic and legend-haunted minds the story must have appeared marvellous, but credible. But such outside entertainment was rare indeed.

Sometimes in the evening I joined a group of village youths in their national game of chin-lone, or caneball. The ball, about half the size of a soccer ball, was woven in open-work bamboo-cane, and was very light. Standing in a circle with their skirts tucked up to free their bare legs, the players strove to keep the ball from touching the ground. Every part of the body could be used except the hand and elbow, and extra marks were earned by difficult manoeuvres like kicking the ball from behind one's back, whirling round off the ground and catching the ball a kick before it dropped. I had rather fancied myself as a soccer player, but amongst these graceful, acrobatic (and tolerant) youths I was plain clumsy. I could often keep the ball off the ground and pass it on to the next player, but that was very elementary stuff.

Never in all my tours did I carry a personal weapon; nor was I received by the villagers other than with great courtesy and friendliness. Once, after I had presented the prizes at a small village school, three venerable old men approached hesitantly from the back. 'They want to tell you something remarkable,' explained my Bench clerk. 'When you were speaking, they all three saw a blue light shining from the top of your head. This is a very auspicious sign.' I laughed. 'Do not laugh, sir,' said Ba Aye. 'These gentlemen are serious. We Burmans believe in such things.' 'Do Bama' – 'We Burmans' – was a phrase often heard; the Burmans had a strong sense of their national identity. Goodness knows what the old gentlemen saw – but so far, touch wood, I have had a remarkably lucky life.

Burmese village houses were simple in design and furnishing. The big main rooms, for living and sleeping, were walled with matting of plaited bamboo and stood on stilts. Underneath roamed pigs, dogs and chickens. The small compounds were swept clean, and decorated by a few shrubs of scarlet hibiscus, oleander or jasmine planted in empty kerosene tins. The whole village would be shaded by tamarind trees, with banana trees and coconut palms round the edge, and sometimes, if it were an old village, a large banyan tree on the outskirts. Some villages still kept palisades or hedges or thorn around them as they had in the old days, and posted kins or watchmen at the gates at night.

Furnishing in the houses usually consisted of a few mats and pots, a large cupboard and a mirror or two, and little else. Rickety tables and chairs might be produced for important visitors, together with dusty tumblers and cups. Hospitality was traditional. Once, walking through the fields, I came on a tiny broken-down shack in which an ancient widow was cooking her evening meal of a little rice. When I inquired conventionally about her health, she offered me with great dignity part of her meagre meal. 'She will be offended if you refuse,' whispered my Bench clerk, so I had a morsel – and sent her a present of food when I got back to camp.

In the rains many villages became seas of mud, with duckboards along the streets to make them passable. But the villagers always managed to keep themselves and their clothes very clean. The village wells, or the banks of a neighbouring stream or river, were the centres of village life, of gossip and flirtation.

Poring over the files in my tent one evening I made a dramatic discovery. Careful reading of the small print in the Village Act revealed, what seemed to me, to be improper use by the Government, over a period of years, of part of village land. I set out my arguments precisely, and I thought irrefutably, and sent the file upwards. It duly travelled up through the Deputy Commissioner, in charge of the District, the Commissioner, in charge of the Division, through the Secretary to the Financial Commissioner to the Financial Commissioner himself, who, together with his Chief Secretary, was the most august and powerful officer in the service, next to the Governor. As Curzon wrote, 'Like the diurnal revolution of the earth went the files, steady, solemn, sure and slow.' Months later I recognized the file, home again! I undid the red tape with eager fingers. Surely my reputation was made as an exceptionally bright young officer! At the end of a long series of minutes I read the culminating remarks, signed by the Secretary to the FC, himself a senior officer. 'I am instructed by the Financial Commissioner', he wrote, 'to say that he regrets that he must decline to grasp the nettle held out to him.' Or, in less urbane language, 'Let sleeping dogs lie, you silly young ass!' It must have been the same sensible administrative instinct which impelled a famous Chief Secretary, when faced with an horrendous problem, to minute neatly, 'Put away for five years.'

One of my tours took me through the poor and remote Karenni hill tracts on the eastern boundary of the district, to visit the people the Burmans called 'the wild cattle of the hills'. Here a primitive form of cultivation, taungya or hill fields, was practised. Each year an area of jungle was cleared, the scrub and the undergrowth burnt, and in the ashes seed was broadcast. After the sparse harvest, cultivation was moved to another plot. For my night's rest a platform of split bamboos bound with creepers was conjured up in a trice. When I went to bed I found two small, threadbare and moth-eaten blankets on the ground by my bed. 'What are these?' I asked my Bench clerk.

He seemed embarrassed. 'Your Honour is trying a land case here tomorrow. These were left by the plaintiff.'

'Slip them back and forget it,' I said, embarrassed myself.

In this pathetic little gesture was the only bribe I was ever offered in my service.

On the foothills were some of the great teak forests for which Burma is famous. In my imagination I had thought tropical forests to be all luxuriant growths, creepers and snakes. But a teak forest in the hot weather is an ugly, dusty world of bare tree-trunks and big dry leaves, with little animal or bird life visible. Often a ground-fire creeps through the leaves on the forest floor, adding smoke to the dust. In the fever-ridden rains, when the Forest firms' assistants had their busiest season, I kept out of the mud and wet in the forests.

In Pyinmana in 1935 to 1937 there was certainly more political activity than there had been in Monywa. But the nationalism was not aggressive. Political parties were getting organized so that they could have their share of the fruits of power, which after the 1937 Constitution was very considerable, and to bring pressure on the British for more concessions. But the atmosphere throughout the district was still one of at least passive, and not particularly discontented acquiescence, to British rule. I never encountered the least personal hostility.

Maymyo

Anyone who got leave in Upper Burma usually made for Maymyo, the so-called official hill station. It was only 4,000 feet up – not to be compared with Indian hill stations – but it had pleasant green rolling country, woods and streams, and it was cool enough to have a blanket at night, even occasionally a fire in the sitting-room. One could dine off woodcock and strawberries and cream, all local.

To get up to this climate after the hellish heat of the plains in the hot weather was in itself a holiday. I believe places can absorb atmosphere from human happenings, in the way that scent lingers in an empty drawer. Indeed this is one of the more plausible explanations of ghosts. Half-way up the steep climb from the plains of Mandalay to Maymo there is a halt where, after the strain of the hairpin bends, motorists of those days drew in to cool the engines of their cars and refill their radiators. So many cheerful travellers, panting for their leave, had stopped there and sniffed the cool air with exhilaration, that the spot seemed full of the spirit of past voyagers as well as present ones. I always wanted to sing when I got out of the car there. I felt something of the same sensation some years later when the little railway climbing up to Simla from the scorching plains stopped half-way up the mountain for passengers to breakfast in an old-fashioned railway waiting-room at Solon, in a temperature cool enough for me to enjoy bacon and eggs.

Up in Maymyo were the Governor's summer residence, official villas, with passable efforts at English gardens, a swimming-pool, carefully cut rides through the woods, a number of Forest firm holiday chummeries, a British battalion, a Burma Rifles battalion, and a well-appointed club with tennis-courts and polo ground. Once a year Maymyo celebrated the gala of Polo Week, during which teams from British and Indian regiments (particularly, of course, the cavalry), from the Police, from the Forest Service, and from the big firms battled for trophies in between dances, tennis tournaments, gymkhanas and other festivities.

I was never good enough at polo to take part in the tournament, but I accepted that for the week the Cult of the Horse was in complete command, and behaved accordingly. I donned breeches and riding-boots, sidled into the bar and listened to the horse-talk. Standing by myself near a group of elegant officers from a smart cavalry regiment (our 'Samurai' at play) I heard them talking of a pony called Grey Ghost. I had already heard a comment on that pony at the next table at lunch. Gazing into my glass I muttered audibly, 'Nice animal, but needs another rib.' There was a momentary hush, followed by a cordial invitation to have a drink. I was in!

Some of the regular Club members found unvaried horse-talk and the rather studied cavalry stance of the visitors a bit of a bore, and the bar for a few days was almost the exclusive property of the polo players. Early one evening the westering sun was shut out by a large bulk in the doorway. I looked up to see one of my great friends from Pyinmana, Gordon Bathgate – a big, portly, red-moustached, bald-headed, Steel Brothers' Forest manager. He had obviously just come in from the jungle, in a sweaty khaki shirt and crumpled khaki shorts hanging below his knees. His large red face looked irritated. The immaculate young subalterns give him a dismissive glance. Bathgate advanced a step nearer in. He gave a prodigious sniff. 'Awful smell of horse-shit in here!' he pronounced slowly.

I could have hugged him.

I met another well-known Forest character in Maymyo. The blue eyes which blazed from his brick-coloured face were intelligent and perceptive; but his contempt for authority, his acid tongue, and his exceptional capacity for alcohol had more than once brought him demotion. The story is told that after the war he left the East and took a comparatively junior job in one of the Whitehall ministries. After a trial period he is said to have marched upstairs and confronted the Permanent Under-Secretary. 'Some bloody fool', he declared, 'advised me to join this bloody Ministry, as it was a new and expanding one. He told me that if I started at the bottom I could soon work my way up. It's too late. All my life I've been starting at the top and working my way down. I can't change now. Goodbye!'

It was in Maymyo that I called on the wife of a colleague to find that she was out and the bungalow was apparently in charge of her very small son. This child, well trained in the conventions of Burmese hospitality, shook my hand and piped up, 'Will you have a drink?' I knew the household well enough to accept, and help myself. The little boy then sat beside me, and, anxious to make suitable conversation with his guest, searched his limited experience for some general topic. Finally, he came up with an important truth, learnt from his mother that morning. Gazing into my eyes he said, gravely, 'We eat marbles, we die!' I did my best to kick this subject around until his mother arrived.

When I told this story to Frank George, my Settlement superior at a later posting, he told me that he had been equally surprised by a small child when he had been SDO at Namtu. This was a mining town in the Shan States, at which in those days there were a number of fairly free-spoken Cornish miners. Frank said he was riding one very chilly and misty morning near the town and came across an ayah wheeling a minute child in a push-chair. Although the child's face was blue and pinched and he was swathed in an enormous scarf, Frank recognized him as the son of a friend.

'Why, hullo!' he said. 'Good morning! How are you, Jeremy?'

The child stared at him for a moment, and then replied with great feeling, and a surprisingly deep voice, 'Christ, it's cold!'

Once or twice in Maymyo I squired the pretty and charming niece of a senior colleague. It took me a little while to spot that I was being rather often manoeuvred into watching polo games in which a certain handsome major in the Frontier Force was playing. It transpired that she had met him on the boat coming out. When he left Maymyo to return to his Frontier post, she looked sad and withdrawn. The gallant major had gone far up-river, and completed his first day's march towards his mountain post, before something clicked in his brain. What was he doing, marching away into the hills, and leaving that adorable girl to the wolves of Maymyo? Quite how he explained it to his brigadier I don't know, but he turned round and raced back hotfoot to Maymyo. At the end of his journey he proposed and was accepted in a matter of minutes. Ethel M. Dell or Maud Diver couldn't have done better.

Just before the Japanese invasion I sat on the Club veranda at Maymyo with an old Army friend (who later had the most brilliant of war records). He told me of a romance with a rather less happy ending than the preceding one. The year before he had been posted in Australia on military duty, and had found himself on New Year's Eve in a bar in Sydney, all alone and not knowing a soul. A couple of kindly Aussies had invited him to come along with them, and driven him some distance out of town to a large, cheerful and boozy party. There he had met the most wonderful girl. He was finally driven back to his hotel by a stranger, but not before great plans had been made with the divine creature, and telephone numbers exchanged.

'The next morning,' said my friend, 'I awoke with a bit of a hangover, but also with a strange sense of excitement and elation. Then I remembered, and leapt out of bed to get my address book. And there, scrawled across the page in rather unsteady writing, was my own name and address. Some disastrous tipsy juggling of books had evidently taken place. I hadn't the faintest idea where I'd been. And though I hung around that bar for several more nights, I never again saw the men who had taken me to the party.'

The British officers of the Burmese Frontier Force and Military Police were an attractive bunch. They were men who had sought remote and adventurous jobs outside ordinary regimental soldiering – some perhaps to work off debts, but mainly to enjoy commands on their own in a change of scenery, and mostly were men of individuality and character. Old Burma hands from those days will remember particularly 'Bonzo' Bowers, the scourge of tigers round Bhamo; 'Tarzan' Learmond, the short, ugly Irishman whose Mounted Police lines in Mandalay were always so spick and span and who, in his kindness, would go out of his way to help whenever he could; Leslie Hurst, the neat, blond cavalry officer who rode so gracefully in the polo field at Chauk and went off to give military advice to the Sultan of Muscat; Jack Haswell, and Bill Waterhouse-Brown, tall, dark and handsome with a beautiful wife to match, who in their turn were kings of Falam, Tiddim and Haka in the remote Chin hills, many days' march from anywhere. They were all devoted to their men – Punjabi Mussulmen, Sikhs, Gurkhas, Kachins, Chins, Karens and

Burmans – and they all seemed happy in their extra-mural soldiering.

Mandalay

The other occasion on which I got away from Pyinmana was when I went to Mandalay to take departmental examinations. Criminal Law and so on were just a matter of study and practice. The Burmese language was a much tougher proposition. The authorities well understood that really good knowledge of the language was essential to an administrator. So young officers, who started on modest pay, got no increments until they had passed their Higher Standard Burmese. This required fluent conversation on any topic, and instantaneous translation from a daily newspaper.

A standing joke in Burmese-language oral examinations was that every now and then a young candidate, unusually fluent in conversation, would make the revealing error of addressing an examiner by the personal pronoun of 'shin', an honorific exclusively used by women to men. Burmese, like Chinese basically a monosyllabic and tonal language, has words which mean three entirely different things when uttered in three different tones. 'Kyaung', for example, can mean a cat or a monastery or a stream. 'Pe' can mean over a dozen things. So it is a difficult language for Europeans to master, and even amongst those who could communicate easily in it there were few who spoke it well. Still, we all had to speak it at least fluently, and this brought us much closer to the Burmese people. In fact, British officials identified themselves closely with the Burmese villagers, and instinctively took their side against landlords and large firms and foreigners generally if there were any reasonable grounds for doing so. In spite of my year's Burmese study in England, it took me two tries and many months before I earned my increment.

Visiting Mandalay was a special experience. There, perhaps for the first time, the mysterious fascination of a totally different civilization and history truly gripped me. I felt the *frisson* which the aromatic breezes of the East sent through Conrad's young men as their ship approached the coast. Mandalay city itself was an ugly, dusty place of wooden houses with corrugated-iron roofs, sprawling down to the banks of the Irrawaddy. But opposite the Circuit House, where visitors stayed, the moonlight (bright enough to read by) shone on the moat, on the high red walls with their carved and gilded pavilions, and on the white gates of the old fort. In the great square within (each side of the square was $1\frac{1}{2}$ miles long) were remains of the palaces and council chambers of the Burmese kings. On the waters of the wide moat floated lotus-lily pads, and on them fell the petals of the gold mohur trees. Beyond the walls stood Mandalay Hill, covered with white pagodas joined by whitewashed steps, the haunt of the famous hermit U Khanti. And beyond that again, blue and remote, loomed the hills of the Shan plateau.

Not much remained of the palace. The space inside the fort walls was mainly occupied by parade-grounds, polo fields and the buildings of the Upper Burma Club. But enough remained of huge teak pillars with traces of red lacquer and gilt to show what the wooden palace must have looked like. Only some fifty-odd years before my visit King Thibaw and Queen Suppayalat, in gorgeous silks, had ruled here as medieval autocrats. They had ruled a world almost entirely cut off from outside developments, a world of white elephants, of princes and princesses and court chamberlains such as I had glimpsed through the zat pwes I had seen in Monywa, a world of 'tinsel and glass' so brilliantly described in Tennyson Jesse's novel *The Lacquer Lady*. Just as for many centuries China had called itself Chung Kuo, the Middle Kingdom, to the Burmans of those times their court was the centre of the universe. Their ignorance of the outside world was almost complete. In 1824, when puny Burmese forces invaded India, their generals carried with them golden chains with which to bind the Viceroy, and orders to advance to England if necessary. When Mindon Min, Thibaw's amiable father, called for a map of the world to have Burma pointed out to him, he was enraged that his country should seem so small. Thereupon his terrified tutor put his hands over half the world and asserted it was Burma. In 1886, when King Thibaw, the last monarch of the dynasty of Alaungpaya, was taken down to the river under an escort of the Hampshire Regiment to be put on board the steamer *Thooreah* en route to exile at Ratnigiri in West India, it was the first time the young

King had been outside the palace walls for seven years.

One or two people, whose lives had spanned both the old and new eras, still survived in Mandalay. I met an aged Frenchman, running a cobwebbed antique shop, who had lived under King Thibaw. And I met too an old Anglo-Indian jade merchant who had first come to Mandalay as stenographer to General Sir Harry Prendergast, VC (a decoration he had won in the Indian Mutiny), commander of the British invading forces in 1885. My friend had then married a half-Greek, half-Burman girl, who had been maid of honour to the Burmese Queen, and who as 'Fanny' had been the heroine of the famous novel *The Lacquer Lady*, referred to above. This girl, Mattie Calogreedy, had originally married a Scots Irrawaddy Flotilla skipper, who died soon after of malaria. She had later had an affair with M. Bonvillein, the French Consul in Mandalay. Aggrieved when her lover returned from leave with a French wife, she gave away to a British agent French plans to supply arms to the Burmans through Tonkin, and added to the British anxieties which precipitated the Third Burmese War.

The old man was in bed, recovering from fever, when I visited Mandalay, but I used to go along in the evening to his dimly lit bedroom, with a half-Shan girl who was a relative of his, to take him some fruit and listen to his stories. He said that Tennyson Jesse, with her novelist's imagination, had got the scene and the atmosphere of the Burmese court extraordinarily right. He should have known, as it seems he told her the whole story. He was vaguely offended because at the end of the book, Tennyson Jesse had married Fanny off to a fictitious Indian curio dealer living in Brighton, instead of to him.

Through the same girl I met another Mandalay original, Seabury Edwards. Seabury was not a member of the normal club-going European community. He held what was for a European a comparatively lowly post in the Customs and Excise Service, and his friends were largely among the Chinese and Burmese and Eurasians. He captivated me. A widely read and gifted talker, with grey hair and a pale, mobile, amused monkey face, he moved around his little bungalow with a large white cockatoo on his shoulder. He also owned a pair of minas with bright yellow beaks and bold eyes. One of them would surprise visitors by muttering from a dark corner, 'Not *you* again!'

Visiting a tavern in North Carolina many years later, I was tickled to see a cocky mina strutting about a large cage. One of the other customers called to his wife, 'Come over her, Mary-Lou, and look at this mina bird!' The bird glared at him, and said in a cross voice, 'I'm not a mina bird – I'm an EAGLE!'

Seabury personally cooked delicious dishes in his French copper cooking-pans. (It was almost unheard of for a European to cook himself.) And he was a brilliant photographer. Pictures taken and processed by him of Burmese scenes and monuments had been reproduced in many of the great papers and periodicals of the world. To close friends he would reveal a different dimension of his art – an astonishing album of explicitly sexual photographs of the very many ladies of all colours and nationalities with whom he had had happy relationships. He had, I believe, actually been married once or twice, and eventually, before he left Burma, he finally married an Anglo-Burmese lady, who in the spirit of Richard Burton's widow, Isabel, in her burning of *The Scented Gardens*, made him destroy his erotic masterpiece.

One of Seabury's sidelines was his work as a talented amateur chemist. When later he moved to Rangoon, he set up as a hobby a private snake-farm, of cobras, kraits and vipers in little open-topped concrete cubicles, with smooth, straight walls and overhangs which the reptiles could not climb up. He and his assistant walked happily among these lethal creatures in tall thigh-boots, and picked up cobras in their bare hands. He explained confidently that when a cobra was at full height, with hood extended, it could strike only horizontally or downwards, but not upwards, so that it was quite safe to pick the snake up from the top. The venom he extracted by making the snake bite into a cup with a tight muslin lid, and the milk, squeezed out when the fangs withdrew, he converted chemically into powdered crystals. These he kept in his refrigerator (along with his beer and butter) and sold later at a good price to hospitals. When I supposed that this was mainly for antidotes, he said no, it was rather for use to clot blood when this was required in operations, or in cases of haemophilia. He explained too that some of his powdered snake venom had great success as an aphrodisiac, and showed me with pride the marks of some of the injections he had made on himself. I politely rejected offers of a sample, which indeed in those days I did not need.

Walking in the garden of his bungalow he frequently carried a large python across the back of his neck. As he talked in his usual joky, excitable way, his right hand steadily unwound the python's tail from his left arm. 'As long as you never let the tail take hold,' he explained blithely, 'he can never get a proper grip of you!'

Seabury, too, in his Mandalay days had much to tell of Burmese legends and superstitions, and he took me one night to see a Mandalay nat-gadaw, a spirit's wife, a woman who danced herself into strange trances and fits, and was seemingly possessed by a Nat.

For me Mandalay was always the heart of Burma. Here in Mandalay one was conscious sometimes of a more restless and aggressive nationalism. Rangoon was in fact the only real city in Burma, but Mandalay was big enough to turn out mobs swollen by thousands of the young undisciplined 'political' monks. However, normally things were peaceful and friendly enough.

4 The Oilfields

Yenangyaung ('Smelling water creek') on the arid banks of the Irrawaddy, in Central Burma, was the cradle of the world oil industry. Oil was first reported here in AD 100. By the 1930s there was at Yenangyaung a long-established oilfield. Not far away, also on the river, was Chauk, a smaller and more modern field. The Government officer presiding over both these fields was called the Warden of the Oilfields, and I had long heard of the legendary Denis Phelips, ICS, who for some time had held the post.

I was excited to learn that I was to leave Pyinmana and proceed to Chauk as Assistant Warden, in charge of Government matters in the Chauk field. The work in Monywa, Sinlum and Pyinmana (as indeed in almost the whole of Burma) was almost entirely rural administration on traditional lines. The oilfields were different. Here was a large European community, mainly of technicians, and an atmosphere of modern progress and efficiency.

On my first evening Willy Armstrong, the gentle and civilized General Manager of the Burma Oil Company in Chauk, drove me round the fields in his open tourer. Over the barren hillocks, cracked by gullies, no human being was to be seen for miles. Lights blazed overhead at intervals, and the pumping machinery creaked and groaned in the shadows below. Forests of tall oil-rigs stood on the skyline. This was a different, inhuman, industrial world, a somewhat ominous and anxious world of the future, not of the past. English administrators and geologists, Scots engineers and American drillers, in charge of Burmese drilling crews, led busy, bustling, active lives dedicated to the winning and refining of oil. Drilling was still considered to have a special mystique, exclusively the secret of Texan drillers. So in the clubs of Yenangyaung and Chauk one met colourful characters who seemed to have strayed in from some other play. 'Whitey' Graves, an old driller who habitually drank a dozen large bottles of beer on a Sunday morning before lunch, 'Blacky' Akers, 'Gentleman Joe' Groves (otherwise known as 'The Senator'), Sam Davis, who never went snipe shooting without a tiffin-carrier full of fried tinned oysters – these were some of the American personalities in Chauk.

In Yenangyaung the area where the drillers lived was known as Whisky Row, while managers' road was called Swank Alley. In the big field the Americans had their own Club, and it was to this dimly lit place that I went on my first night in Yenangyaung. I did not think that anyone knew who I was, or even noticed me. I fell into conversation at the bar with a pleasant girl, who took pity on a lonely stranger, and we had a few drinks together.

The next morning I presented myself to my new boss in his office. A sunburnt and genial bachelor, whose famous and deafening laugh announced his presence a long way off, he had been an Oxford boxing blue, and still looked tough and wiry. He received me politely, but excused himself to read a note from Eric Bradshaw, the senior Government geologist, which had just arrived for him with a flagged copy of the *Oilfields Manual*, the Bible of local regulations. He looked somewhat put out. I found out afterwards that the note read: 'Dear Denis, I was glad to see last night that your new Assistant is already acting in accordance with the footnote to Regulation 4.' The footnote in question read: 'Warden includes Assistant Warden in all his activities.' Everyone in the American Club had, of course, been watching the new arrival closely, and had been highly amused that he had spent his first few hours chatting up the Warden's favourite lady.

Incidentally, one of the entertainments of the oilfields was Eric Bradshaw's story of how, as a student in Dublin, he had, for a bet, got a billiard-ball into his mouth, and, unable to get it out again, had to travel to hospital by tram with a crowd of boozy and interested Dubliners.

Making my initial tour of the fields with my new chief, we came upon an immensely tall watch-tower. 'Good view of the whole field from up there,' said Denis. 'Care to go up?' I assented apprehensively. The metal ladder was vertical, with oily rods set alarmingly far apart. I clung convulsively to each greasy step as we went higher and higher, until we reached a square hole in an oily wooden platform. Somehow I got up. The view was indeed panoramic, but I was thinking of nothing but the first stage of the way down, scrabbling with my fingers to cling on to the slimy platform while my legs sought the first slippery step below. I dislike heights anyway, and must have been quite pale by the time we reached the ground.

Years later I said to Denis, 'That was a cruel test you put me to on that bloody watch-tower. I suppose you were well used to it?'

'Never been up before,' he answered. 'I was shattered when you agreed to go up. I've never been so frightened in my life!'

I soon learnt that Denis was uncrowned king of the oilfields. The motley crew of oilfield workers adored him. The Burmese knew he understood them (he eventually married a Burmese) and would fight for their interests. An efficient and experienced administrator, he was also the most amusing and stimulating of companions. He could drink and play poker with his American pals all night, but when next morning he sat as a magistrate he brooked no nonsense from any boon companion who came up before him. 'Gee, Denis!' and 'Aw, hell, Denis!' met silencing fines for contempt of court. A kind and generous host, his bungalow was open house and friends from outside Yenangyaung often moved in to stay without even consulting him first. His was one of those rare personalities whose arrival on the scene lit up the occasion – a game of tennis, a supper party, or just a drink at the Club became an event of infectious hilarity, touched with fantasy. When Denis's famous laugh was heard in the distance people would smile and say fondly to each other, 'There's Denis!', and everyone would feel jollier at once. Underneath the humour and the *bonhomie* was a more private personality – an agnostic and rationalist, sensitive to pain and death and fearful that the compound arithmetic of human population was leading to disaster for the world, a subject on which he corresponded pessimistically with other neo-Malthusians. But I met no one who enjoyed more the daily exercise of living.

Official meetings of the oilfield executives somehow metamorphosed themselves into the Zinnia Luncheon Club. New members of the Club were called seedlings, and Denis, the Chairman, was always referred to as Hsin Byu, the White Elephant. No one who worked in the fields in Denis's heyday will forget what fun it all was, including the trouble and dangers.

Part of the general good humour stemmed from the nature of oilfield work. Many people in their lives struggle with vague, formless and often insoluble problems. An oilfield engineer usually had a precise problem, which with ingenuity and professional skill could be solved. A drilling bit stuck down the hole, a pipe to be guided in a new direction, a new piece of tackle to be devised, a core of earth to be analysed; these were immediate absorbing practical challenges by which the professionals became as obsessed and boring as golf players or fishermen can be about their respective pastimes. I could see what Einstein meant when he said, 'People like chopping wood because they can see immediate results.'

I got the smell of oil in my nostrils too. Years later I visited the great producers of Texas, the rigs on stilts of Lake Maracaibo in Venezuela, the seaside fields of Kuwait, and the unlikely swamps of south-eastern Nigeria, and I was always excited to be in the old and strangely unchanging atmosphere.

Later I was to serve for a total of seven years in the United States. But the first Americans I met, the cheerful, generous, open-hearted roughnecks of the American Club at Yenangyaung, gave me an abiding affection for the people. Before my day, the American Club had had even more of a Frontier atmosphere, with pistols fired off in the bar. And in the archives of the Burma Oil Company there survives from those days a cable so succinct and so clear in its message that I have often quoted it to junior officers inclined to verbosity in official telegrams. It came about as a result of a visit by a Scots director's wife to the oilfields. So shocked was she to find many of the drillers living with Burmese girls that she got to work on the BOC Board when she returned home, and inspired a circular to all staff that women other than wives must be put away at once. A meeting at the American Club of the vital technicians in the new craft produced a cable to the Head Office in Rangoon. It read (I bowdlerize slightly): NO SEX NO OIL.

The new regulation was quietly forgotten. In my day, living conditions had much improved and many drillers had their wives with them from the States.

The mystery of the craft began to dissipate too. In the early days the hard-won experience of the Texan drillers was precious. I have been sitting in the shade of the rig, chatting drowsily with a somnolent old roughneck, when he suddenly leapt to his feet and barked new orders to his drilling crew. His trained ear had caught a faint new note in the sound of drilling, which told him of trouble far down the hole. Similarly, when drilling was being done by the old-fashioned cable tool, a gnarled but sensitive hand on the cable could interpret from the vibration what was happening deep in the earth below. But scientific knowledge was overtaking pragmatic experience, and it was found that young Scots engineers could be trained in reasonable time into perfectly good and less expensive drillers – better, in fact, than some of the illiterate and not very experienced men brought in by their pals in Texas to enjoy the high pay. And then the more experienced and intelligent of the Burmese crews began to show that they could do it too.

However, while it lasted, the small American colony of Texan drillers was an exotic growth, unlike anything else in Burma, and it gave life in the oilfields a novel and amusing spice. Their great pastime was poker, and since they had plenty of money and not much to spend it on, the stakes were high. Sometimes the players in the 'Big Game' would sit down after coming off morning 'tower' on a Saturday and play more or less straight through to the start of morning 'tower' on Monday. A month's pay would go west with a few cheerful oaths.

Although work in the heat and dust of the arid and barren ravines was hard and sometimes dangerous, there were recreations available such as could be found in very few other places in Burma. The clubs had tennis- and squash-courts, and excellent swimming-pools; there was a film show once a week, and gramophone dances on Saturdays; staunch expatriates played cricket on matting wickets (their wives providing traditional teas with cucumber sandwiches); and amongst the rocky nullahs golf was played with Scottish intensity, on 'greens' made of sand bound into a fairly firm surface with a mixture of crude oil. Frankie Bestall, our Irish police superintendent (whom I afterwards met as British Consul in Houston, Texas), sailed a specially rigged little junk on the swirling waters of the Irrawaddy. We also had polo, and shooting trips, and picnics to Mounts Popa and Pagan.

Within visiting distance were the deserted temples of Pagan, one of the world's most remarkable religious cities, many miles square and containing nothing but thousands of derelict pagodas. A royal capital for 250 years, Pagan was now a ghost town abandoned since the Chinese invasion of the thirteenth century. The Burmese kings of that era had rashly executed the envoys of the great Kublai Khan, and retribution, if slow, had been stern. To me as a young man this immense area of deserted, and for a large part not very distinguished monuments, struck me as a waste of human effort, which could have been better used to dig wells and canals or to make roads and bridges. But travellers have felt great tranquillity in this place.

My nice modern bungalow and the civilized amenities of oilfield life led me to invite my sister in England to stay. Before she went home she had met her future husband in the Burma Oil Company. When she arrived, she complained that there was no mattress on her bed, nor curtains on her windows. I assured her that I had for some years slept comfortably on a webbing charpoy topped by a plaited bamboo mat; curtains had just not occurred to me. Other British wives on visits soon gave her support, and the comforts of my bungalow rapidly improved. I was encouraged to have my first large dinner party, and to invite a number of married couples. My old drunken mugh (mugh = top-grade cook), who had fed me for years on stringy chicken, goat chops and caramel custard, sometimes twice a day, had been discovered by my sister to have in his repertoire a wide range of *cordon bleu* dishes, learnt before he was sacked as assistant cook from Government House. Crockery and cutlery were as usual borrowed from neighbours, and with my sister as hostess the great dinner went off very well. For dessert the cook, exhorted to do his best to honour the lady guests, surpassed himself with a pudding which contained everything – meringues, cream, fruit, spun toffee, the lot. On the top, piped in cochineal icing, lay his idea of an appropriate greeting: GOOD NIGHT MADAM.

Any monotony of diet I had got used to in the days before my sister arrived was, however, surpassed by the regime I encountered during a trip to some outlying wells on the other side of the river, under the supervision of an enormous Canadian driller with a Burmese wife. I was a little embarrassed at being accommodated in a spare room, from which the only exit was through the nuptial chamber, and not altogether put at ease by my host's cheerful bellow of 'Don't mind us, son!' I ate with my host, while his wife cooked separate and delicious Burmese dishes for herself. My host and I had the same menu morning and evening every day: a large plate of chili con carne (from a tin) and a vast slice of lemon meringue pie (made by his wife), washed down by several bottles of beer.

'Don't you eat anything else?' I ventured to ask.

'No.'

'Why so?'

'Because', was the uncompromising reply, 'these are my favourite dishes.' It was not surprising that he weighed well over 20 stone.

In the oilfields themselves the Burmese were pretty much in the background. Apart from a few young Burmese graduate engineers and Labour Relations officers, the oil company Burmese (several thousand of them) were almost entirely manual workers.

A curious relic in this community were the twin-sas (well-eaters). Before the British came a small amount of crude oil was recovered for unrefined use by an hereditary clan of twin-sas, who dug shafts of up to 100 feet into the ground, lowered one of their number, equipped with an air-pipe and a very primitive sort of tin diver's helmet, into the depths of the shaft, and winched up buckets filled with crude oil by the diver. It was a dangerous task, and by tradition only a close relation manned the windlass and controlled the diver's air-pipe. The twin-sas still carried on their primitive extraction in my day, legally secure in their privileges, surrounded by a forest of modern oil-rigs, some over wells pumping thousands of barrels a day.

It seemed to me sensible enough that outsiders with infinitely greater geological and technological expertise should come in to extract the earth's resources for the world's use, providing they kept the country's laws, paid good wages to the workers, and paid suitable revenues to the Burmese Government.

Colonialism and imperialism were not yet words of world-wide infamy, and I suffered few pangs of conscience. The British were swapping capital and skills for a share in resources. They were taking profits out of the country, but they were creating the profits in the first place – a trick the Burmese after Independence never learnt on the same scale. The Burmese workers were very well looked after, with good accommodation, water and sanitation, medical and welfare serivces, as well as educational and recreational facilities. They were by Burmese standards very well paid. Nearly 10,000 in number, they added up to the nearest thing Burma had to the nucleus of an industrial proletariat, and hence they began to attract the involvement of young Communist students from Rangoon University. As in other countries, the very fact that they were well-paid élite workers made this work-force the more eager for a greater share of money and privileges. For the first time in Burma I sensed ominous underground political stirrings. For the first time I came across crude leaflets with drawings of blazing torches, and hammers and sickles, carrying echoes of the teachings of Marx, Lenin and Mao Tse-tung. Although I did not know it at the time, among those behind the trouble and new-style propaganda in the oilfields was a young Communist student called Thein Pe, with whom I was to co-operate during the war against the Japanese.

Strangely enough, some of the most anxious moments of my time in the oilfields did not arise from local labour disputes, or from protests against the Government. They came from a racial explosion of the indigenous Burmese against the Kalas, the foreigners from outside, who at this juncture were identified with the Indians, and particularly the Muslim immigrants from what is now Bangladesh. That explosion derived from the same sort of pent-up racial and economic resentment which has, throughout history, led to pogroms against hard-working immigrants – such as the massacre of Chinese in Indonesia after the First World War. It had happened in Burma before, in 1930 and 1932. Readers of Maurice Collis's *Trials in Burma* will remember descriptions of grinning Burmese in Rangoon, with flaming tow on long bamboos, scorching Indians down from their hiding-places at the tops of trees, to dispatch them with their dahs on the ground.

In 1938, the spark that set off the explosion was an article in a Burmese paper in Rangoon which raked up from some seven years back a criticism of Buddhism in a book by an obscure Muslim village schoolmaster. Bloody anti-Muslim riots in Rangoon (in which over 200 Indians were killed), exploited by politicians who wanted to embarrass the party in power, were inflamed further by the Burmese press. As the newspapers reached out into the country, the troubles spread like ripples from a rock thrown into a pond. It was obvious that the ripples would reach us soon.

Together with the Indian officer in charge of the Mounted Police in Chauk, and the oil companies' management, rapid plans were made to forestall the trouble. At the height of the danger the companies concentrated European women and children in a group of easily defended (and evacuated) bungalows on a bluff beside the river. The most prosperous Indian shopkeeper demanded a heavy police guard on his premises. I demurred. Feeling like a military commander, I decided not to split up our small force into guards for separate buildings. I ordered that the main police units should be posted on the small hillocks surrounding the town, from which a good view could be obtained of the whole town. With motor transport and horses the police could be speedily moved to whatever quarter might be threatened. Contrary to my plan, however, I found a substantial guard outside the big Indian store. The Indian police officer in charge, bearded and turbaned, and an old polo friend of mine, evaded my eye. I did not challenge him. Perhaps his idea was the better one anyway; and I sensed that the shopkeeper had, so to speak, bought a great many tickets for the Police Ball.

As most troubles broke out after dark, we imposed a curfew and arranged with the oil companies to provide us with lorries carrying searchlights, with which constant police patrols were kept up all night. And as the villages with the worst criminal record lay across the river, we arranged for launches with searchlights to patrol the river at night. Leaflets warned everyone that rioting would be sternly dealt with. We had several anxious and watchful days, but all worked well. In the larger and more difficult towns of Yenangyaung, where the new Warden Tom Atkinson was in charge, all hell broke loose, and this was brought under control only by the courage and leadership of the Warden.

In due course the inevitable Government Commission of Inquiry toured the country, analysing the reasons for the trouble, and checking on how it had been handled. The Warden was rightly commended and received a decoration. I searched with modest pride for some comment on my elaborate and successful precautions. I found it. It was laconic. 'Mr Glass', it said, 'was lucky to have been in such a quiet district.'

This had been a flare-up which died down. But there were more lasting troubles. The early strikes and processions had been reasonably good-humoured. I stood on a chair on one occasion and harangued a large crowd of workers apparently in a nasty mood and advancing on some of the BOC offices. In my fluent, but far from correct Burmese, I begged them to go home and send me a deputation in the evening, so that we could really discuss their grievances without any incidents. To the astonishment of the police, they went home.

We had many menacing processions, but I can only recollect one occasion in Chauk when a crowd began to break windows and damage property. After going through all the gobbledegook of reading the Riot Act, I authorized the police to charge with their bamboo staves. The crowd ran, but there was one Burman whose pride forbade him to do so, and he walked away from the police with a slow and defiant step. I had an uneasy sense of witnessing a foul at soccer when he received a whack across his towelled turban.

The longer the troubles dragged on, the more the tension grew. There were some ingenious tactics behind the strikers. Entrances to the company's offices and workshops were blocked by crowds of girls, looking pretty and fragile, lying in the road across the gateways. Illegal processions were headed by crowds of small schoolboys, whom the police could not very well handle. Counter-tactics were devised. In the early hours of the morning the entrances and driveways of company buildings were covered with a black and sticky oil mixture, from which no ladies' clothes would easily recover. And Frankie Bestall enrolled fifty Burmese constables' wives as 'special constables', armed them with slippers and set them on the schoolboys. The children broke and fled, not in fear of being hurt, but from a male chauvinist shame (strong in the Burmese male) at the idea of being smacked by a woman.

Dr Ba Maw, the Prime Minister, came up to investigate, and I drove him around the oilfields alone in my car. He was cool and analytical. 'Mr Glass,' he said, 'we must try and distinguish how much of these troubles are labour troubles, which perhaps can be solved by negotiation, and how much political troubles stirred up by people who, for nationalist or party political reasons, want trouble for its own sake.'

I had naïvely supposed them to be almost entirely straight labour troubles. But Dr Ba Maw was right. There was a new feeling in the air. In my previous posts in Burma I had, of course, been aware of the Burmese pride in their country, their religion, their customs and institutions, and like all Englishmen had enjoyed dealing with people who took it for granted, in a relaxed way, that they were as good as you were. But on the whole people seemed to accept British rule without obvious resentment or apparent expectation of early changes. The intensified national self-consciousness and the appearance of the slogan of 'Lutlat-ye' or 'Freedom' came in significant part from the University of Rangoon, and from the Radical Party who defiantly called themselves Thakins (which, as noted earlier, was the Burmese equivalent of Sahibs, and the usual honorific by which Burmese address Europeans). Young men began to question not whether the British administration was efficient or just, but why it was there at all. Most of the Burmese work-force in the fields were concerned with rates of pay. But the mere fact of the confrontation seemed to the young Thakins a symptom of revolt against 'foreign exploitation', and they came up from Rangoon to stir the pot. They even arranged an Oilfield Workers' March to Rangoon to reinforce their organizations there. What Dr Ba Maw knew, too, was that egging on the student Thakins and the oilfield workers was his unscrupulous rival, U Saw. U Saw's party paper *The Sun* had been one of the instigators of the anti-Muslim riots. And U Saw aimed, by manipulating the Thakins (against whom he turned sharply when in power) to stir up yet more disorder and trouble for the Ba Maw Government. U Saw was hell-bent on the premiership, which he eventually got.

Once again in the job of Assistant Warden I was a sort of Pooh-Bah. I was the local Industrial Safety Inspector and

Commissioner for Workmen's Compensation, and as such had to inquire into the cause of accidents. Crude oil in itself is not particularly flammable (though when it does catch fire the huge black pillars of smoke are unmistakable). However, when oil vapour collects on low-lying pockets, great danger is present, and smoking in the fields was a serious offence. Sometimes workers fell off rigs. One man fell some 70 feet, but, guided by his guardian angel, hit the mud slurry in the sluice at such a lucky angle that he escaped quite unhurt (though he spent some days in hospital recovering from shock). My first accident case, the day after I arrived, was a difficult one. A Burmese public bus, careering too fast round a corner on a road through the fields, had met a large company lorry ferrying an open section of a huge pipe. The sharp edge of this pipe had cut through the top of one side of the bus and sliced off the tops of the heads of the front passengers as if they were boiled eggs for breakfast. The bus-driver was at fault, but the case ended with substantial *ex gratia* compensation to the families of the deceased.

I was also Chairman of a local committee for dealing with inter-company disputes. In earlier days competing oil companies drilled wells as close as possible to their rivals' boundaries. Hills in the older parts of the fields had dense forests of old rigs. Scientific drilling also made it possible to control the deviation of the drilling pipe far below the surface, and cause it to drift into adjoining areas. So a periodic committee was attended regularly by the drilling superintendents from all the companies. In my day the companies of any significance were reduced to the Burma Oil Company (the giant), the Indo-Burma Petroleum Company (a rather dashing subsidiary of Steel Brothers, whose great pride was the prolific field on the banks of the Irrawaddy at Lanywa, opposite Chauk), and the smaller British Burma Petroleum Company. The drilling superintendents were as tough a bunch of men as I have ever come across. Each had to read out the past two weeks' drilling log, detailing every well within a certain distance of other companies' territory (e.g. depth and angle of drilling). The details were in technical language, and gabbled at the speed of a Texas cattle auctioneer. I protested mildly that I couldn't understand a word they were saying. 'Don't worry,' was the reply. 'We understand each other, and that's what matters.' I was just there to hold the ring and intervene only if there were a dispute, which was seldom.

In the absence of the Yenangyaung chaplain I took my turn in reading the prayers at the non-denominational service in Chauk Church. I vetted all the plans for new workers' village settlements proposed by the companies.

As Revenue Officer I supervised the inspector who regularly 'dipped' the huge petrol reservoirs to measure the contents and determine the revenue for locally refined oil. Much crude oil, of course, went by pipeline all the way down to the refineries at Syriam, near Rangoon.

As President of the Municipal Committee of Chauk Town, I managed its finances, safeguarded the welfare of the local Burmese inhabitants, and improved the sanitation and maternity facilities. My Burmese municipal colleagues seemed grateful, and just before I left passed a resolution to name a street 'Glass Street'. I was flattered; and on one of my last trips round the town I set off in search of 'Glass Street'. I found it. It was on the very outskirts of the town, about 30 yards long, and more or less a gully of mud. I was also touched to receive from a Pongyi to whose monastery I had been of some assistance an enormous black lacquer vase. On one side in gold lettering it bore his name, U Nanda, while on the other, also in gold, was the inscription 'Goodbye Mr Glass', another memento I had to abandon when the Japanese arrived.

As senior local Magistrate I had, as well as trying cases, a special overall responsibility for law and order. The most trying part of the oilfield troubles was night-time fires on the oil-rigs. My phone would ring, after which I would struggle into my clothes and join the police and the company's fire-brigade to see how bad it was and what could be done.

When I finally left Burma on home leave, I was sleeping on the first night out in a cool comfy cabin on the home-going steamer. Someone in the next cabin rang for a steward, and the ringing of the bell penetrated my dreams. Half-asleep, I was up, into my clothes and out into the passage before I realized it was not the phone calling me out to an oil-rig fire.

5 Home Leave

For a young bachelor, after four years or more in the backwoods of the East, his first home leave was an exhilarating time – exciting from the moment of boarding the steamer. The clean, white starched sheets on the bunks, the polite Goanese stewards, the gathering in the bar of a mixture of friends and new faces, chattering happily, the release from the pressures of work and responsibility, together with the prospect of months of pleasure ahead, built up into a bubbling euphoria.

On this leave I went by steamer to Calcutta, and then did the long railway trip across India to join a P & O liner at Bombay. In those days, before air-conditioning, a first-class passenger could arrange for a huge block of ice to be placed in a tin bath under the fan in his railway carriage. As the dust from the Indian plains seeped in through the windows and the ice melted, an unattractive pool of mud formed on the floor. At night the window-shutters had to be secured against the naked and oiled thieves who might clamber in the dark along the side of the speeding train.

It is odd how 'the potency of cheap music' can so clearly mark times and places in one's memory. The tunes of this leave started with a glamorous cabaret singer in the Taj Mahal Hotel in Bombay singing 'A-tisket, A-tasket, I've Lost My Yellow Basket' and 'A Nightingale Sang in Berkeley Square'. Later in my leave, when I attended a 'Commem' Ball at Trinity, the band played 'Jeepers, Creepers, Where D'You Get Those Peepers?' and 'When the Deep Purple Falls over Sleepy Garden Walls'. These tunes always recall vividly to me the summer of 1939.

A long sea voyage is a wonderful way to start leave. Tired and sick passengers recovered steadily, in time to enjoy themselves when they landed. Shipboard life on steamers plying east of Suez had not changed over many years. Deck quoits, deck tennis, skittles, swimming, brisk walks round the deck, and dancing in the evening provided the exercise. Meals were gargantuan, and the menus cunningly devised to look even more varied than they were. By the end of the voyage we identified a 'Crimean War' pudding. A solid plum duff, it appeared successively on the menus as Alma, Balaclava, Inkerman and Sebastopol puddings.

And drink was cheap. I heard a steward, after receiving an order from a senior major with a very fruity complexion, remark to a colleague, 'Blimey! *Annuver* double gin! It's like feeding jujubes to a helephant!'

And there were the usual shipboard flirtations. I watched with interest the rivalry of two young subalterns for the attention of a graceful blonde. Leaning back on the rail one evening, well aware of how the pose accentuated the curves of her figure, she was approached by one suitor, and said yes, she would very much like a drink. Some minutes later the young man returned bearing a silver tray, with two long glasses clinking with ice, white napkins, and little bowls of salted nuts, to find his rival had slipped in with *his* offering and was drinking and laughing with the lady. The face of suitor number one was expressionless. He stood silent for a moment, taking in the scene and looking at the girl. Then in a slight and graceful movement he dropped his tray over the rail into the Indian Ocean, and strolled away. I was entranced. 'What style!' I thought. By the end of the voyage he had won.

Standing on the top deck one evening and looking down at the passengers on the main deck, I chatted with the First Officer, veteran of many such trips. 'By the end of the voyage,' he mused, 'I can usually tell if a couple, who shouldn't be, are sleeping together. Early on they become inseparable throughout the day. Then all of a sudden they cautiously avoid each other much of the daytime, and I guess they are in each other's company all night.'

Travelling home after a visit to relatives in Rangoon, a chatty elderly lady found her deck-chair next to that of a pleasant-faced, sympathetic-looking, middle-aged gentleman, and soon began to tell him of her trip. She had much enjoyed herself, but her parting had been a little clouded by worry about a favourite niece (one of the most beautiful girls in Rangoon). 'She is in love with a handsome man in one of the firms, who has no money, so marriage is difficult. And all the time she is being pursued by, and badgered to marry, a nasty old man – a judge, I believe.'

'Madam,' said her companion sadly, 'I *am* that nasty old man.'

One fellow-passenger was unhappy and withdrawn. This was a Garhwal Rifles major, who had been seconded to the Burma Rifles. He had an honest and likeable face. He told me one night that he had been in command of the troops which had fired on a large crowd of violent demonstrators in Mandalay a few weeks earlier. His detachment was small, and the crowd, headed as usual by young political monks, was of over 15,000 people. Completely out of hand they threatened to overwhelm his soldiers. About a dozen had been killed in the shooting. He was sure it had been right to shoot. But he could not sleep, thinking of that scene. After the volley, for what seemed to him an interminable and nightmarish time, the crowd did not break, but stayed solid and screaming in front of him. Then suddenly they realized that the bullets were real, and they broke and ran. This was the only occasion I remember in my time that troops fired on a Burmese crowd. Violent demonstrations ceased at once, and Burma remained quiet in the early years of the war.

Certain moments on the long voyages to and fro between England and the East linger in the minds of all who have travelled this road. There is the moment when one wakes suddenly in the night to hear the whole ship creaking and groaning as she fights through dirty weather. There is the strangely poignant moment when, leaning on the rail at night and looking at the black ocean, one sees another passenger ship, lights ablaze, passing silently by in the opposite direction. For outward travellers there is the morning when the ship's officers all appear in tropical white uniforms and the hatch-covers begin to give off the tarry scent of baking canvas; and over the side there are flying fish shimmering over the warm waters of the Indian Ocean. And there is the moment when the ship is motionless in harbour, without the accustomed throb of the engine, and one lies in one's bunk listening to the distant noise of cranes loading and unloading cargo, and to the fussy hooting of tugs and launches, and watches the sunlight, reflected off the water, rippling lazily on the cabin ceiling. And for travellers of my generation there was the recurring reassurance at so many ports of the presence of the Royal Navy – pinnaces hurrying about, brass gleaming and smart, cheery, white-clad sailors.

As we approached Marseilles we had a settling up of poker debts. A conservative and rather nervous player, I had nevertheless had a run of luck. One of the subalterns confessed that he just did not have enough spare cash to pay me. 'Tell you what,' he said, 'I'll give you my poshteen.' I was more than satisfied. This was a garment he had brought down from the North-West Frontier, of a type not then often seen in England – a long sheepskin coat with the wool inside and a goatskin collar. With a hairy green Tyrolean hat I had somehow acquired, I greatly fancied myself in this outfit, and much looked forward to the effect it would produce on my friends back in England.

At Marseilles I handed over my luggage to a Cook's man to put on the train to Switzerland, and set off for a drink in the town. On my return I found him, clearly a bit sozzled, sitting hopelessly by my luggage. Before I could speak, he raised his hand. 'I should explain something,' he said, 'I am *not* the Cook's man. We live in the same lodgings. He is ill, so I borrowed his hat to see if I could do myself a bit of good. But', he added sadly, 'it's all too complicated.' I collected a porter, managed to get all my gear on to the right train, and took my new friend off for a couple of quick drinks before we left. He seemed vaguely disappointed on parting that I didn't tip him.

My leave started with my parents, who at that time, owing to my mother's asthma, were living in a flat in Montreux. I was away a few days skiing, and on my return I could not see my prized new poshteen. 'Oh, that horrid thing,' said my dear mother. 'It smelt so badly I gave it to a Swiss shepherd!'

After exile, London seemed just as good as I expected it to be, its attractions seen for a few moments at least with all the impact of novelty. Just to travel in a clean, brightly lit, red London bus was a thrill. And on my first night in town I met old friends everywhere I went. After five years' absence I was pleased to find in one of my favourite pubs the same old layabout sitting cadging drinks in the corner of the bar. He recognized me at once. 'Hullo, old boy,' he said in his languid voice. 'Been away?'

As my leave wore on, the first fine careless rapture wore off. Old boon companions were married, and hard at work all day. After the initial reunion there was less and less in common to talk about. I found myself spending my time with other men on leave. Those were the days when it was still the custom for those on leave from the East to write their names and whereabouts in a book kept specially in the bar in Hatchett's in Piccadilly, so that friends could contact them.

In my club in Piccadilly I met Dudley Logan, a Bombaing friend from Pyinmana. He told me he was bored with the mud and slog of timber firm life and was going to get out. He was, however, fussed at the difficulty of getting another job. 'Don't worry,' I said lightly, 'there'll probably be a war soon and we'll all join up and get killed.' In his case this turned out to be all too true.

My ICS colleague Peter Knight from Baluchistan and I (both Class 1 magistrates) decided to do something professionally interesting, and, armed with a personal letter from His Majesty's Commissioner of Prisons (Patterson, who had once run a Borstal in Burma), we visited a number of British prisons, including Dartmoor and Wormwood Scrubs. At the latter place I suffered an embarrassment. On the strength of the Commissioner's letter, we were being shown around by the Deputy Governor, and asking all the right serious questions, when, as we passed one cell, the inmate bounded to the bars. 'Hullo, Leslie!' he called cheerily. He was another old friend, apparently in prison for putting out the lights in a night-club and pinching a diamond necklace off an elderly lady's neck.

I called in one day to see Dr Davis, my old supervisor and history tutor from the School of Oriental Studies. He gave me a long interrogation on Burma. I had to admit that politically things were not going too well. The increased nationalist pressure towards independence was understandable. But some of the leading nationalist politicians were unattractive characters, failures in other walks of life, underlining Samuel Johnson's dictum that 'Patriotism is the last refuge of a scoundrel'. 'Parliamentary democracy' had produced not parties differing in principle, but politicians constantly regrouping their followers, concerned mainly with power and the fruits of power, and when in opposition prepared to adopt almost any tactics to embarrass their opponents. Freedom of the press had permitted cheap little journals to foment violence, bloodshed and racial hatred. Political interference with justice and impartial administration was on the increase. I was for speeding up the process towards Burma ruling itself, but I was beginning to doubt the suitability of parliamentary democracy for a country like Burma. 'Adversary politics' seemed to be a luxury for a country with few experienced leaders. Dr Davis had an academic's reaction. 'Take a year's study leave and write a book about it!' he suggested – an idea which did not tempt me.

Waiting for a bus in Chelsea, I met an old school friend, James Hartung. Seeing I was bored, he took me off on a round of little drinking clubs, which London was full of at that time. If I remember rightly, I must that night have joined seven clubs as a 'life member' for a trifling sum. James was about to join a territorial unit in Chelsea as a lorry-driver. The next time I saw him was in the uniform of a major in the Royal Engineers in 1943, bargaining in a Delhi antique shop for a handsome lump of lapis lazuli.

Peter Knight and I and another friend also took a car over to Norway and Sweden. Again, amongst other frolics, we visited some prisons, and I still remember what a good idea it seemed in Swedish prisons to let the inmates keep budgerigars in their cells. Towards the end of this trip we called on the uncle of a Swedish acquaintance who had given us his address as a poste restante for our mail. To our surprise, we were met by a smart launch with a crew, and taken over to a private island. Our host, it appeared, was a Swedish ambassador on leave. This was July 1939, and he talked of the coming war. We hoped that the war-clouds would somehow move over. But he was positive.

'Which side will Sweden support, sir?' I asked him.

'Why, we shall be neutral of course, but many of our business-men will help Germany.'

'Who will win?'

'You can see round my house the books and pictures that show I am a sincere Anglophil, but I am sorry to say I believe the Germans will win.'

'Why do you think that?'

'Well, I have two nephews – one educated in Germany, determined and disciplined, and very industrious, able to take over the running of the family factories. The other, your friend, was educated at Oxford. He does not care to work, and spends most of his time out in a sailing-boat with a bottle of wine and a blonde.'

'I think you may be wrong, sir,' I said. 'If the war comes, the Germans will already have been going flat out for some time. The British haven't started yet. They are fresh. And when they do get started I think they will surprise you.'

My defensive remarks proved to have substance. Some of the wildest and most irresponsible of my Oxford friends covered themselves with glory in the war.

When I came on leave I had felt vaguely that it was about time I found myself a wife. But in England this turned out to be far from easy. My parents had then no fixed base in England, and I had no ready-made social circle. Girls I had known before were nearly all married. In London I met one or two entertaining urban butterflies who would have been unhappy and quite out of place in an up-country Burma district. I seriously thought of approaching the Dean of Women in London Univeristy for help in finding a suitable spouse from the latest crop of graduates. But somehow this seemed a bit cold-blooded, and anyway I doubted if my initiative would be sympathetically received by the Dean.

Towards the end of my leave my money was running out and boredom setting in. People in England were not really interested in India or Burma. The feeling was beginning to grow in me that in Burma was the real life, that was where the challenge and the comradeship lay. Before my leave was up I was recalled there, and, together with hundreds of Indian Army officers and reservists, I was waiting in York for embarkation on a big convoy from Glasgow when war was declared. I was actually inside a garage where a middle-aged mechanic was working on my car when the Prime Minister said the fateful words on the radio. The mechanic did not stop his work or look up. 'Well, here we go,' he said in a flat voice, reaching for another spanner.

The next day we sailed from Glasgow, guarded by warships.

On the *Duchess of Bedford* I found my old boss Bernard Binns, a veteran of the First World War. 'Listen to me, Leslie,' he said, 'there are a thousand officers on this ship and hardly any stewards. Life is going to be pretty uncomfortable with them.

But there are also a much smaller number of warrant officers, who will have a separate mess and look after themselves much better. As civilians no one will mind or notice if we attach ourselves to the warrant officers' mess.' It was good advice. 'By the way,' he said one evening, 'no one in the ICS is being released for the services at present, and as Commissioner of Settlements I have asked for you to join me in the Settlement Department.'

6 Settlement

The Field Season

After my brief brush with industry in the oilfields, Settlement work took me right back into the heart of rural Burma, the scene in which 90 per cent of our administration operated. As Philip Mason has pointed out in his autobiography, *A Shaft of Sunlight*, our Indian Empire was 'the last of the pre-industrial empires', with more in common with the empire of the Moguls than with more modern examples. The produce of the land had for centuries been the main source of Government revenue.

The Settlement and Land Records Department made and kept the most detailed and accurate maps and records of all the cultivated area of Burma. Based on these large-scale maps (16 inches to the mile) and their careful soil classification, on random harvesting of crops, on inquiries into the cost of agriculture (ploughing oxen, seed grain, implements, hired labour, etc.) and on the distance from the market, a land revenue rate was recommended for all types of crops in the district covered. The basic rates, later varied on a sliding scale following, for example, the price of rice in Rangoon, would hold good in theory for thirty years. The Settlement Officer, with his troop of surveyors and assessors and clerks, after two or three years' work, wrote a sort of Domesday Book for the district in which they operated, called a Settlement Report.

November to April, covering three months of 'cold' weather and three of 'hot', was the 'open season' in which field-work took place. From May to October there were the 'rains', during which the Settlement party withdrew to its headquarters to digest all the information it had collected, and to write up the statistics on which the final recommendations would be based. In the open season the Settlement Officer spent much of his time camping in a tent, or in a zayat or in a dak bungalow. Inspection of the kwins, as large field units were called, started very early in the morning. Shway Ba used to wake me while it was still dark by softly waggling my big toe. It was the Burmese custom to wake people gently, for fear that one's leipbya or butterfly spirit, released in sleep, might not have time to get back into one's body again. The Burmese had some odd ideas about the human spirit. When a Government servant died, it was still in some areas traditionally believed that his spirit could not be free to go until a superior officer had signed written permission for the dead man to resign from his post. I have solemnly signed such eerie release notes.

The tradition of the Department was that one arrived at the fields a little before daylight, even before the village cocks started crowing, at the hour which the Burmese describe as 'when there is light enough to see the lines on one's hand', and at which, as one unrolled the kwin maps, the first rays of the rising sun should come over one's shoulder to illuminate the map. The morning, which started crisp and dewy, but grew hotter and hotter, was spent trudging round the fields (usually in thick boots to minimize the risk of stepping on a Russell's viper) accompanied by elders from the local village, and checking the soil classification maps and holding registers.

When I first started Settlement work, a paddy-(rice) field looked to me just a regular flat field, the same all over. When I was more experienced, the contours stood out more like a range of mountains. Basically, fertility depended on water; and the practised eye could mark how the water normally circulated through the fields, which in slightly higher and off-course areas were starved, and which, in the hollows, were liable to be swamped. The feel of the soil in the less well-watered areas indicated its suitability for sesame, tomatoes, ground-nuts, cotton, millet, maize, chillies, and so on, while the silt-enriched watercourses grew tobacco in the dry season. The main crop was of course paddy, and Settlement Officers grew to know intimately the whole process of growing it: the repairing of the kazins, the low earthworks which kept the water in the fields; the broadcasting of the seed in the nurseries; the emergence of the pale green shoots in the nurseries changing to surely the purest and brightest green in the world; the slow churning of the fields with ploughs drawn by bullocks or water-buffaloes; the armies of cheerful women who transplanted the shoots to the main fields (with tradition-sanctioned ribald jokes and gestures if men approached during this operation); and the checking of the water-flow. Then after a longish gap came the harvest, reaping with small hand-sickles, threshing with slow-moving bullocks, and winnowing with large trays of plaited bamboo-cane, measuring by standard baskets, and transport to the collecting-point.

Sitting on the ground in the sunshine of a late afternoon at harvest time, back against piles of paddy straw, listening to the rhythmic shuffle of the golden grain in the winnowing trays, and savouring the strong scent of ripe, sun-baked crops, I felt close to rural communities throughout the centuries. *Fortunatus et ille deos qui novit agrestis* I had learnt from Virgil at school – 'Fortunate too is the man who has come to know the gods of the countryside.' There is deep contentment to be found in the last stages of a successful harvest. And it is the more real when one has followed the farmer's trials throughout the year – the hard manual labour, the threats from insects, wild animals and diseases, and the uncertainties of the weather, 'the long drawn question, between a crop and a crop'.

The Settlement party checked all these operations at each stage with great care. The hardest work was the checking and if necessary reclassifying of all the soil classification maps. Irritated by political attacks on 'unfair' assessments made by 'inefficient' Settlement parties, I persuaded a local Burmese member of the National Assembly to come out to see the work. We met at dawn, and I gave him a full morning's walking the fields in the baking sun. As we relaxed with curry and beer he asked me plaintively and sincerely, 'Mr Glass, does your *mother* know you have to work so hard?' We had no more complaints about sloppy work by the Settlement party.

In a later incarnation, when I was on the staff of Field-Marshal Sir John Harding during the EOKA troubles in Cyprus, I was titular boss of Lawrence Durrell, then the Government Press Officer. One evening after several bottles of Cyprus wine in a little wine shop in Kyrenia, Larry, who thought I had always been in the Foreign Office, lashed out at me with some contempt. He himself had had his hard times, and earned his living at one stage as a waiter. 'You', he declared, 'have never done a real day's work in your life!' He meant manual or physical work. I gave him a short description of life in the open season in the Burma Settlement Department. The next morning he sent me a copy of a little privately printed edition of his poems. Inside was written, 'Mea culpa, Larry', the most graceful of apologies. To my sorrow, somewhere on my travels the book has disappeared.

The morning's slogging in the fields was followed by a bath (hot water from kerosene tins has a distinctive metallic scent), brunch, and a nap. I lost count of the number of bottles of Rose's Lime Juice Cordial I finished in an open season. It was always my first thirst quencher as I collapsed, drenched in sweat, into my canvas camp-chair.

In the early afternoon there was a discussion with the local elders about all aspects of cultivation. After tea, when the cool of the evening began, I would put a handful of cartridges in my pocket, take my dog and gun and wander round the fields on the edge of the jungle, where the jungle fowl would venture out to feed, or walk quietly through the upland scrub listening for the partridge calling from the bushes, or peer up into banyan trees for green pigeon. This was genuine shooting for the pot and brought me many a tasty camp meal. The fun of this sort of shooting was doubled by one's having a gun dog. I received my Springer bitch as a small puppy, scarcely weaned, when I was off on tour. In the evening I was wandering round the camp with a gun, and shot a partridge which fell into a thicket. I had marked the spot, but simply couldn't find the bird. Then I thought of Sally, fetched her, putting the little scrap in my pocket, and walked back to the thicket. I put her on the ground and sat back to smoke a cheroot. She picked her way slowly about and suddenly went rigid. Sure enough, under the tall grass in front of her, was the bird. Rarely can a gun dog have started its working life so early.

Tropical night fell as if suddenly a curtain had been drawn. Each evening I ate a solitary dinner by the light of a Tilley pressure lamp, usually reading a book in front of me on a folding wooden table lectern. One hand manipulated a fork, and the other turned the pages. I must have read all the Penguins and Pelicans so far produced, on whatever topic.

Sometimes some villagers turned up for a chat round the fire; but in any case I was asleep on my camp-bed by 9 p.m. each night.

THARRAWADDY

I did my initial Settlement training under a more senior ICS officer, Frank George, who was doing the Settlement of the famous district of Tharrawaddy. Frank was a spare, scholarly figure in owlish spectacles. His appearance was utterly deceptive. When on leave, he climbed mountains, sailed and explored the farthest recesses of Greenland. Indeed he had missed sailing with us on the *Duchess of Bedford* at the beginning of the war because he was in Greenland and couldn't be reached in time. Oddly enough, as a small boy I had always been interested in the exploration of frozen lands, and one of my heroes had been Ernest Shackleton. As a special treat, way back in 1920, my mother had taken me to hear him lecture, and even managed to get me (completely tongue-tied) on the platform to shake the great man's hand. I had been enormously impressed by the fact that when during the lecture he described the agonies of thirst he and his comrades suffered on their epic boat trip from Elephant Island to South Georgia, he had had to stop and take a drink from a carafe of water on the table. As a small boy, one of my favourite topics for crayon drawings was the multicoloured aurora borealis crackling behind 'winter quarters' below Mount Erebus. And later a mutual friend at Oxford had brought to our digs Gino Watkins, the dashing young Arctic explorer of those days. Gino had talked of his trips and tried to teach us how to crack a long seal hide whip. So I was able to follow Frank George's stories about tundra moss and rolling kayaks. Frank's vade-mecum was a wonderful pocket volume produced by the Royal Geographical Society called *The Explorer's Handbook*, which told you how to survive anywhere in the world. A trained statistician, he took me in hand and told me simple facts like the difference between a 'mean' and an 'average', and the validity and limits of 'random selection". Erudite in literature, he quizzed me in the evenings with such questions as 'What was the name of the Indian in *Moby Dick*?' He had read geology at Cambridge and never moved without his hammer, and he had a lecture on local rocks ready for me by dinner. He introduced me to chemical tests for soil analysis, and to the principles of ecology, and at all points tried to keep me to a standard of accuracy beyond my normal bent. Not unnaturally, after he left Burma he joined the UN Food and Agriculture Organization in Rome. We became and remained great friends.

I saw Frank a couple of years or so ago, long retired. He had just returned from sailing (at the age of seventy) through an especially turbulent area of the ocean from Iceland to the Solent, with the veteran mountaineer and sailor Harold Tilman (rising eighty). I saw him again in London the next year and asked him what he was doing. 'Looking for Tilman,' he said. I had read that Tilman with six young companions had vanished on his latest trip between Rio and the Falklands. 'Here in London?' I inquired. 'Yes,' he said. He had on retirement taken on navigation as a hobby, and became editorial consultant to the Royal Institute of Navigation. He explained that he was poring over charts of currents in the seas where Tilman had disappeared, trying to calculate where a disabled ship could have drifted to, and where rescuers could most profitably search. He could have added, like Alonso in *The Tempest*, 'The sea mocks our frustrate search on land', for Tilman was never found.

Tharrawaddy district was notorious as the cradle of the Burmese Rebellion of 1930, when Saya San, a fanatic monk, persuaded his followers that, tattooed with his cabalistic signs and wearing his charms and amulets, they would be impervious to bullets. I still possess a Tharrawaddy 'silver bullet' acquired by Jim Lindop in the Rebellion, and given me by his widow. It unscrews to show inside two tiny carved figures of a Buddha and a nat (spirit), and some black threads bound by silver tags. The peasant who had carried this talisman had thought himself invulnerable.

Modern Burmese writers now refer to this Rebellion as an important nationalist milestone, an act of desperate resistance to the foreign occupier. No doubt there was something of this in it, though much of Burma remained unaffected. Saya San found many peasants in a mood for protest, as the slump was causing Indian money-lenders to foreclose on mortgages into which the Burmans had lightly entered. Any student of Burmese history will also recognize one of the regular and frequent appearances of a 'pretender' to the throne (often a man with authentic links with the Royal House; King Bodawpaya had 166 children and 433 grandchildren), ambitious to rule in glory.

Saya San, a monk-magician, a necromancer and alchemist, called himself the Thapannakate Galon Raja, 'the Dragon King', set up his 'palace' in a bamboo hut in Tharrawaddy, donned royal regalia, and paraded under a golden umbrella. He ordered his 'generals' to raise an infantry brigade to be called 'The Shield of Royalty', and artillery batteries to be known as 'The Invincible Thunderers', and then carried on as if these formations actually existed. He kept a diary in which he recorded his second coronation thus: 'My second coronation was solemnized this day in a stately cave, a lovely place forty cubits long and thirty cubits wide, garnished with figures of Nats, Dragons and Animals, not the work of man but of nature. This day the Earth shook, the Moon eclipsed and two Suns rose together in the East.' Another of his proclamations reads: 'There shall be tribulation. The Burmans still wander on the mountains, and the Kachins on the plains. The sky shall be overcast with rain. The cities shall flow with blood, and the Paddy Bird [the British] that slew the Hunter [King Thibaw] shall be slain by the Dragons [the Galon rebels].' Saya San and his peasant following were not far removed in time from the medieval world in which his fantasies could flourish.

Dacoits and bandits joined in the disorder, and it took over a year, and extra troops from India, to put down the rising, in 1932.

To be Deputy Commissioner of the rebel district of Tharrawaddy only a few years later was a tricky assignment. Always a violent area, it averaged, with a population of $1\frac{1}{2}$ million, eighty murders a year. The Government had appointed Dick Richards, who succeeded remarkably in getting the trust and affection of his truculent charges. A kind and straightforward man, purged of pettiness by his experience of the horrors of Gallipoli and the Somme, he loved Burma and the Burmese. He did his best for them, and they knew it. I can still see him, squatting by a camp-fire, in relaxed companionship with village elders, a cheroot between his teeth, occasionally grunting out some question about the crops or cattle, or laughing at some ribald village joke. He did his job so well that he was kept on in this difficult post long after he had merited transfer. He was at heart a writer and a poet, and is the author of a number of slim volumes, mostly about his beloved Burma. He is a dedicated fisherman and a lover of cricket. Sometimes in the unlikely arena of a dusty field outside Tharrawaddy he conjured up a cricket match, mainly with Indians and Anglo-Indians. I am an erratic cricketer, but on this occasion I hit one blow in which everything seemed to click perfectly, and the ball disappeared far off in a grove of mango trees. Like Betjeman's golf shot, it was 'a glorious sailing bounding drive'.

After the game an old Indian merchant, one of the few spectators and a passionate aficionado of cricket, approached me solemnly. 'Sir,' he said, 'yours was the biggest hit I have seen in Tharrawaddy. The ball landed in my mango grove. With Your Honour's permission I propose to erect a small commemorative masonry pillar!'

If ever a future archaeologist comes on this little monument, there must be long odds against his guessing what it marks.

Dick and his wife Cynthia were kind and generous hosts to Frank and me when we were in from the fields. When we planned to repay this hospitality we pondered on what special delicacies we should order from far-off Rangoon. The definition of items as 'luxurious' relates closely to their scarcity. The main dainties I remember we ordered were cold-store kippers, cold-store butter, and two bottles of sloe gin.

In the northern part of the district there were some foothills and not uninteresting country. In the south were the interminable flat paddy-lands of the Irrawaddy delta. Trudging round these drab fields was a chore. There was little shooting, except the odd snipe from railway track borrow-pits, and the climate was damp and sticky. Lying awake one lonely night in a gloomy, sour-smelling, bat-infested dak bungalow, listening to the high pinging of a mosquito which had somehow got under my net, I thought, What the hell am I doing here? I must be mad.

This sort of mood afflicted all of us from time to time, most often perhaps in the damp and mildew of the rains, but also at the end of the hot weather when temperatures rose in Upper Burma to over 110 degrees. This was the classic syndrome of the young English 'civilian' exiled in the East, of whom Alfred Lyall wrote in the 1880s:

> And he lies as thy scorching winds blow
> Recollecting old England's sea breezes
> On his back in the lone bungalow....
>
> With the sweets of authority sated
> Would he give up his throne to be cool?

In such a mood one April, thinking of the green hills on the Welsh border, and the daffodils blooming, and the cuckoo calling beside the trout streams (and now I live here and it really *is* like that), I sent this disgruntled parody of my favourite poet of the Marches to my friend Peter Knight in India:

> In summertime on Popa
> My love and I would sit
> And watch the mangy pi-dogs
> Amid the flies and shit,
> And spray ourselves with Flit.

Young civilians in the mofussil (provinces) had in truth little female society. In most up-country stations there were a few British wives, but the young girls who came out from England in the cold weather concentrated, for the most part, in Rangoon and Maymyo. In some stations there were Anglo-Indian girls, often very attractive, but unspoken conventions limited these friendships. Some British officials married Anglo-Indian and Anglo-Burmese girls, and very charming they could be; but in those days it was definitely not the done thing, and young officials were dissuaded from such a venture. There were then few, if any, educated Burmese girls in most up-country places. The village girls were, of course, charming and friendly creatures – neat and dainty, scented with jasmine, fragrant thanaka powder, and the coconut oil from their hair. The Government frowned on any official having a Burmese mistress, though this was not unknown. This opposition was not so much a question of Victorian morals as the Government's understandable obsession against possibilities of corruption.

However honest the officer, there would always be the danger that his Burmese girl could, unknown to him, take bribes and promise to try to influence him in some case or another. Again, some officials married Burmese wives and lived happily with them. Burmese women were amongst the freest in the world, and many were excellent businesswomen. But few transplanted easily from their native soil.

Although some young officers came out from Britain married for their first tour, this was not particularly well viewed, as it barred their posting to some of the more unpleasant places and was thus not fair to their bachelor colleagues. In fact, few of my colleagues married young. By and large for several years we were starved of female companionship of our own sort. Most of us were well over thirty and pretty mature before we married. The wife of one colleague complained to my wife years later, 'I sympathize with anyone who has married an ICS officer. They are so damnably self-sufficient.'

MANDALAY

Before *le cafard* had really got me, however, I was posted to run my own Settlement Party to do the Settlement of Mandalay district – one of the nicest districts for such operations in the whole of Burma. Mandalay city was a fascinating and comfortable base. Along the Irrawaddy there was a great variety of agriculture, lakes in the north with duck shooting, partridge in the foothills, jungle fowl and woodcock higher up, and in the paddy-fields outside Mandalay some of the most fabulous snipe-shooting in the world. Also near Mandalay was the famous small area of paddy-fields which, like some classic French vineyard, produced taung-deik-pan, an incomparable small-grained rice which commanded a high price from rice connoisseurs even outside Burma. And closer in still were the neglected royal mango orchards, where big yellow mangoes grew in the same garden as long red ones and a variety of green ones. Up in Maymyo, which was also in the district, some of the main crops were asters and strawberries, grown in the fields of Anisakan for the Rangoon market.

In high good humour I drove along the canal, north-east of Mandalay, which ran along the base of the Shan foothills, to the airy bungalow at the headworks. Canals and irrigation channels, however small compared with the vast works in India, brought me happy memories of my childhood and my father. As a cool breeze came off the headworks weir, I drank a solitary bottle of excellent Mandalay-brewed beer and felt the joy of being alive. Bernard Binns had showed me how to cool beer on tour. The bottles were put in a canvas bucket filled with straw and drenched with water. The bucket was then hung in the hottest sun. Regular watering kept evaporation going and the end-product was nice cool beer. I met the same principle at work in 1943 in Delhi, where the grandest and most expensive hotels were still cooled by a primitive and traditional form of air-conditioning. This consisted of kuskus tatties, long curtains of straw and fibre hung over the entrance doorways which were kept constantly wet by a minion standing by. Evaporation from these screens, besides producing a rather depressing dank smell, cooled the entrance halls.

The countryside near Mandalay, last seat of the Burmese kings, was tradition-ridden and haunted. Groves near the canal were said to be inhabited by nats, spirits of heroes and princesses, dead in combat or by misadventure or suicide. Farther up the Irrawaddy a malicious female nat controlled a whirlpool. If the Tungye Thakinma, the Tungye Lady, didn't care for you, she could turn your boat over. Even educated Burmans were nervous sailing past this spot. The zat pwes in the village dramatized stories of kings, wise men, magicians, ogres, generals and slaves taken from a medieval world which had actually existed here within living memory. And away to the east the Shan plateau had its own ancient traditions and its hereditary princes, the 'Sawbwas', 'Lords of the Sunset', who still kept some sort of civilized court.

One young Sawbwa, Sao Hkunhkio, the Sawbwa of Mongmit, had in his student days in England acquired an English consort. Mabel, Mahadevi of Mongmit, came from a comparatively modest family, but she was born a queen. Tall, slim, blonde and serious, she had a quiet dignity and strong sense of duty. Anyone who marries a husband of a different language and culture finds that one of her greatest trials is her husband's family, and Mabel faced many jealousies and intrigues in her court. But she supported her husband with love

Burmese Minthami or dancing girl

Outer wall and moat of Mandalay Palace

3 Timber elephants

4 A Twinsa, traditional Burmese shallow-well oil worker

5 Winnowing paddy

and courage, and when the Japanese overran Burma she stayed with him. Both of them survived the war.

Mandalay city itself was haunted by past glories and cruelties. As short a time ago as 1856, at the founding of King Mindon's new capital, pregnant women had been buried alive under the posts of the main palace, so that their ghosts would ever be on guard against intruders. In the old Frenchman's shop in Mandalay I found a life-sized wooden statue of a Burmese warrior, the paint all gone from the surface of pale, weathered wood. He was carried round on a bullock-cart with my baggage, and each night he stood in front of my tent. My servants and the Settlement clerks approved. I was under special and magical protection.

North and east of the canal headworks lay real jungle, in which I sometimes took a day off. Before entering the forests for shooting, an old Burmese hunter, his long hair twisted into a top-knot, and with blue-tattooed thighs, who came with me, shed his sandals and insisted on obeisance to the nat of the forest, with a little oblation of gin. All the Burmese people had originally come down from the mountains of Tibet and China, and their pre-Buddhist animism (still strong in the present hill tribes) lingered on. Fear of certain 'nature nats' was widespread. There were, for example, believed to be in certain rivers little creatures with elephant-like heads, local kelpies, who could drag down a traveller and his horse to a watery doom.

One night of the full moon, in a remote dak bungalow near the canal, I was woken by a loud shaking and rustling of leaves from a large banyan tree close to my window. I got up and went on to the veranda to see what the cause was, and became aware that all around the tree was quiet and still. The breeze, if that is what it was, was extraordinarily local. Lights began to appear in the servants' quarters, and I could hear excited voices. One voice was hoarse and incoherent. When Shway Ba appeared with a hurricane lamp he said, 'The cook is very drunk and frightened. He says there is a nat in the tree.' The cook was indeed screeching drunk on local liquor. Soon the tree was still.

When I was on leave I told my father about this incident. He said that in India he was woken in a dak bungalow by a noise as if all the crockery and furniture in the bungalow were clattering about. He ran out and found the leaves of a big tree outside quivering and trembling. This sort of happening was well known at this spot. He was told that the bungalow was once lived in by an alcoholic old lady, who was now in an institution. The phenomenon in the old house was said to coincide with particularly manic fits suffered by her in the institution. Burmans generally believed firmly that this shaking of leaves denoted a nat in the tree. They even believed there were three sorts of tree nat: Akakasoh, who lives at the tops of trees; Shekkasoh, who lives in the trunk; and Boomasoh, who lives in the roots.

A river flowed through the trees beyond the headworks, and there were pools full of fish. Lying by the river one afternoon, tired of fishing, I heard a clear whistle, and soon after saw a pair of otters playing in the water close by. They were obviously having fun for fun's sake. Another time I saw a family of mongooses gambolling in the sun. And high across the forest clearings ungainly hornbills flew wobbling, always looking about to overbalance. Sometimes a splash marked not a fish but a big lizard, a put, swimming away. Snakes were rare. I once shot a hamadryad, a king cobra, surprised by my dog. Poised to attack, it reared 3 feet into the air. I made off fast after killing it, before its mate arrived. But throughout my time in Burma I saw very few snakes.

The most famous place for hamadryads was Mount Popa, the extinct volcano, sacred home of the Mahagari nats, which rose sheer from the flat plains round the oilfields. There one could see the graceful and chilling ritual in which the Burmese snake-charmers, men and women, ended their dance by bending slowly foward and kissing the huge cobras, allegedly without having first removed their poison fangs. The danger seems to have been real, as every now and then there was a fatal accident. 'Cam' Fraser, the Mrs Malaprop amongst the Scots technicians in the oilfields, once shook his companions by warning an American tourist of the dangers of Mount Popa. 'Madam,' he said, 'take care up yon hill – you'll be likely attacked by haemorrhoids!'

Our field headquarters was in Mandalay itself. Another young bachelor, Geoffrey Thomas, working in the Settlement of a neighbouring district, and I lodged when we were in Mandalay with the senior judge of Upper Burma, in his spacious bungalow. Geoffrey was a short, merry, black-moustached Welshman, known for some reason as 'The Orphan', whose *joie de vivre* often set him off on spontaneous escapades. When I went out with him in his car in Mandalay one day to post some letters, he suddenly got the bit between his teeth and drove hell for leather 50 miles up the hill to Maymyo, where, after borrowing a change of clothes and some money, we spent a cheerful weekend.

One of our special friends in Maymyo was the legendary 'Beaver' Barton. This middle-aged, rotund, bearded character fell into no normal Burma category. Left behind by some Cambridge University expedition to Indonesia, he had fallen for South-East Asia and never gone home. He seemed to have private money and lived with two excellent Chinese servants in a flat over a shop in Maymyo, where he kept open house to selected friends. His hospitality included amongst other drinks an astonishing selection of obscure liqueurs. He spoke several languages, and his conversation when not ribald was often donnish and sophisticated. He disappeared mysteriously from time to time, and rumour had it that he was somehow connected with Intelligence on the China border. Certainly later in the war I met him again, still unaccountably wearing his beard, but dressed in the uniform of a major of the Royal Engineers. He was living with an attractive red-headed hairdresser in a rather unsalubrious quarter of Calcutta, and still sometimes disappearing mysteriously. He kept well out of conventional social circles in Maymyo. Once a general's wife, determined to pin down this mystery man, set off to collect from him a contribution for some charity. 'Beaver' was warned by his friends. When the lady rang his doorbell 'Beaver' appeared, smoking a vast cheroot. 'I didn't expect visitors. But won't you come in?' he said politely. He was stark naked. The lady fled.

The Orphan and I envied his life of eccentric self-indulgence, and enjoyed his company. One evening in his flat, Geoffrey, his judgement dulled by wine, invited the 'Beaver' to come to a grand garden party shortly to be given by the Judge for all the notables of Mandalay, and to bring with him the equipment to make his famous punch with fifteen ingredients. Back in Mandalay good sense returned. We concocted a telegram to

Barton in Maymyo: REFERENCE YESTERDAY'S INVITATION ON NO ACCOUNT REPEAT ON NO ACCOUNT COME.

It was too late. On the morning of the party a large dilapidated open tourer drew up, the back seat full of bottles, and the boot containing a large iron cauldron. Quite what went wrong will never be known. Perhaps Geoffrey in his nervousness tipped in one of the wrong bottles – but I have never witnessed anything like the result. At one moment the Judge's guests, Burmese and Europeans, all in their best clothes, were chattering brightly on the lawns in front of his house. A few minutes later a scythe seemed to have been swept through several groups of the party. Many of the most distinguished visitors had to be supported home, and the distraught Judge spent most of the night writing abject letters of apology.

The next morning we had one of our recurring scenes at breakfast. The Judge, looking pale and sighing heavily, said that he regretted that we must find other accommodation as soon as possible. His decision was final

Our life with Judge Alan Gledhill, the kindest and most conscientious of men, was a sort of Burmese version of an Aldwych farce of those times. Geoffrey and I, young and feckless, were the Ralph Lynn and Tom Walls types, and Alan, mild, balding, mature and responsible, strove like Robertson Hare to keep the train on the rails. When after some shenanigan or another which the Judge felt quite out of keeping with a judicial establishment, we had one of our eviction ultimatums, Geoffrey would catch my eye and lean back in his chair. 'Wouldn't think of it, Alan old boy,' he would say. 'How lonely you would be! Having us here is very good for you, you know. We keep you young and jolly. But for us you'd fade away!' By the evening we would be sipping the Judge's excellent cocktails of Mandalay rum, cane sugar and fresh limes, and our host's furious protests of the morning would have been shelved yet again.

In spite of the apparent austerity of Buddhism, the Burman is a somewhat reckless, pleasure-loving character with a strong sense of humour, and he approves of the same characteristics in others. Even when there were hot political passions seething in

Mandalay bazaar, Geoffrey was welcome there at all hours, drinking and joking with some of the Government's more voluble enemies, and flirting with the political Thakinmas. Where indiscretions by a more stuffy officer might spark off a howl of protest in the Burmese press, the officers they liked were shown wide tolerance. The officers whom the villagers recollected were remembered not so much for their administrative acts as for their personalities. From the distant past many recalled the Kya Ayebaing, the Tiger DC, who kept a pet tiger under his bungalow, and shared some of his pet's qualities. Then there was Williamson, an officer whose eccentricities had under them the safety-net of a comfortable private income. Reprimanded for slowness in coming when summoned by his Commissioner, and told that in future he should come *at once*, whatever he was doing, he answered a later summons by being borne in slung on bamboo-poles, naked in his tin tub. One of the best-loved of officers was Bernard Swithinbank, a tall, angular Etonian and scholar, who used, when bored with paperwork in a senior post, to stalk off alone, with a Shan bag over his shoulder, to wander for days through the villages, in order to recapture the feel of the people he was administering.

Best remembered by the Burmese of all British governors was Sir Harcourt Butler, a plump, jovial figure, indiscreet in words and actions, who liked racecourses, good living and grand tours, and unconventional friends. He was lucky in that his regime coincided with a period of prosperity. Sir Charles Innes, the gaunt and austere Scotsman who succeeded him in the increasing economic gloom of the early thirties, remarked sadly, 'After the Lord Mayor's Show, the dust-cart. And I am the dustman.'

One day in 1941, Alan Gledhill told us that there were some Indian Congress detainees shut up in Mandalay gaol. I got permission to go to see them. They were young, educated and bored. They gave me a polite welcome. I remember thinking with surprise how much more 'English' they seemed than the Burmans one met in Mandalay. I promised to get them some books, and indeed sent them in a large parcel. Except in Rangoon I did not very often see a Burmese house with a bookcase in it.

Recess in Rangoon

By special dispensation Bernard Binns arranged that my party should in the rains spend its 'recess' in Rangoon. Of all places in Burma Rangoon was the least Burmese. The largest rice port in the world, its commerce and industry were dominated by the people who had built it up from what a couple of centuries back had been a small fishing village – the British (especially the Scots), the Indians and the Chinese. In Rangoon were the headquarters of the Government, the High Court and the Parliament of Burma, but it was pre-eminently the haunt of the expatriate businessman on whom so much of the country's prosperity depended.

Binns kindly offered to put me up until I found accommodation. On my first night with him, after a long spell in the 'jungle', I went out to enjoy the bright lights. In the early hours of the next morning, as I drove up the road lined with senior officials' bungalows, I thought that a cautious and quiet return would be prudent. So I switched off my lights and my engine, and coasted silently in the dark into my chief's drive.

The next morning I was awakened by one of the house servants. 'Binns Thakin would like you to have breakfast with him,' he said, in grave tones. Out on the veranda the white-haired Binns Thakin was sitting, shoulders hunched, gazing morosely out at his lawn. A hoopoe, its black-and-white wing feathers shining in the sun, unfurled its crest at an emerald-green bee-eater, and pecked at the grass. Beyond, in the middle of a once magnificent bed of scarlet cannas, my host's especial pride, sat my car.

Most of the official villas in Rangoon has passable gardens. The Indian malis did their best with such flowers as could survive the climate – cannas, zinnias, balsams, coxcombs, bougainvillaea, marigolds and the inevitable 'stockus and flockus', as the malis pronounced stocks and phlox.

I was in time forgiven for my car in the cannas, and more than once, in the old aroma of gin and menthol, we repeated our late-night choruses of Monywa, ending by tradition with 'And Boney's on the sea, said the Shan Van Vaugh!'

'Golden Valley', where many officials lived, had little damp corners populated by frogs, and my most abiding memory of night in Rangoon in the rains is the loud, incessant and cheerful croaking of the frogs.

In 1940 my sister came out and married her Burma Oil Company fiancé in Rangoon. The wedding reception was held in Bernard Binns's garden. Her husband was almost immediately commissioned into Burma Army Signals.

Bernard had played a large part in getting a 46-pound paddy measuring basket, of standard specific dimensions, laid down as the only legal measuring basket – a move for the protection of the jungle peasant selling to city slickers. He was a passionate advocate of land reform (probably the most important task in Burma) and drafted the original Bills which the Burmese Parliament finally adopted. Between 1937 and 1941 Burmese ministers brought into law a Tenancy Act, a Land Purchase Act and a Land Alienation Act, and made some advance with agricultural credit and land mortgage banks. Frank George and I used to argue with Binns about his use in drafts of the term 'fair rent'. We said that 'fair' was a moral and relative conception too vague for a legal document. He said that there was a commonsense consensus on what 'fair' meant in the circumstances of Burma. I forget how the argument was resolved.

For a young bachelor the recess in the rains in Rangoon allowed a pleasant and relaxed life. Unlike work in the districts, office hours were regular, and time after office was one's own. I played soccer for the Gymkhana Club team, and golf on the lush course at Mingaladon. There was at that time a separate Burmese Golf Club, at which, however, reverence for the Royal and Ancient was no less sincere than at Mingaladon. Burmese members like my friend U Kyaw Min, who on a visit to Britain had actually played a round at St Andrew's, were jokingly entitled to be addressed within the Club as 'Haji' (the title gained by pilgrims who have visited Mecca).

Mixed bridge, tennis, the cinema, dancing, moonlight parties at the swimming club and sailing club made Rangoon life socially more amusing than life up-country. Some of the urban wives were refreshingly witty and bitchy and irresponsible. And there was even some night life. The most respectable of Rangoon night spots was the Silver Grill. Gentlemen were admitted only if they were wearing a dinner-jacket. Burma 'black-tie rig' incidentally was on the Calcutta pattern of black dinner-jacket and cummerbund and white trousers, as opposed to the (in my eyes somewhat smarter) Punjab rig of black trousers and white dinner-jacket. As I lived some way out, and never knew when the spirit would move me, I kept a suitcase with some spare dinner-clothes with my friend Pete Arratoon, the Armenian owner and manager of the Silver Grill. A short ex-boxer, with a cauliflower ear and a husky voice, he was a good and wise friend. Sometimes, bored by the 'imported' cabaret (this was the era when blondes, clad in long, wispy dresses of fuschia colours, did elaborate 'adagio' dances with slim, dark partners), I would join him and his cousin in the private cubby-hole. They would often while away blank spots in the evening by playing draughts. I recall the cousin complaining, 'I'm tired of playing with you, Pete, you always win. Can't you give me a handicap?'

'Sure, I agree to a handicap.'

'Now we'll have a better game. What's the handicap to be?'

Pete made a magnanimous wave of his hand. 'I'll play you left-handed!' he croaked.

One night, driving down to the bright lights through blinding monsoon rain, I hit the outer wheel of a rickshaw. The rickshaw-man was shocked though not hurt, but the police decided to prosecute. Conviction for dangerous driving would have done me no good at all.

The Commissioner of Police, Rangoon, Mr Prescott, was a Scot of rugged and dour integrity. He had little love for the ICS and thought this a good opportunity to make an example of a young member of the service. I decided to beard him in his spacious office, on entering which I noted that his face looked more like granite than ever.

'I have a request to make of you, Mr Prescott, about a driving case I am involved in.'

'Oh, yes?' he said, his eyes already glistening with the pleasure he would get in smacking me down.

'I have seen the police papers –'

'You shouldn't have!' he interrupted.

'– and the prosecution says "the accused then drew up outside the Montparnasse".'

This was a much lower grade night-spot beyond the Silver Grill, frequented by drunk sailors, though graced with a dignified and noble-featured Red Indian 'bouncer', the flotsam of a bankrupt travelling circus.

'As you know, Commissioner, the Montparnasse is not a very nice place. My intention was to visit the Silver Grill – indeed my car was near to that entrance. I should be obliged if for the sake of my reputation you could have the police record corrected.'

He stared at me in silence for a moment, and then even his eyes crinkled with the faint hint of a smile. 'All right,' he said.

In fact the Magistrate (a Chinese) found that my offence lay in the range of minor offences which could legally be 'compounded' by a suitable payment to the aggrieved party. The rickshaw wallah was more than satisfied with his recompense, and the threat to my career was lifted.

Both in Maymyo and Rangoon I made friends with Army officers and dined formally in regimental messes – those of the Burma Rifles, the King's Own Yorkshire Light Infantry and the Gloucestershire Regiment, and was refreshed by the orderly ritual of mess night, the pipers of the Burma Rifles, and the excerpts of Gilbert and Sullivan from the regimental orchestras. The officers' nicknames had a schoolboy cruelty. One of the more homely subalterns was known as 'Rosebud'. Another, better looking, was always called 'Cherry'.

'Why so?' I inquired.

'Oh, don't you know, old boy. Short for Cherrapunji – wettest place in the world!'

I checked: the rainfall at Cherrapunji is about 400 inches a year.

I came across in the Gloucesters an old friend of mine from school and Oxford, where he had had a considerable reputation as a beer drinker. Once in a railway train I got talking to a private in his regiment. 'Do you known Captain A?' I asked. 'Oh, yes! We always ask for him as Prisoner's Friend!' The captain was killed later in the war, and I thought that remark would have made an epitaph he would have liked.

One of the big communities of Rangoon was the Chinese. They kept very much to themselves. But in Rangoon I sampled the delicate nuances of classic Chinese cuisine, in a banquet of thirty-five courses given by a Chinese friend. Tradition demanded a sip of plain tea between each course to cleanse the palate, but on this occasion we must have lost some of the subtleties of flavour, as our host provided each guest with a large bottle of whisky and one small bottle of soda.

There was also a choice of Chinese restaurants in the city, where the food was good, and each male guest was waited on by his own little Chinese girl, who cracked sunflower seeds for him with her teeth, fed him with delicacies on chopsticks, and wiped his face and hands with perfumed towels. A meal was a delightful and civilized ceremony. The young lades were, however, like the Bunnies in the Playboy Club in London, not to be touched by the customers.

On fine evenings in the rains the Chinese would fly kites from the high bunds round the royal lakes, after covering their kite-strings with glue and powdered glass, and betting on who could first saw through his opponent's kite-string.

More than half the population of Rangoon were Indians – the dock labourers, the mill workers, many office staff, lawyers, doctors, merchants and traders, the last categories including some very rich men. Indians paid more than half of Rangoon's taxes. Across the Bay of Bengal loomed a powerful backer for Indian interests.

The one place in Rangoon where all communities met on a cheerful and equal basis was Kyaiksakan Race Course. The Burmese are inveterate and passionate gamblers, and it raised immediate misgivings if one saw a sub-treasury officer in the crowd.

In one district a visiting Commissioner announced a spot check of a sub-treasury. The sub-treasury officer solicitously placed the Commissioner under a shady tree and brought him some tea, while he went off to open the building. After rather a long wait the Commissioner went to find out the cause of the delay. The sub-treasury officer, who had for long been borrowing large sums of Government money for his betting, had this time been fairly surprised. Consequently he had thought fast and logically, rapidly cleaning out the strong-room of all the remaining money he could lay his hands on, and departed for ever.

A friend who recently visited 'socialist' Rangoon tells me that one of the first notices to be seen on arrival reads: *Import of All Gambling Paraphernalia Strictly Forbidden.*

I remember after the war sitting on a houseboat on the Nile at

Cairo and being told a story by an old ICS colleague of mine, from another province, who had also ended up in the Diplomatic Service.

'When I was a junior,' he said, 'I was on the Governor's staff in the capital city. I made friends with one of the ADCs and we really lived it up – well beyond our means. One day we faced the chill fact that we were both very seriously in debt. Disaster loomed ahead. So we decided to go for broke. One of our friends had a racehorse which he had long assured us would win at the next meeting. We sold everything we could, borrowed more, and we put our all on the horse to win. If it lost we planned to send in our papers.'

'What happened?' I asked.

'It won,' said my friend. 'We paid off all our debts and had some money in hand. That very evening I proposed to the lady you know as my wife.'

'My God!' I said. 'It must have been exciting watching the finish of that race!'

'Watching the finish?' said my friend. 'You must be joking. I was downstairs in the loo being sick!'

The old Indian Empire was a horsy world. So it came as rather a shock to many old-timers when, in 1935, an ex-submarine commander, Sir Archibald Cochrane, VC, who turned out to be a notably unhorsy man, was appointed Governor of Burma.

I remember the tragic faces of his ADCs in Maymyo. 'Would you believe it, old boy? He takes us for long walks every afternoon on the golf-course. My legs have got so muscular I can't get into my polo boots!'

Watching the Rangoon races on the great day of the Governor's Cup, Sir Archibald moved his gaze to an aeroplane in the distant skies. 'Ah,' he murmured to the horrified lady sitting next to him. 'At last something to look at!'

Amongst the senior officials who occupied comfortable armchairs in the Pegu Club, the oldest and most selective club in Rangoon, was a Director of Public Instruction who had the distinction of being warned off the Rangoon turf. When I told a colleague in India about this, he countered with a story of having once accompanied a distinguished DPI on a visit to a big Indian girls' school. The school had been given little warning of the visit, so that they did well to think up a suitable literary slogan for their welcoming banner. In their haste some slipshod needlework on the banner was excusable. The DPI had a province-wide reputation as a ladies' man, and to my friend's deep delight the lettering read: *Welcome Sir X! The Penis Mightier than the Sword!*

An unexpected visitor to Rangoon was an old friend from my prep-school days – 'Peter' Brooke, then the 'Raj Kumar' or heir apparent of his uncle, the White Rajah of Sarawak. He was meeting his blonde and attractive young wife-to-be, and, owing to some difference of opinion with his uncle, wanted to marry her in Rangoon. I drove him around to a number of clerics in the city in pursuit of a special licence, which he eventually obtained. 'Why don't you join me in Sarawak when I take over?' he asked. 'Say as Minister of Finance?'

Things did not turn out well for him, as after his uncle died in 1941 the Japanese took the country, and the Colonial Office took over Sarawak entirely after the war. He now lives in Sweden in a community devoted to meditation and the study of UFOs, and communication with 'beings' in outer space, about which he occasionally writes to me.

The lakes of Rangoon were amongst its most attractive features. Little islands, pleasant for evening picnics, caused strange currents and wind eddies, so that small-boat sailors who could manage here became very adept at sailing indeed. On one island lived a somewhat mysterious figure out of the mainstream of Rangoon society. He was an ex-officer of a British regiment with private means who had taken up residence in Burma. It was told of him that when he was a young officer he had heard that Queen Suppayalat, the tigerish last Queen of Burma, was still alive, after returning in 1917 from exile in India, and was living in a small villa in the outskirts of Rangoon. He sent a message to ask if he could call on the old lady, and received the answer that she would receive him if he would approach her in the traditional way to approach the Burmese royal throne – that is to say, crawling on the ground with two palms together in the respectful salute called the shiko. No doubt to her surprise, he agreed. After he had made his reverential entrance, the ex-Queen said, 'That is enough, Captain. Come and sit by me', and a chair was produced.

The Bishop of Rangoon in those days was the great and good George West, who had an MM from the First World War, and a noble reputation as a grass-roots missionary in the poor Karen hills. In his simple goodness he reacted sympathetically to the message of Moral Rearmament, which was riding high at that time. In my old district of Yamethin the DC had been bemused by a visit from the Commissioner, who had got the bug and been converted to 'absolute honesty'. He was meticulously reimbursing the Government with petty sums for Government notepaper he considered he had used improperly, and refunding carelessly calculated overestimates in his claims for travelling expenses, and he urged all his subordinates to search their consciences over such matters.

George West upset one of his staff who was trying to get an administrative decision out of him, by telling him to go and have a 'quiet time', and see what guidance he got from God.

'I stood in the corridor for a bit,' the clergyman told me with glee. 'When I returned, the Bishop said, "Did you get guidance?"

'"Very clear guidance, sir!"

'"Good. What was it?"

'"To go and ask the Bishop!"'

It was this same clergyman who slightly embarrassed some parishioners he was showing round his new bungalow. 'This is the drawing-room. This is the bedroom where my wife and I sleep.... And this', he added with sombre pride, 'is the little room where I sleep during LENT!'

Although Rangoon had such large populations of Europeans, Indians and Chinese, it was impossible not to sense that this was the capital of Burma, since over the city floated the great golden spire of the Shwedagon Pagoda, the most revered shrine of Theravada Buddhism, of which the original nucleus was certainly standing there in the fourteenth century. Steep flights of steps under ramshackle roofing, and flanked by colourful stalls of tinsely toys, candles, flowers, gold leaf, incense and religious trinkets and souvenirs, led up to the great platform. There before a wide variety of gold, silver and marble statues of the Buddha and shrines to traditional nats, festooned with flowers, men and women knelt or squatted and murmured what by Buddhist teaching were not meant to be prayers, but clearly often were. In theory it was useless to pray to Buddha in Nirvana – in his perfect rest he could not be disturbed for help. From time to time gongs sounded, or a pongyi wandered round. Children played beside their mothers; all was informal and casual, something very much part of the normal life of the Burmese.

Sometimes on a fine night if I were at a loose end I would call Shway Ba or my driver and say, 'Let's go up to the Shwedagon.' Shedding socks and shoes at the entrance, we would wander quietly around, soothed by the atmosphere under the towering golden bell of the pagoda. No one questioned or resented the presence of a European, as long as he showed respect for his surroundings.

Nearby was a big conglomeration of pongyi kyaungs, or monasteries. It was easy to enter a monastery as a novice, and particularly in cities like Mandalay and Rangoon among the disciplined and devout monks were young men, arrogant and greedy, who traded on the monks' special position, and often criminals on the run from the police. The cry of 'insult to religion' was so dangerous and inflammatory that some of the Rangoon monasteries in Goodwin Road were virtually 'no go' areas so far as the police were concerned. And there were political nationalist monks as dedicated to Burmese nationalism as Irish or Greek priests to their causes. At one stage monks of this sort used to roam the streets with canes, beating Burmese girls for wearing their attractive traditional coloured skirts, instead of pinni, the drab, pale, biscuity-pink homespun cloth which extreme nationalists declared (in imitation of the wearing of khaddar by Gandhi's followers) should be the uniform for all patriots in Burma.

The habit of defying authority is difficult to drop, and not long after General Ne Win's coup in 1962, fourteen years after Independence, the General had to arrest nearly 150 monks – something the British would not have dared to do.

At moments when Burmese nationalism was on the boil, such as during the student strikes, the terraces and platform of the Shwedagon were taken over by excited crowds, and the whole area buzzed like a vast swarm of bees. However, the centre of modern Burmese nationalism was, as mentioned earlier, the University of Rangoon. Attractively laid out in Burmese architectural style in parks and lakes, the University, with a high standard of British, Burmese and Indian academic staff, strove to make young Burmese men and women into an élite of Western-type graduates. Vote-catching Burmese politicians continually lowered the standard of entrance.

Rangoon in fact brought one up against the hard political realities of burgeoning nationalism, which could pass one by in many rural areas up-country. The average up-country Burman was a small farmer, and most farmers were busy men who accepted life and got what they could out of it as it was. Up-country, too, the foreign presence was fairly unobtrusive. The great majority of the officials, magistrates and policemen with whom the villagers had to deal were Burmans, increasingly influenced by Burmese ministers in the Government in Rangoon. The number of Europeans in Government service in the district was, in contrast, steadily diminishing. The rural Burmese had a strong in-built nationalism, but in their conservative tribal memories there were still some thoughts of the tyrannies of the last Burmese kingdom, from the 'Independence' of which tens of thousands of Burmans swarmed south to be subjects of the foreign British Empire. It still meant something for the peasants to say, 'Under the British we sleep in peace.' Throughout most rural areas there was still a pretty general, if fatalistic, acceptance of the Asoya, the Government, and the 'wind of change' was still only a gentle breeze.

The students of the University, deliberately educated by the British in the literature and history and political philosophy of freedom, had no such memories of the past. This new generation of young patriots looked forward, and looked for early change.

Apart from some senior administrative officers there were few highly educated Burmans up-country. But in Rangoon there were Burmese High Court judges, lawyers and doctors, and the older generation of politicians like Sir Paw Tun and Sir Htoon Aung Gyaw. U Myint Thein, who afterwards became Chief Justice of independent Burma, was a charming and intelligent man in whose house I dined, and who is happily still alive in Rangoon. The ablest Burmese officials were in the Secretariat. And it was good to talk with the Burmese members of the University faculty.

I remember a senior Burmese don, who knew many British officials well, sighing and saying to me, 'I live in two worlds.

When I talk with my friends the British officials I know that they are honourable men, thinking in their own way of what is best for this country, and working towards it. Many of them are doing jobs we Burmans cannot yet do. And then I listen to my students, sincere young men, many of whom have never met a British official, who believe that the British are greedy and tyrannical "capitalist" oppressors, and that the problems of the country would all be solved overnight by Lut Lat Ye [Independence]. There seems no communication between these two worlds.'

Dr Desai, a quiet old Indian historian from the University, said to me, 'I think the British rule efficiently and honestly. But I do not think any country should ever rule another country.'

So used was I to the idea of the British Empire in those days that his remarks seemed to me novel and vaguely subversive. It made me stop and ponder. Certainly the British would hate any other country to rule them and would die to stop it; and certainly no country should rule another country permanently. But in a world where different areas developed at different speeds, and in which some were weak, backward, corrupt and inefficient, was not some outside intervention almost inevitable and perhaps beneficial? Did not history teach that power abhors a vacuum? Anyway, my job was to make the best of the actual situation as it was, not to moralize on the rights and wrongs of the past. With which pragmatic and not very profound thoughts I went off to play football with those stalwart Karens Saw John and Saw Belly.

The student strike of 1936 was the first of many demonstrations, and the excited students, fed by their parents, camped for three months on the platform of the Shwedagon. In 1938 an oilfield workers' march, organized by the small Thakin Party, ended in Rangoon, where the students joined them. The resulting fracas ended in a student, Ko Aung Gyaw, dying after a police lathi (bamboo staff or baton) charge. I was in Rangoon when his bloodstained shirt, the martyr's symbol the students craved, was borne dramatically round the streets.

In fact, like the monks, students found it difficult to abandon the thrills of violent opposition to the Government even after Independence in 1947. In July 1962 troops fired on the students, killing seventeen and wounding thirty-nine. General Ne Win, the Head of State, burnt down the Students' Union building and closed the University for over a year.

But up to the war student politics, although active, did not seem to be of major significance. For years the big national political parties, the old GCBA (the General Council of Buddhist Associations), the Myochit (Nationalist) Party, the Sinyetha (Poor Man's) Party, with widespread grass-roots networks and their own 'mass organizations', had struggled for power against the British and against each other. The recognized national leaders, those with first-hand practical experience of administering the country, were such men as U Chit Hlaing, U Ba Pe, U Pu, Dr Ba Maw and U Saw. After 1937 the fruits of electoral success were substantial. Elected Burmese ministers had effectual control over practically all internal affairs of the country.

The political leaders were also manoeuvring for position, so that they would be in power and take over when the British eventually left. Naturally all parties strove to be the leaders in trying to get maximum concessions from the British on the speed of constitutional advance. And naturally when the war started they demanded a promise of freedom after the war as a condition for Burma's co-operation with the war effort. Sensing that the real struggle for power would come when the British left, political party leaders began to form their own private armies, somewhat on Blackshirt lines: the Dahma (Tough Sword) Army of Dr Ba Maw, the Galone (Dragon) Army of U Saw, the Green Army of U Maung Maung. Although anti-British feeling was not widespread, there was a sense in the air that 'The Time of the Changing of Kings' was perhaps not so far off. So, at a time when their own power to influence events was getting less, the British administrators were faced with more problems of disorder and departure from the principles of government they had tried to uphold.

To the leaders of the big national parties the students were pawns to be used when in opposition to embarrass the party in power. At the 1937 general election the small Marxist-influenced Thakin Party, which had a number of adherents in the student body, won only three seats in the House of Representatives of 132 members. No one could thus have foreseen that the young men who were to form the first

Government of independent Burma in 1947 were mainly to be students drawn from the Thakin Party.

I enjoyed the comparative sophistication and variety and comfort of Rangoon, and the change of society. And yet it was with relief that I returned to Mandalay for the next open season. Up-country officers developed a camaraderie and pride in their work and responsibilities which was accompanied by the usual affectation of despising those who were 'pen-pushing' in the Secretariat. Many officers alternated between the Secretariat and the district, but some clung rather adhesively to Rangoon.

Once, when two of my colleagues were on leave and touring the Tate Gallery, they came on a painting by Stubbs, *A Horse Frightened by a Lion*. In this picture the animal, with staring eyes, leans rigidly back, his hooves plunged deeply into the ground.

'Doesn't this remind you of someone?' asked one friend.

'Who?'

'Isn't it very like Tomkins when he was told he was being transferred up-country from the Secretariat?'

To be fair, many of our brightest brains were in the Secretariat, and on them fell the biggest responsibilities for policy-making and finance, and the constant strain of keeping pace with Burmese nationalist politics and the Burmese Parliament. Political parties consisted largely of changing combinations of individuals banding together in the pursuit of power rather than groups projecting substantially different policies. By 1941 there were no less than twelve identifiable parties. At one stage U Saw was jealously regarding U Pu, who was a short-time Premier after Dr Ba Maw. The Secretariat jingle ran:

> I saw U Saw watching Pu
> And Pu saw I saw U Saw!

Anyway, I was glad to be going up-country again. In my next recess I would have to write my Settlement Report, my Domesday Book, and much hard work remained to be done. One tradition in the Department was that each of the customary two parts of the Report should be prefaced by an appropriate literary quotation. Freddy Pearce, a famous Settlement Officer, had prefaced his Part II, which was comprised mainly of statistics, with lines from Gilbert and Sullivan: 'Merely corroborative detail to add artistic verisimilitude to an otherwise bald and unconvincing narrative.' A comment rather near the bone. I had already chosen my fly-leaf quotation: 'A' babbled of green fields'. I knew that exacting standards would be applied by my superiors, and I had already learnt my lesson (which I have never forgotten) from a minute by Sir Bernard Binns when he submitted to the Government of Burma the Report on another district written by one of our most able colleagues. 'This Report', he wrote warmly, 'is the best Settlement Report I have read in my career. But, considering that Mr B was given an extension of two months in which to finish it, it should have been half as long.'

In fact, as things turned out, all the long hours of work put in by me and my party came to little. I never wrote the Report.

7 The Japanese Invasion

> Summers and Winters had gone – how many times?
> And suddenly the Empire was wrecked.
> The Imperial army met the barbarian foe,
> The dust of the battlefield darkened the sky and sea,
> And the sun and moon were no longer bright,
> While the wind of death shook the grass and trees
> And the white bones were piled up in hills.
> Ah, what had they done – the innocent people?
>
> Li Po, AD 759*

The war in Europe had by now been going on for some two years and had affected far-away Burma but little. A number of young men from Forest, oil and other firms had been released for military service, and were training at the Maymyo OCTU. Later on, civil servants who were not released did some rudimentary military training with the tough little miners of the KOYLI. But we were neither militarily nor psychologically prepared for war. For years we had been taught to believe that Singapore was an impregnable bastion, guarding our area of South-East Asia. Little effort was made to involve Burmese popular support in a war which did not seem likely to threaten them directly.

Then suddenly came Pearl Harbor. And one evening on 10 December 1941, when I was eating my solitary dinner in a Forest bungalow, I heard the chilling radio announcement of the sinking of the *Prince of Wales* and the *Repulse*. Before long the

---

* Li Po, translated into English verse by Shegayashi Obata (New York: E. P. Dutton, 1928).

Japanese were on our borders. On 23 December Rangoon was bombed, and again on Christmas Day. Settlement seemed even more remote from the war than district administration. I could no longer stand fiddling about with kwin maps. Denis Phelips from the oilfields was now Secretary of the Defence Department, and he arranged that I should come at once to Rangoon to help out where help was needed.

Rangoon city was almost at a standstill. Japanese anti-personnel bombs had slain many of the Indian manual labourers on whom the city depended, and their poorly paid comrades had little reason to risk their lives further. I found 'Orphan' Thomas already at work with a fleet of lorries, clearing corpses from the streets.

I was given a miscellany of jobs. I was made Assistant Controller of Civil Defence, under Dickie de Graaf Hunter, who had just come from England with recent experience of similar work in the blitz. With the projects for building more air-raid shelters in mind I was also made Controller of Building Materials, basically bricks; and through my contact with the oil companies I helped in the organizing of petrol dumps laid down by the companies on the roads going north from Rangoon. In my spare time I helped Daw Mya Sein, a gallant Burmese lady, set up a depot for the issue of free rations to such of the population that remained. I remember searching through the *Prisons Manual* to discover the statutory minimum prison rations, to use as a guide for the quantities of food to be issued from the depot.

Dickie de Graaf Hunter, the Controller of Civil Defence brought out by the new Governor, Sir Reginald Dorman-Smith, was a cool and elegant young man who had come too late to an impossible task. He did what he could. Watchers nearer the border signalled the spotting of Japanese aircraft bound for Rangoon. These were plotted in our headquarters, and winking coloured lights shone to show their approach. But not much else could be done about them except sound the sirens. Even if there had been time to build underground shelters, Rangoon's water-table was too high to allow digging to any depth. But slit trenches were rapidly built.

In further raids on Rangoon we learnt the great sense of security to be found in an ordinary slit trench; and from then on our eyes were always on the look-out for a ditch to dive into.

I was invited to stay in Rangoon with my Pyinmana predecessor, Gordon Apedaile, tall, taciturn and efficient. Amidst the general horrors Gordon was bitten by his horse, which was suspected of rabies, and he was duly packed off to the Pasteur Institute in the city to start his series of injections. On his way home after his first jabs he heard the drone of Japanese bombers overhead and dived for a nearby ditch, which proved to be an open sewer. While crouching under a culvert for the raid to pass, he read his instructions from the Pasteur Institute: *No alcohol – and avoid all excitement.*

There was not much anti-aircraft artillery available to defend Rangoon, or indeed many fighter planes. A few RAF pilots in slow out-of-date Brewster Buffaloes did their best. But the main air defence came from the American pilots of the Air Volunteer Group, 'The Flying Tigers' formed under Colonel Chennault to fight for the Chinese. It was wonderfully exciting to gaze up into the sky and see the AVG tear into a Japanese bomber formation. They shot down many aircraft, but were outnumbered by the persistent waves of Japanese bombers and Zero fighters.

One evening in the Silver Grill I made friends with a young AVG pilot. When I tried to insist on paying for my round of drinks, he turned on me in a sudden fury. 'I get paid a lot of money for this job,' he said. 'At least let me get some fun out of spending it while I can!' I heard he was killed shortly after.

Then came the alarming report of a disaster to the 17th Division, opposing the Japanese in the south-east. As the division fell back on the only bridge across the Sittang river, the bridge was destroyed by our side with two British brigades still on the wrong side of the river. Stories began to leak back of confusion and inefficiency, and for the first time the nasty possibilities of the Japanese invasion began to sink home. On 15 February 1942 came the shattering news that Singapore had fallen. Historians may consider this date only second in significance in its context to 2 January 1905, when the Russians surrendered Port Arthur to the Japanese.

Amongst my various jobs I helped with some broadcasts on the situation to the rest of Burma. At one stage, the Governor, Sir Reginald Dorman-Smith, who had succeeded Sir Archibald Cochrane, declared bravely that we would hold Rangoon. Since in the event we did not do so, he was afterwards blamed for misleading the people. But he was acting on military advice, to prevent the morale of the city being totally destroyed. The Governor was blamed too for leaving by plane with his family and personal belongings. He did not do this until 4 May 1942 (just a year since he had arrived in Burma), when the fall of the entire country was unavoidable. In fact, he was ordered to leave by Churchill personally, and his exit seemed to many of us sensible enough. In the early stages of the invasion the District Officers in Tavoy in the far south were ordered to stay put to help their districts. The Japanese not unexpectedly put them straight into gaol for the rest of the war, and consequently the order was cancelled for other districts. In times of disaster and failure there is always search for a scapegoat, and the Governor had the bad luck to be selected. Some Army PR officers even admitted afterwards that they deliberately tried to shift the blame on to the Governor.

Reggie Dorman-Smith, tall and dark-moustached, was a relatively young man, only forty-two years old. He was a debonair and cheerful personality, articulate and intelligent, possibly with a hint of flashiness. A politician himself (he had been in the Cabinet as Minister of Agriculture in the UK), he understood the top Burmese politicians of that era, and they liked him. Had he been in Burma at the time and in the place of his predecessor, I think he would have been an outstandingly successful and popular Governor; whereas the silent and indomitable naval VC might have been more to the taste of the services in time of war. Not that Dorman-Smith was without imagination on the military side. Noel Stevenson, a Frontier Service officer, had, even before Japan declared war, started training Kachin guerrillas. The Governor, hearing of his scheme, ordered him to Rangoon and gave him the task of organizing levies throughout the hill country. Some senior military officers did not take kindly to this civilian interference in their special sphere. When the Japanese arrived and started pushing back the 17th Division towards Rangoon, Stevenson, who had some of Wingate's fanaticism and caused the same hackles to rise on the same sort of staff officers' necks, prepared a raid by his irregulars to wreck the airfield of Mae Sariang in Siam before the Japanese could grab it. It was all too amateur a plan for the Army to accept. But in the event the hill levies played a most valuable part in the war in the next three years.

Every Japanese air raid increased the steady stream northwards of the city population, and more and more institutions ground to a standstill. One afternoon I joined in a bizarre and melancholy foray to shoot all dangerous animals in the zoo, as all their keepers had decamped. Tigers, panthers and poisonous snakes were killed, and the deer released in the park, except for one which we shot for fresh meat. When we had gutted the poor beast, we threw its entrails into the lake, and great fish thrashed and swirled in the course of their unusual meal.

Flames began to take hold of part of the city. As warders and nurses began to sidle off, criminals and lunatics were also released, so that at least they would not be caught by fire or suffer starvation behind bars. One night, driving alone through deserted streets by the light of burning buildings, I had a puncture. As I changed the tyre I had a macabre sensation of being watched. I turned and saw a small group of lunatics gazing vacantly at me and my car. I am still haunted by the memory of the flames and the shadows, the long, empty Chirico-like streets, and the silent, crazy watchers.

By now arrangements were being made to evacuate Rangoon and destroy everything that would be of particular value to the enemy, such as dock installations and the refinery at Syriam. I was at this stage earmarked for the party of 'last ditchers' who would carry out the 'Big Blow' and be evacuated by sea.

Meanwhile, I had moved into the Burma Signals' mess, with my brother-in-law Dick Kemp, who later in the war rose to Lt-Colonel as CO of the Headquarters Signals of the 14th Army. Seeing a particularly large blaze in an empty quarter of Rangoon one evening, I said to Dick, 'That's the hell of a fire. Let's go down and enjoy it.' So we took a couple of bottles of Buckfast Abbey Tonic Wine, retrieved from some crates on the docks (for whom *could* they have been intended?) and drove my jeep down to the fire. The wind was blowing hard away from our vantage-point, so we could get as close as the heat would allow us. The giant red-and-yellow flames, making such a roar that we could hardly hear ourselves speak, climbed and twisted skyward. It was shamefully exhilarating. All we lacked was a portable gramophone playing 'The Ride of the Valkyries'.

At the last minute before the Big Blow I was given more duties in connection with the up-country petrol dumps, and I left Rangoon by car in a military convoy with John Drysdale of the BOC, who was as usual cool and precise, and faintly amused by events. We were the last civilians to leave Rangoon before the Japanese cut the road on 7 March, with the road-block which nearly trapped General Alexander and his staff. Our first stop was Prome, where I found Bernard Swithinbank, the Commissioner, supervising the evacuation. He told me of the suicide a few days before of Fielding Hall, a young ICS colleague, and showed me the note he had left behind, pathetically trailing off in despair: 'I know I made a bad mistake. I thought I was doing the right thing. I am....'

As was usually the case, it was the most conscientious, the most sensitive, the nicest of men who had reached the point of taking his own life. 'The wicked', as the Bible says, 'flourish like a green bay tree.' Fielding Hall was steeped in the Buddhist tradition of the old Burma. His father had written one of the best known and most sympathethic of all books about Burma, *The Soul of a People*. Working under conditions of tremendous strain as Under-Secretary in the Home Department, he had received news that the Japanese were nearing Rangoon. As many of the warders and attendants had fled, and more seemed likely to do so, on his own initiative he had released the criminals and lunatics. In fact, the news was erroneous. The Japanese were still some days away. He was reprimanded for an impulsive and premature action. In ordinary circumstances he might have shrugged it off, but over the last week he had 'supped full of horrors'.

Later when I got to Mandalay I heard that another colleague had shot himself – Dugald McCallum, my friend and exact contemporary, whose wedding I had attended before we left England. Like Fielding Hall he came from a family with long Burma traditions, and had been born in the Shan States when his father was Commissioner there. A romantic and idealistic Scot, it was not simply the destruction of the orderly and just administration, for which he and his father had laboured, or the fearful injuries to the land and people he loved, which had sickened him. He was at heart a pacifist and a hopeful believer in

'The Parliament of Man, the Federation of the World'. I do not know what last straw broke his back, but I had talked to him enough times in the past to know how repulsive to him was the very idea of war.

On my way up-country I heard that my old post of Pyinmana had been left in flames by Japanese bombers. More than once on this trip I saw the bloated victims of bombing.

At Yenangyaung preparations for 'scorched earth' were in full swing. The final destruction team were hurriedly given commissions in the Army, in case they were captured by the Japanese. Foster, the demolition expert brought in from outside, looking cool and professional in neat white shirt, shorts and stockings, prepared charges to blow up the power-station and millions of tons of crude oil. The BOC engineers closed down the wells, plugging the larger one, and chopping up bits and drills and shafts. 'I feel like a cavalryman ordered to shoot his own horse,' said one of them to me.

Meanwhile Robin McGuire, the current Warden, was supervising the evacuation by plane of the remaining women and children, which included the families of civilians as well as of the military. I spent two days helping with this task. Since the car I was driving had defective brakes, we hit the back of a military truck, and from then on up to Mandalay (where I got a new vehicle) we had to stop at very short intervals to put water into the leaking radiator.

Soon after we left, the Japanese did another of their constant infiltrations and envelopments, setting up a road-block north of Yenangyaung which trapped our forces. After a bitter battle the road was cleared, with the help of Chinese divisions coming down from the north-east. There is no doubt that the Burma Government, and particularly all the Burmese Ministers who regarded China as Burma's traditional enemy, were most reluctant in the early stages to let Chinese troops in, in case they never left again. Some Chinese formations were adept at avoiding fighting, but others fought well, and the 200th Division under General Lo held Toungoo on the Sittang axis in the west for thirteen days.

When I got to Maymyo, to which the Burma Government had retreated, I found things comparatively peaceful. True in the Club I found tired and wounded officers of the KOYLI, a bit more serious than I remembered them before, but with spirits undaunted. Walter Baxter, tall and dark, with a bandage round his head, was standing on the lawn in just the position in which he later portrayed the chief character of the sad and successful novel about the campaign which he wrote after the war, entitled *Look Down in Mercy*.

And while there I found my old friend from school-days, Mike Calvert, now Acting Commandant of the Bush Warfare Training School. Mike was a red-faced, cheerful tank of a man, who had both boxed and swum for the Army. In his head for years had buzzed the bee of a novel form of warfare, fast-moving and highly equipped columns, supplied from the air. He was soon to become famous as a Chindit leader, perhaps the youngest brigadier in the Army, with a DSO and bar. Later in the war his Brigade Major said to me, 'Little did I realize that one of my duties as Brigade Major would be to walk with the Brigadier through the jungle, well ahead of the column, carrying a bag of grenades for the Brigadier's personal use.'

'Come and meet a new man in my line of business,' invited Mike. I met a lean and untidy lt-colonel, with a sombre gaze and the scar of a gash across the throat. 'Do you speak Burmese?' he asked at once.

'Yes.'

'I would like you to join me tomorrow. I am off to take a look at Prome.' (Prome was 250 miles south.)

'But Prome is probably in Japanese hands by now.'

Coldly, 'I know.'

'Well ... I must report to the Burma Government first and get permission to join you. I'll go up at once.'

My petrol duties were over, and I expected at this stage to be released on military duty, which seemed obviously to have priority.

The Chief Secretary wouldn't hear of it. 'The DC at Monywa [now the last but one district on the way out of Burma to India and clogged with refugees] has had a complete breakdown. You must go immediately and take over.'

The Colonel took the news badly. But there was nothing for it, and I rapidly packed for Monywa.

Years later, when I was a Counsellor in the British Middle East Office in Beirut, I told this story to Sir Edwin Chapman

Andrews, Ambassador to the Lebanon. 'I knew Wingate well,' he said. 'I was the political officer with the escort he commanded, taking Haile Selassie back to Ethiopian territory through the Italian lines. One of the Emperor's rasses gave me some curved Ethiopian knives as a memento, and I passed one on to Wingate. After the successful Ethiopian adventure Wingate, who had a strong sense of destiny, waited impatiently for the call to take up some vital war command. The authorities seemed to have forgotten him, and low and dispirited he paced up and down his Cairo bedroom in increasing frustration.

'One night an officer in the next room heard the pacing interrupted by a heavy fall, and went in to find Wingate had cut his throat, with his curved Ethiopian knife.

'His attempt to kill himself was unsuccessful, and in due course George Steer and I went to the hospital to see him. He was sitting up in bed with his throat bandaged. He had lost a lot of blood and for once his eyes weren't bloodshot, and his gaze seemed clear and sensible.

'"How come you failed, Orde?" I teased him. "You usually succeed at anything you put your hand to." "You are right," he replied, "I've been giving it a lot of thought. As I pulled the blade across, my muscles tensed up and pulled my jugular away. Next time I will sit in a hot bath and relax, and I will not fail."'

The officer I saw in Maymyo had a fully healed scar. But his eyes were fanatical again.

As I packed my gear at Maymyo I heard the drone of Japanese bombers approaching Maymyo. Since the Japanese had caught most of the remaining RAF aircraft on the ground in Magwe on 21 March, and the AVG were pulling out, the Japanese had more or less roamed the sky unmolested. This meant not only that ground forces had little defence against air attack, but that, since we had no air reconnaissance of our own, it was impossible half the time for us to know where the Japanese forces were. As the drone grew louder I thought, This is no place for me, leapt into my car and set off down the hill to Mandalay en route for the Chindwin. As I drove along I heard the crump of bombs behind me. Half-way down the hill I could see Mandalay. Another wave of bombers was approaching the city. I pulled into a wayside village and asked for the headman. 'How are you, Thugyi Min?' I said in Burmese. 'Big trouble this war.'

He agreed.

'Bombing in Maymyo, and bombing in Mandalay – not good to be in either place just now.'

Again he agreed.

'Tell you what – have you got a shot-gun or two? I have some cartridges and my own gun. What say we have a shoot to pass the time?'

'Good idea, Thakin.'

It is entirely in character for the Burmese to seek distraction and amusement in times of trouble and disaster. In a moment my car was covered by a camouflage of bamboos, beaters were summoned, two rather rusty shot-guns appeared and off we set. The villagers were delighted when we shot a barking deer, which I left for them, with the gift of a box of precious cartridges.

'We'll be back, Thugyi Min,' I said as I left the headman's village – and I am sure he believed me.

In the late afternoon I drove into Mandalay through the acrid smoke of smouldering buildings, and past remains of trees standing like big sticks of charcoal. One large tree stood like a black cross against the sky, and I remembered with a jolt that it was Good Friday. I found the DC looking worn and ashen-faced.

'I'm on my way to take over Monywa,' I said. 'Can I stay the night?'

'Of course,' he said, 'but I don't know if I can find you anything to eat.'

'I've brought dinner,' I said, producing two brace of jungle fowl. 'I saw you being bombed, so stopped in the woods and had a quick shoot.'

'My God,' he said, shaking his head, unamused.

I knew even at this late stage, walking alone into a Burmese village, that I would be treated in a friendly and courteous manner typifying the attitude of the Burmese people to the Japanese invasion. There was no nationalist uprising behind the British lines, and moreover I came across no anti-British manifestations anywhere in the countryside. A small group of activist students from Rangoon University came in with the Japanese Army. Yet the ordinary up-country peasant saw with bewilderment and apprehension the collapse of the Asoya (the Government) he was used to, and felt no particular sympathy for the invaders.

Throughout their history the Burmese villagers had feared the dangerous and turbulent 'Time of the Changing of Kings'. This time of tribulation for them came from events beyond their control. 'Ah – what had they done – the innocent people?'

Unpacking in the DC's bungalow in Monywa I felt that my Burma days had come full circle. Here I was where as a new trainee I had dutifully sat up all night singing with Bernard Binns. And as in the finale of a panto the entire company began to assemble. 'Orphan' Thomas, who had escaped from the last district he evacuated on a shunting engine, turned up as cheerful as ever. Our old host, Alan Gledhill, who as a judge could very well have carried straight on through Monywa, did what many of those streaming through did not do – he offered to stay and help, an offer which was gratefully accepted. Most of the many people pouring through Monywa did not stop a minute longer than they needed. Our compound was full of abandoned transport and possessions of all descriptions. Then in the last few days we were joined by Ian Wallace, a brother Settlement Officer and one of the best linguists in the Service, who had wound up a long string of districts on his way up, by John Fann, a burly Irish DC, and by Bernard Binns himself, his bottle of Carew's gin firmly under his arm.

When I arrived I found large camps of Indian refugees awaiting transport to take them up-river to Kalewa, a nearer jumping-off place for the overland trek to India. For these, rations had to be provided, sanitation arranged, and inoculation against cholera carried out. A small and devoted band of subordinate officers, Burmese, Indian and Anglo-Indian, worked day and night to keep the refugees rationed and on the move. A couple of Indian sub-assistant surgeons, a very junior form of medical officer, carried out inoculations and simple first aid into the night. And twice a day hordes of refugees were packed into some of the eleven stern-wheelers of the Irrawaddy Flotilla Company's Chindwin fleet and sent up-river.

Bernard Binns as usual had the right slant on things. We had all seen acts of great gallantry, in particular that of a police Officer and one of the best linguists in the Service, who had wagon from a burning train at Monywa station and pushed it to safety. We had all seen acts of great devotion to duty and great coolness and efficiency in the face of danger and disaster. There would no doubt be some recommendation for awards and medals. 'I will only recommend those who draw less than a thousand rupees a month [£900 a year]. Anyone who draws that or more [which covered all DCs] is *expected* to behave well,' said Mr Commissioner Binns.

One day in the third week of April an officer with the insignia of a lt-colonel came into my office.

'Good morning,' I said. 'What can I do for you?'

'Oh, I'm the new Military Commandant. The military are taking over the administration, and I'm to be in charge of this district.'

'First I've heard of it,' I said. 'But anyway, here's the office. What shall I do?'

'Just carry on, old boy,' said my new friend. 'I think I'll have a gin in the bungalow.'

He looked as smart and clean as if ready to go on parade, and was utterly unperturbed by the military situation. In the British way he did not accept defeat as anything more than a temporary set-back and 'a bit of a bore'.

As we sat under the tamarind trees in the evening, sipping whiskies and sodas, I said that messages from my headmen reported Japanese forces only three days' march away. 'Impossible, old boy,' said my friend. 'Take it from me, there are no Japs that side of the river.'

News reached me that my sister, with a unit of the Women's Auxiliary Service (Burma), which was working in the Burma Army HQ cipher staff, was stationary in a train not far to the north-east. This seemed too close to where the Japanese would soon be, and I sent a message to warn her. Whether the message had any effect, I don't know, but all the girls got away.

Meanwhile British forces began to arrive in Monywa and all the big Irrawaddy Flotilla boats were commandeered for the Army. After desperate appeals we were allowed the boats for the refugees for one more day, and working without a stop we arranged for double trips to take as many of them as possible (close on a thousand on each boat) as far as we could up the river. The ones who couldn't get on were in despair, and wept and wailed and besieged my office. Most hysterical were some upper-class Indians and Anglo-Indians whom I had urged to leave when I first arrived, but who had dillied and dallied hoping that things would turn out all right, and that they wouldn't have to leave their homes and possessions.

I had been going hard, day and night, for some time. That night, without warning and without consciously feeling particularly strained or distressed about things, I found myself alone in my bedroom sobbing noisily and bitterly and quite unable to stop. After drinking the best part of half a bottle of neat whisky straight down, my sobbing fit stopped abruptly.

I had told the Military Commandant that my information was that the Japanese were two days, then one day away. On the third day (30 April) we were sitting outside the bungalow when shots whistled through the trees from the other side of the river. 'Japs,' I said, as we crouched below the bund.

'Must be just a nuisance party,' said my friend.

At that moment the wind brought us the rumble of tracked vehicles from over the river. 'Largish nuisance party?' I inquired.

Throughout the day more British troops began to trickle into Monywa and take up positions on our bank. We made plans to depart that night.

For years an ancient steam-launch had chugged across the Chindwin as a ferry, and this we commandeered for the civil party in the DC's bungalow. An Indian senator from Rangoon with three companions surfaced to say he was about to arrange to buy the launch for his party. 'Come with us, by all means,' I said, 'but the ferry is now Government property.' (The syrang or boatman received proper compensation.) We fixed a sampan alongside to accommodate a few more evacuees, and filled the boat with such stores as we could find, and into a basic issue of knives, spoons and cups. I went upstairs in the bungalow at dusk, hoping that no bullets would find their way through the flimsy matting walls, and had a bath. At least I'll start this trek clean, I thought as I donned my tough Settlement boots for the march to India.

After nightfall we set off. The Indian syrang was used only to going across the river and not up it, and before long we were stuck on a sandbank between the Japanese and British forces, waiting to resume battle by daylight. The Indian lascars slid

6 Japanese generals march into Government House, Rangoon, to sign surrender documents, 1945

7 Return to Rangoon by Sir Reginald Dorman-Smith, 1945

8 General Aung San's successful trip to Britain, January 1947. Front row: Thakin Mya, Mr Attlee, General Aung San, U Tin Tut, Lord Pethick Lawrence. Just behind Aung San is U Saw (hatless), instigator of Aung San's assassination later that year.

9 Lord Mountbatten calls on U Thant, Secretary-General of the UN, in March 1948. The author is between them. On the left is Admiral Brockman.

into the water and tried to scrape away the sand from the propellers with planks. It seemed to take for ever, and some of us impatiently joined them in the dark water and dug and scraped. At last we were afloat, and after backing we set off up-river with a shower of sparks from the funnel. There were some desultory shots from the far bank, and we were away.

By dawn we were far up the Chindwin in jungly, beautiful and lonely country. We began to relax and take stock of our position. We had stores for several days, and decided to sail up as far as we could before disembarking. Suddenly a Japanese plane appeared. It swooped down, took a look at us and turned away. Our ancient craft still flew the Islamic green flag, with sword and sickle moon, of the syrang; and those of us wearing khaki had tried to conceal themselves under the deck of the boat alongside. We hoped we looked in no way military.

To our dismay, the plane turned and came back, and flew low over the water quite near our boat. We could see the two airmen in goggles staring at us. Then once again the plane turned away. This time it climbed high, turned and dived straight down at us. We were sitting ducks out in the middle of the river, with nothing to hide behind, no slit trenches. I think we all thought we were finished. Strangely, in the seconds of the dive I did not think so much about being killed myself as of the horrors of being left in the middle of nowhere, surrounded by dead and dying companions and unable to do anything to help them.

But for some reason the plane did not open fire at us, and this time it turned and made off for good.

For a long while no one spoke. And then an Anglo-Indian police sergeant croaked, 'I'll make some tea.' He made buckets of it, very strong and very sweet. I have never appreciated any refreshment so much.

Farther up the river we got a lift from a larger cabined launch, captained by 'Chindwin' White of the Irrawaddy Flotilla Company, who afterwards earned fame by his bravery in assisting 'Elephant Bill' in his work for the 14th Army. At Kalewa (the base from which in peacetime Frontier Service officers started their long marches up into the Chin hills) we found the IFC stern-wheelers now beginning to ferry across the retreating British forces. Without these vessels the extrication of our armies would not have been possible. All these vessels were scuttled in due course.

Thus ended a famous era of river transport. Already the side-paddle steamers, which plied between Rangoon to Mandalay and went northwards on the Irrawaddy, had been sunk at Mandalay. These great Clyde-built steamers, capable of carrying a thousand deck passengers and hauling freight barges along with them, had for long dominated the waterways of Burma and advanced the comfort and prosperity of its inhabitants. Even before the annexation, their Scots captains had been respected figures in Upper Burma. When the fall of Mandalay was imminent John Morton, the local Company manager, led a team after dark which scuttled the historic fleet with bursts of Bren-gun fire at the hulls of its steamers under the water. The river near Mandalay is still full of wrecks, for silt soon made them unsalvageable. In all, 550 of the Irrawaddy Flotilla Company's 650 vessels were denied the enemy.

At the little village of Sittaung, some hours north of Kalewa, we disembarked and started on our westward march to India. We had been three days on the river from Monywa. Three more days' march on rough jungle tracks would take us to Tamu, and another six days or so, mostly on steep tracks up the hills (which rose to 5,000 feet) to Imphal, where we hoped to find some transport for the last stretch to the railhead at Dimapur. There were eight to ten of us in our particular group, including one Anglo-Burman woman. En route we were joined by an English Forest officer's wife.

It was the end of the hot weather, and the jungle was exceedingly hot and dusty. One evening, still thirsty after finishing my water ration, I came upon a stagnant pool, green and slimy, under a big tree. Reasoning that perhaps my body could drink through my skin, which could filter out impurities, I sat in this noisome pond up to my neck for half an hour, and came out much refreshed.

Walking with us were scattered little groups of British soldiers dispersed from their units in the general confusion. They had been fighting continuously in the heat of the hot weather without any respite since the Japanese invasion had started four months before. They all had their arms, and none of them seemed to accept that they had been defeated.

A battalion of the KOYLI and another of the Duke of

Wellington's Regiment had suffered so many casualties that they had been combined into one battalion. This, we heard, had not been a success. In between fighting the Japanese these units had scrapped with each other. We saw young soldiers with slogans round their bush-hats – *Once a KOYLI always a KOYLI!* and *Up the DOOKS!* It was clear that regimental spirit was perhaps the most powerful element in the fighting morale of the British soldier.

Lying on the ground in the jungle one night, unable to sleep, I got into conversation with a young soldier nearby. 'What are you fighting for?' I asked curiously. 'Democracy? Our country? Your family?'

He seemed puzzled and embarrassed by my question. 'I suppose,' he said at length, 'for the "kids".' By which he meant his mates in his regiment.

> Oh, passin' the love o'women,
> Follow me – follow me 'ome.*

Gradually we came out of the jungle into steeper and more barren mountains. Occasionally we passed the bodies of fellow-travellers. On one corner, when after a succession of steep, slippery slopes the road seemed to have reached the top, round the bend in the road rose the steepest and most forbidding slope we had yet met. At this corner more than one traveller had given up the ghost. Any hint of pride in the exercise of walking over the wild hills from Burma to India was quelled by the fact that over this route went whole Indian families – including old men, delicate women and children. In fact we were lucky to have got through on a comparatively short route, before the rains really struck.

Janet Lindop (later Humble) wrote a vivid account (unpublished) of the walk-out. Amongst many moving stories she recorded this incident:

> I remember one distracted man, an Indian coolie with his wife who was dying of smallpox, and two small children. He

---

*'Passing the love of women' was the biblical quotation (2 Samuel 1:23) Kipling adapted in his poem 'Follow Me 'Ome' to express the British soldier's intense loyalty to his comrades.

was torn between his love for his wife and his hurry to get himself and his children to safety. Later in the day he passed us, walking very fast, with one child on his shoulder and the other trotting behind. ... We came across one incredibly old and frail Indian woman, stepping slowly with the aid of a long staff. There is one, we thought, who would never make it; yet weeks later she passed our camp near Imphal, still walking at the same pace. Jim personally went and lifted her up on to a lorry to take her down to the railhead. He said that although she was so tall she was light as a feather.

One stout and elderly Irrawaddy skipper, who had no doubt peered at the ever-changing patterns of the river from his bridge for years, a glass of whisky at his elbow, without having had to walk more than a few steps at any time, was pushed and hauled along the trail by his faithful Chittagonian crew. They made it. But, weakened by the virulent local malaria, the old man died on arrival.

Refugees who had left it too late were overtaken by the monsoon rains in the more northerly route through the Hukawng valley. The most tragic stories are told of that Via Dolorosa on which all the girls of a convent school are said to have perished, and many thousands of others.

Professor B.R. Pearn of Rangoon University was later commissioned to write an official report on the mass exodus of refugees into India. Whether he recorded too many horrors for public morale in wartime, or whether he was too critical of the lack of reception arrangements by the Government of India, I do not know, but his report was not published at the time. There is little doubt that many Indians were fleeing at least as much from fear of what the Burmans would do to them, with the British gone, as from fear of the Japanese.

At one stage on our route, when we were getting short of food, we were happy to come across a Bombaing rice depot, laid down originally to supply the Company's own evacuating staff. This was presided over by a cheerful young Anglo-Burman, Norman Goldberg, whose courage and enterprise on dangerous border patrols later in the war won him an MC and bar. Plain boiled rice was our mainstay, a diet sometimes enriched by the luxury of a potato or a hard-boiled egg. We once managed to buy a basket of eggs in a Naga village, where we found physical types different from anything we had known in Burma, tall men with the noble features and *gravitas* of Red Indians.

I trudged much of the way with Ian Wallace, a wry and imperturbable Scotsman, and we sustained each other by interminable, if amicable, bickering. As we walked, we adapted a rhyme from our childhood:

> Up the airy mountain, down the rushy glen,
> Off we trip to India, for fear of little men.

The sound of any aircraft sent us diving off the path into the jungle, but we arrived with all our party intact and in reasonable health at a reception-point in Assam. The first British troops we met there were a Scots regiment. Fresh-faced, alert, smartly dressed, and wearing cocky glengarries, they gazed with curiosity, and I thought with some disapproval, at the bedraggled refugees who streamed past their outposts.

From now on we were transported by lorries. These heavy vehicles were driven along precipitous tracks by young Indian drivers, with arms and legs as thin as sticks, and only a few weeks' rushed training. As we swung round the more dangerous bends, we could see a graveyard of wrecked lorries far below. Our man did us splendidly. That night while we slept, our lorry was hijacked, but luck in due course brought us another with just room to climb in, and this carried us to the railhead at Dimapur. The boredom of a long wait there on the open platform was broken by a flight of Japanese bombers overhead. Surely, I thought, they *must* bomb the railhead, but they flew on, presumably to another target.

As we talked with other evacuees on the platform, we heard news of the deaths of many friends. Jim Wallace, Dugald McCallum's brother-in-law, a major in the Burma Rifles, had been killed blowing up a bridge as the Japanese attacked. An unusual combination of polo player and novelist, he had become increasingly interested in Buddhism, and when I last talked with him he had decried the material world and praised the aim of reducing human wants and desires. As a keen believer in all sensual pleasures, I had managed only non-committal noises in reply. Brigadier Roughton, who had visited me on the mountain tops of Sinlumkaba, had had fatal heatstroke during the fighting round the oilfields. Girling, who had brought a Burma Rifles unit to Chauk in the riots, had been killed in the fighting, as had Raymond Hall, an old friend from Steel Brothers. Grigson, tall and angular, an old Bombaing friend, had been killed by a bomb at Shwebo, and Jack Murphy, a handsome and jovial judge, had been killed by a bomb on the route we had just travelled. On the same route a deeply depressed Forest officer had slipped away from his friends into the trees and shot himself.

We were to hear of more deaths. Gemma Monk, a charming auburn-haired girl I had ridden with in Maymyo and entertained in the oilfields, and who had recently become engaged to one of the Governor's ADCs, was killed as a Japanese fighter strafed the plane in which she and her aunt were about to leave Myitkyina airfield. Her aunt survived, but was forced to serve out the war as a domestic servant to a Japanese officer. Noel Whiting, a dilettante European living in the hill resort of Kalaw, where he was captured, was another who became a domestic servant. He was for a time 'butler' to a Japanese police commandant, whom he described as 'very pleasant in many ways, and who in the evenings sometimes asked me to sit down and talk'. The civil prison camp in Tavoy to which Whiting was later moved was much less agreeable.

But we were safe, out of danger, and on a train to Calcutta. I had to admit to myself that that was what really mattered. A few days later the liquid portcullis of the north-western monsoon slammed down behind the retreating British Army, and India was safe for a season.

At the Great Eastern Hotel in Calcutta we were told no rooms were available. I suspect our bristly chins and dirty appearance had something to do with this. At the Grand Hotel three of us were accommodated in one room, and throwing away our worn and sweaty clothes we had glorious showers. As we dried ourselves, I said, 'Listen, boys, this is a unique moment in our lives, and we should enjoy it. Just for the moment we own *nothing*. All our wordly goods were left to the Japs, and we've just thrown our clothes and boots away. We don't have a single bloody material possession – marvellous!'

My friends saw the point, and we lay happily naked for a

couple of hours in long chairs, sipping whiskies and sodas under the swishing fans.

In the evening, at last clothed from the hotel shop, we went off for the treat we had promised ourselves on many occasions on our trek – a good dinner at Firpo's Restaurant. When it was served, none of us could eat more than a few mouthfuls. Maybe our stomachs had shrunk as a result of our austere rations. Or maybe the strains and sorrows of the last few months had at last caught up with us.

This is where this little memoir should logically end. We were over the border from Burma, and none of us would ever again see quite the same Burma as we had known. For many reasons that era was irrevocably gone. And that was the light-hearted era of the days of my youth which I have been trying to recall before it is quite forgotten. When we did return, a young Forest officer, saddened by the destruction of war in the forests where he had served, started his first dispatch to headquarters with a quotation which summed up the feelings of all of us: 'How green was my valley! And how sad it is now.'

8 India 1

The Far Eastern Bureau

The next three and a half years in India were an interlude, and in many ways another story. But my connection with Burma was maintained throughout the period of exile. None of us doubted we should be going back.

SIMLA

Most officials on escaping from Burma made for Simla, where the Burma Government had set up its headquarters-in-exile. I had another reason for going, which was that my sister was there, waiting anxiously for news of her husband in the Army. To anyone who had been brought up on Kipling, Simla was the materialization of a familiar dream. The town clung precariously to the sides of the same mountains; the jhimpanis propelled the same rickshaws; lights flashed from the same buildings and hotels; subalterns still rode with their colonels' wives to see the dawn or sunset on Jakko Hill. Monkeys leapt noisily about on the tin roofs; the acrid smell of charcoal and hookah tobacco drifted up from the bazaar; and nostalgia took me back to the hot weather that my sister and I, as small children, had spent with my mother in the little Himalayan hill station of Chakrata.

I remembered as a little boy moth-hunting at night with my father in the woods 'down the khud', wild roses by the path, the trousers of the hill women, the fresh smell of pine-needles, and the hint of snow on the breeze. I remembered the spiked collars the Sahibs' pet dogs wore as a guard against the greedy leopards which lurked in the jungle round the town, and the young British officers on leave laughing and teasing me on the tennis-court at the little Club. I had in fact been born in an Indian hill station.

In Simla I stayed at a pleasant old-fashioned hotel with long wooden verandas, Costorphan's. For my first breakfast I startled the khitmutgar (head waiter) by ordering a steak and a pint of beer. The cool air, the relief of being safe, the excitement of new experiences, had given me a ravenous appetite. I met many friends from Burma, taking a little leave and getting their future postings organized. A Simla custom was for a siren to sound each day at noon. For the first few days the reaction of the Burma refugees was to look round nervously for the nearest slit trench.

The Burma Government, apart from making arrangements for its refugees, started planning at once for return. The Governor set up a Reconstruction Department under Eric Arnold, which spent long and dedicated hours planning a British version of a new and better Burma. A few stalwart ministers and officials had followed the Governor out. Sir Htoon Aung Gyaw remained as Governor's Adviser; Sir Paw Tun, an ex-Premier, and his family were out. U Kyaw Min, one of the most senior Burmans of the ICS, soon became one of the sights of Simla. A somewhat rotund figure, he spurned the use of rickshaws, but found the steeper slopes difficult to manage; so he hired two strong rickshaw-men to push his back while he puffed up hill.

On the train up to Simla I had travelled with two colleagues of my sister's from the Women's Auxiliary Service (Burma), the daughter of the Commissioner of Moulmein, and her cousin, a young war widow. I saw a lot of them in Simla, and before my leave was over I was engaged to Pamela Gage, widow of Lt Eroll Gage, RN. Walking with her one day down the narrow winding Mall, we met two ladies in Burmese dress. One of them rushed up to me, threw her arms round my neck and addressed me in rapid Burmese.

'What does she say?' asked my fiancée.

The other Burmese lady translated: 'She says she used to live with your master!'

It took me a little time to explain that my friend was the Burmese wife of Gordon Apedaile, the ICS colleague who had put me up in Rangoon during the last weeks before evacuation. She could speak no English, knew virtually no one in Simla, and was overjoyed to see someone she knew well and could talk to.

Among other friends we found in Simla was Tom Atkinson, my old chief in the later days of the oilfields, who went straight off to be DC in the Frontier hills and, refusing treatment in the despair of delirium, died of pneumonia at his post a year later; and tall and handsome Peter Banks, of the Bombaing, recently married, who soon afterwards was killed (before his son was born) fighting with the Chin levies on the slopes of Suanglangsu Vum. The story of the hill-tribe levies and their exploits against the Japanese is one of the least-known stories of the war. Famous amongst the levy officers were 'Stooky' Seagrim, of the Burma Rifles, who was executed by the Japanese after giving himself up, on the far side of Burma, to save reprisals against the Karens; Eric McCrindle, of Macgregor's Forest Division, with whom I had toured near Pyinmana, also killed in Karenni; and Harold Braund, of Steel Brothers, who wrote a vivid account of the dangers and hardships of campaigning with the Chin levies.

DELHI

My own appointment was less heroic. From my frustrated post up in Mandalay I had submitted to the Government in Rangoon a number of memoranda on what I thought should be done about war propaganda, on which I had long had a bee in my bonnet. This was perhaps the reason why I was selected as Head of the Burma section of the Far Eastern Bureau in Delhi. The Bureau was run by the Ministry of Information in London under the direction of the Political Warfare Executive, and had charge of British war propaganda in South-East Asia and the Far East.

Delhi was two cities: New Delhi, formally laid out with modern public buildings, self-consciously designed to fit into India (which they didn't quite do); and Old Delhi, with the Red Fort, bazaars and crowded streets, which had grown naturally from its native soil.

I got a room in Old Delhi in Maiden's Hotel, the hotel from which two English girls, up in Delhi for some social week or another, had cabled their alarmed father, SEND FOUR HUNDRED

RUPEES OR CAN REMAIN MAIDENS NO LONGER. After some days a letter reached me which had been chasing me around. It was an invitation from Sir Gilbert Laithwaite, the Viceroy's Principal Private Secretary (whom I had never met), to stay with him until I could find somewhere to lodge in Delhi – a very kind gesture to a young stranger, and an opportunity I could not miss. When I rang Gilbert to accept, he assumed I had just got off the train. Disingenuously I did not disabuse him, but I had great difficulty in dissuading him from sending an official car to the railway station to fetch me. I stayed with him three or four days before announcing I had found lodgings at Maiden's Hotel, and thus had a unique opportunity of seeing the glories of the court of the 'Lat Sahib' during the twilight of the British Raj. Clemenceau had said the last word, in that ancient countryside, on Edwin Lutyens's imperial buildings: 'What magnificent ruins they will make!' Lord Linlithgow, an enormously tall Scottish nobleman, presided over affairs with imperturbable dignity and courtesy. Laithwaite, the Jesuit-trained official, and Linlithgow, the Scots Presbyterian landowner, made a formidable combination. This team, so inseparable that the Government of India was sometimes referred to as the 'Linlithwaite Government', ruled one-fifth of the human race for seven and a half onerous years.

My main impression of the Residence was of large numbers of immaculately clad Indian servants moving silently about. Below were the two massive buildings of the Secretariat, and still farther below the great Avenue, and the official bungalows laid out on a precise plan and gradation of type of dwelling, so that the moment any official in Delhi told you his address it was possible to make a good guess at his rate of pay.

Gilbert was exceptionally kind and hospitable, and we have remained good friends ever since those far-off days.

After my wedding in Bombay my wife and I eventually lodged with an ICS colleague, Bill le Bailey, Deputy Commissioner of Delhi, in a large, comfortable, old-fashioned bungalow in Old Delhi. We were joined next year by our baby daughter Julia, born in Simla and the third generation of my family to have been born in India. After the war it took a good deal of research to establish that my grandfather (who had worked most of his life in India) had been born in London in about 1824, before Julia and I were permitted to register as United Kingdom citizens. Julia had a magnificent ayah, a robust hill woman in trousers, called Diwarkoo. When she sang lullabies to the baby I could hear some far echoes of my own infancy.

>Gussuli, Gussuli Tunda
>Hamara Baba Punga
>Gussuli Gussuli Hogya
>Hamara Baba Sogya.
>
>(The baby is warm,
>My baby is naked.
>The bath is over,
>My baby sleeps.)

Also in Old Delhi was the Cecil Hotel, full of people working in the city. Pamela and I were having tea one day in the grounds of the Cecil with an old Forest officer from Burma, who worked in GHQ drawing maps of little-known tracks through the Burmese jungle, one of which was later used by our forces to recapture Maymyo. There was a sudden alarming swoop of wings and a table-napkin covering the sandwiches was whisked away. Our friend's expression did not change. '*Winter's Tale*,' he said in a flat tone. 'Act IV, Scene 3, line 23.'

When we were finally able to find the plays of Shakespeare we looked up the reference. It read: '... when the kite builds, look to lesser linen'. I don't know how long our friend had been waiting for such an opportunity.

Bill le Bailey was a large, cheerful, noisy bachelor. From time to time he flew into spectacular rages with his office and household staff. To see him and his huge red-bearded Pathan khitmutgar standing eyeball to eyeball and bellowing over some domestic difference was a sight to behold. Bill was another whom Indians liked and trusted, and to whom they therefore gave a wide licence they would hardly allow to many of his colleagues. He was a kind and considerate host. His periodic dinner parties worked up to a routine climax. His 'party pudding' was a delicious affair of fruit and cream, shut in at the top by a hard toffee lid. Giving this lid a powerful whack with a spoon, 'I declare this pudding open!' he pronounced triumphantly, while dazed guests picked pieces of toffee and fruit from their hair or corsages.

Every day I rode a bicycle to the Far Eastern Bureau offices in Connaught Circus in New Delhi and back. The FEB had been started in Singapore under Rob Scott of the Foreign Office, and was just getting going when the Japanese took Singapore. Rob, an expert in Chinese and Japanese, was captured and given a particularly bad time by the Japanese. He survived, and after the war refused to give evidence in war crimes trials against his gaolers, since he understood the Japanese compulsions for their actions. Other evidence convicted them, but, in one of the oddest incidents arising from the war, his ex-gaolers asked as a special honour that Rob Scott should attend their execution.

Amongst the team being hastily assembled in Singapore was John Proud, an Australian who escaped to join the Psychological Warfare team in the Pacific as a Commander in the Australian Navy, and whom I was later to meet in Cyprus as Director of the Cyprus Broadcasting Service during the EOKA troubles. Rob Scott had also enrolled in Singapore two Australian journalists, Ted Sayers and John Galvin. Neither was an expert in South-East Asia, but they both understood the object of the exercise and escaped to India to get FEB moving again. Experts on broadcasting who escaped from Singapore were E. Alington Kennard, previously Editor of *The Straits Times*; Eric Robertson, a Scot who reached a high position in the BBC after the war; and Peggy, the Australian girl who became his wife.

Our first Director was Paul Butler of the Foreign Office (he became Sir Paul before he left). He was a tall, thin, distinguished-looking man with grey hair, gentle and precise in his manner. He knew the Japanese intimately. His great contribution was to assemble a team of experts who really knew the languages and peoples of the area – Harold Braham and Henry Hainworth on Japan, Alec Adams on Thailand, Rawlings on Malaya. The Japanese section was particularly strong. Trevor Legatt, who had then the highest judo rating ever achieved by a non-Japanese, had lived Japanese-style in Japan, and was expert not only in the language but as a calligrapher. Marjorie Biddle, a tall, dark woman with a baffling squint, who had long lived in Japan and had married the Japanese surrealist poet Nishiwaki, was a brilliant artist and caricaturist, able to reach into Japanese emotions. Marjorie also had a private sketch-book, which she kept under lock and key, containing cruel caricatures of people in Delhi she didn't particularly like.

In the Burmese section I had Daw Mya Sein, a Burmese lady distinguished as a public figure and writer; David Morris, an eccentric Australian Buddhist, whose knowledge of Buddhist scriptures enabled him to produce a weekly Buddhist sermon or fable for the radio; four Burmese writers or translators, Maung Khin, Ba Saw, Aung Thein and a charming young lady called Ma Tin Nu; Kinch, the old schoolmaster who could illustrate any Burma scene with a few quick strokes of his pencil; and Streenivasan, a young South Indian schoolmaster, born and brought up in Burma and educated at Rangoon University, who had been helping the Burma Defence Department with war propaganda before evacuation. 'Streeni' afterwards had a successful career in India. He rose to be a brigadier and Director of Public Relations in the Indian Army. After leaving the Army he was Director of News at All-India Radio, Controller of Government Advertising, and Chairman of the Indian Board of Film Censors. He has twice been to visit me in Herefordshire in recent years. We worked closely with the Burma Section in All-India Radio, of which the chief Burman was U Khin Zaw, an exceptionally cultured young man, dedicated to the preserving of the folk-music of his country, who also had a team of Burmese helpers.

The London and supervising end of FEB was in the hands of Vere Redman, previously Press Attaché at the British Embassy in Tokyo, who had had a long and intimate experience of Japan. He had survived internment and rough handling by the Japanese (made worse by the fact that he was a diabetic), who suspected all Japanese linguists of being spies.

Paul Butler got a good machine going, but in the end apparently did not satisfy the London chiefs of the Political Warfare Executive that he was a sufficiently imaginative and aggressive 'psychological warrior'. Somewhat aloof, he did not often make jokes. But I remember driving back with him from a cocktail party for the Press of Delhi given by Sir Frederick Puckle, the genial Secretary to the Government of India in charge of Information and Broadcasting. I was defending Sir Frederick's regular cocktail parties as essential for his job, with so many foreign correspondents in Delhi.

At this, Paul Butler leant back in his seat. 'Ah – I see,' he said, 'many a pickle makes a Puckle!' He smiled to himself, clearly pleased with this *mot*.

John Galvin was the most tempestuous of Paul Butler's henchmen. A short Catholic Irish-Australian of demonic energy and sweeping financial imagination, he habitually thought in much bigger terms than the rest of us. I believe that when he joined FEB in Singapore he was the modest press representative of a press picture agency. In Delhi he began to concern himself with the technical side of broadcasting, threw himself wholeheartedly into this vital new field, and eventually flew home to London and by sheer force of personality persuaded Brendan Bracken to provide £13 million in order dramatically to increase the scope and strength of overseas broadcasts from Delhi. I believe he learnt from this wartime experience that, providing you have the nerve, it is no more difficult to think in terms of very large sums of money than in smaller ones. So, after the war, he progressed from purchasing war surplus stores to textiles in Hong Kong and tin mines in Malaya, with his own cargo shipping line thrown in. He ended a multimillionaire, owning a huge ranch in California, and eventually appeared in the *Guinness Book of Records* as a result of his receiving from the US Inland Revenue the biggest recorded personal tax demand in history. My wife and I stayed with him on his ranch in 1959. He was a generous and unassuming host, unfailingly loyal to old friends.

KASHMIR

I had been in hospital twice with bacillary dysentery, and some unpleasant gastric malaria, after walking out from Burma, and when I succumbed to an epidemic of jaundice which swept GHQ, New Delhi, I was granted sick-leave. Consequently Pamela and I, with our baby daughter, set off for Kashmir. There are two places in my life which have surpassed my expectations: Venice and Kashmir. After a long, hot drive over barren mountains, the descent in the evening light into the Vale of Kashmir was to discover Shangri-La. Like the Moguls, we appreciated the country doubly for having come from the furnace heat and dust of the Delhi hot weather. Green grass, flowers, poplars, deodars, gleaming water and the mountains beyond were balm to the spirit. And our houseboat was waiting on one of the lakes, brightly lit, with a courteous khitmutgar in spotless white waiting to serve us dinner.

In the morning little boats drifted up to our windows to sell fresh fruit, vegetables, flowers and sweets. A venerable lace-seller called 'Mister Butterfly' gazed with interest at Julia kicking in her cot. 'I have some of those,' he remarked politely. We swam from a houseboat moored in the middle of the lake; gliding in shikaras, the Kashmir gondolas, we visited Mogul gardens which sloped down to the lake through cherry blossom and roses and water channels flowing over shallow terraces. The voices of carefree subalterns of bygone days could be heard behind the names of shikaras and shops. We travelled in a shikara called 'Love on Springs' to inspect a furniture shop bearing the name 'Cheerful Chippendale, the Worst Carpenter in the World'. When the delights of Nagin Bagh and Srinagar palled, we took our houseboat staff and lorries to camp in tents and fish in clear mountain streams – we caught more trout each day than I have ever done before or since – or pony-trekked up the mountains.

Many years later, as Adminstrative Counsellor with the British Embassy in Washington, I had to try to persuade the District of Columbia Engineer Commissioner to let us build a new chancery in an area designated as residential. The Commisioner and I stared at each other for a moment before laughing aloud. He had been on leave in the next houseboat to ours on Nagin Bagh. I believe our memories of Kashmir helped ease the passage of the building permit.

BACK TO DELHI

After some time Sir Paul Butler was recalled to England and we waited for some great new chief. In the end no one came. John Galvin looked after the finances and the expansion of broadcasting, and Ted Sayers, a solid and cautious character, kept the show together. This arrangement meant that the 'country experts' were given a pretty free hand, which suited all concerned.

Our targets were various. The Japanese broadcasts, given extra vitality by Alington Kennard, were partly aimed at the Japanese mainland itself. Other broadcasts were aimed at Japanese troops, for whom the FEB Japanese section concocted both strategic and tactical leaflets. Marjorie Biddle, for example, painted, in delicate Japanese style, different Japanese leaves and flowers, which, accompanied by a line of classical Japanese poetry, were designed to arouse homesickness and melancholy in the Japanese soldiers overseas. I don't know how successful this was. But one leaflet, I cannot remember whether it was an FEB leaflet or not, sent a little chill down my spine. It showed falling cherry blossom. Underneath was a haiku – 'A fluttering cloud of cherry petals... and there comes, pursuing them, the Storm'.

We learnt a vital propaganda lesson from one particular leaflet produced by the Japanese to arouse homesickness in our troops. The picture on this showed an old-fashioned English cottage with roses round the door. The caption read something like this: 'A smell of cooking comes through the door. Someone is singing "Home Sweet Home". Can it be the wife?' This was not so *very* far off target, yet it was comical and, if anything, likely to boost the morale of our troops.

The lesson we learnt was that propaganda aimed at a foreign people can be effective only if it is channelled through nationals of their own country, and that anything which they feel is not quite right, for whatever reason and however hard it may be to explain, should be scrapped forthwith. We therefore gave a very free hand to our Burmese translators to put over the required ideas in whatever words they thought would work best. We tried to ask ourselves what it was we wanted the readers of our leaflets to do or not to do. Then we went along, so far as we could, with our target's inborn emotions and prejudices, putting only in the tail the argument intended to persuade them to do what we wanted. We did not criticize or decry the people we were addressing – Burmese villagers, or Burma's National Army, or Japanese soldiers. We implied always that they were decent, honest, brave people misled by bad leaders. It was General Iida (never the Emperor) and Dr Ba Maw whom we pitched into. I was shocked, at the time of Suez, to see British leaflets designed for dropping in Egypt depicting Egyptian troops as comical and cowardly.

We made a lot of fun of Ba Maw in our cartoons, which was not too difficult. But it seems that he at least made some effort to prevent the 'Japanization' of Burma. The Japanese sensed his reservations. In one of the more extraordinary stories of the war in South-East Asia, some right-wing Japanese officers incited a naïve and fanatically patriotic Japanese civilian to assassinate Ba Maw, whom they suspected of being in touch with the British. The attempt was bungled, and the assailant and accomplices were tried by the Japanese, but not too savagely punished.

Our Japanese script was often written, or rather painted with a brush, by Trevor Legatt. He was a perfectionist in all he did – judo, chess, piano or Japanese lettering. I have seen him, brush in hand, practising for hours, indeed for days, a single stroke of a single letter, over and over again. I learnt from him that judo was not just a wrestling skill but a form of mental and physical discipline. His script was finally accepted by Japanese as not only written by a Japanese, but by a high-grade Japanese calligrapher.

In the early stages of the war it was virtually impossible to take Japanese prisoners. Such was the Japanese military code of honour that a soldier would far rather kill himself than be captured. Overrunning a Japanese position meant finding a dead soldier in every foxhole – some blown up by their own grenades. So we were at one stage lent a Japanese-American, a 'Nisei boy', to help with our work. I thought of him as a Japanese on our side, and one day I made one of those thoughtless cracks one made about Yanks (and that they made about us). He turned quiet and left the room. Trevor admonished me, 'You must remember that though he looks like a Japanese he is in his heart a true-blue American.'

Trevor was a tall, rather gangling figure. He told me he had been outsize at school and bullied. He had taken up judo to work out the resentment which had built up inside him. Once he knew he could defeat any man he met in unarmed combat, he felt exorcized, and I found him to be the gentlest and mildest of men. He said that at the Berlin Olympics of 1936 the Nazi

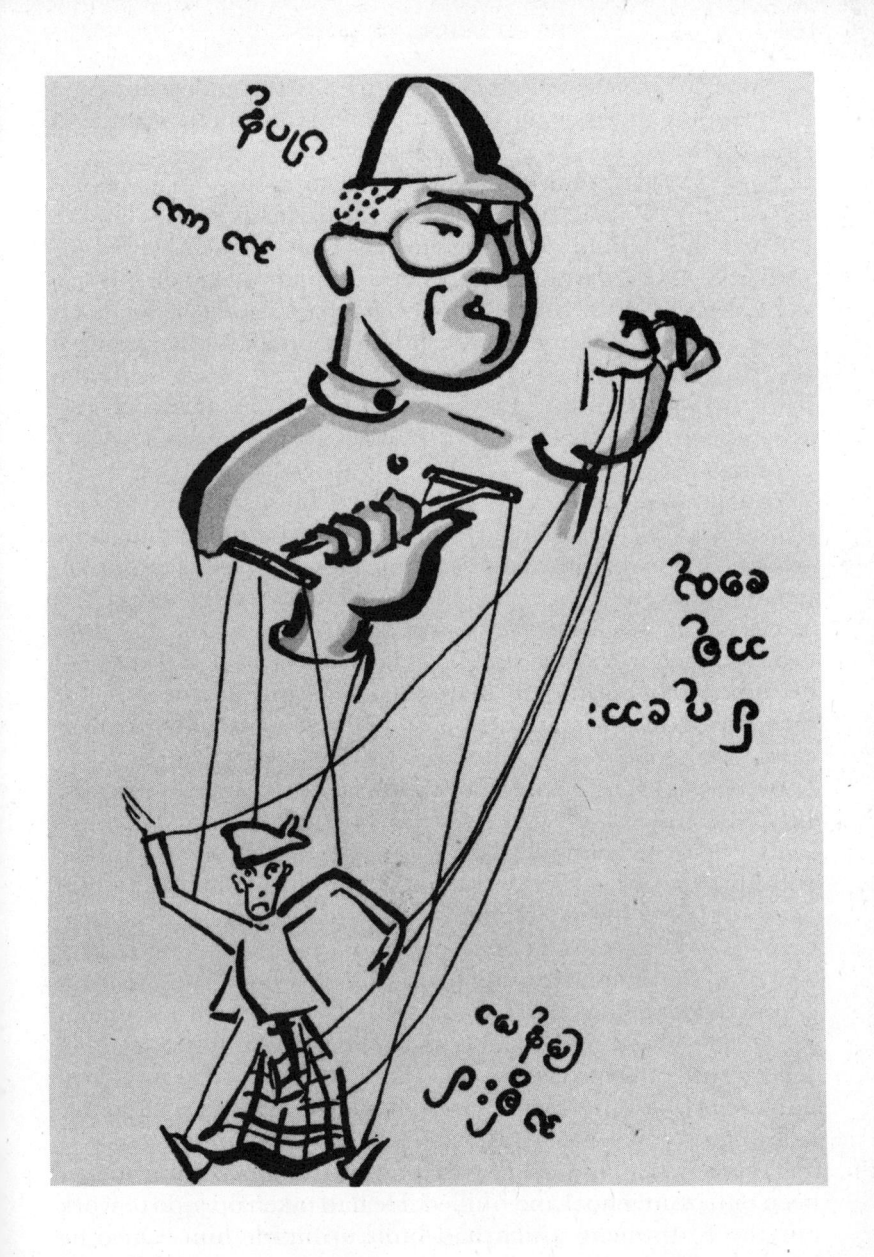

British aerial propaganda leaflet: Dr Ba Maw as a Japanese puppet

athletes used to watch him in order to try to find out the secret of his training and diet. What they made of their observation of him, I cannot imagine. In wartime Delhi he usually wore an open-necked shirt, and he walked with a slight stoop. His normal meal was a poached egg and a glass of milk, usually taken while he was reading some volume of poetry or philosophy. He started to teach me chess, and, just to demonstrate the difference of class between us, asked me at the beginning of a game to choose which particular square I should like to be mated on. I chose the most unlikely square I could think of, and in due course my king was humiliatingly shepherded on to that very square for the *coup de grâce*.

In our Burma section one task was that of helping in the preparation of some of the radio scripts for U Khin Zaw, who was responsible for the main radio output. We by no means always saw eye to eye with one another. I reckoned that All-India Radio overseas broadcasts were paid for by the British Government and therefore should put out a strictly British policy line. U Khin Zaw, while whole-heartedly anti-Japanese, reckoned that AIR had some independence, and took a line sometimes more likely to please Burmese nationalism in forecasting post-war developments. After long argument we came to an amicable arrangement. On the whole, under the light control of his British supervisors, his approach prevailed.

We were never sure how many listeners there were who could hear the broadcasts. A few educated Burmese and, as the war wore on, more Burmese at the top in the Government and in the Army, had sets capable of picking up Delhi. But at that time there were few sets in the villages, and indeed the Japanese made it illegal, on pain of death, to possess a set capable of long-range reception. It was the villagers at whom we mainly directed our leaflets, and above all our weekly serial newspaper *Lay Nat Tha*, 'The Spirit of the Wind', a name devised by U Khin Zaw.

In the early days it was difficult to know what to say in Burmese leaflets. We had been beaten by the Japanese, and we were still doing badly in the war and were very much on the defensive. Promises of early victories might turn out to be hollow. So we concentrated on stirring up the Burmese national spirit against the Japanese. One of our earlier leaflets showed General Maha Bandula (who, as a Burmese historical hero,

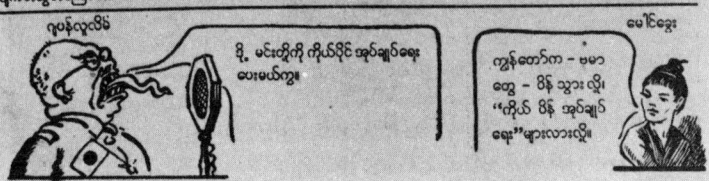

British aerial propaganda: front page of the weekly Burmese newspaper, *Lay Nat Tha* (The Spirit of the Wind)

ranks as Nelson or Wellington does in Britain) clad in his traditional armour, making a rude and defiant remark in idiomatic and allusive Burmese to a modern Japanese officer.

A while after a consignment of these leaflets was passed to the RAF some of the bundles were returned, with the caustic comments of a senior officer to the effect that he didn't feel like risking the lives of his crews to drop this sort of stuff. I therefore wrote a note to Air Chief Marshal Sir Guy Garrod, apologizing for not having accompanied each new leaflet with a full explanation of what the RAF were being asked to drop and why. I explained the care taken in deciding the theme, and the attention paid to every detail in the picture, and to every word of the text. The result had to be passed by at least six different Burmese, as being likely to stimulate the intended reaction in a Burmese mind, before it was accepted. I went into detail on the special significance in this particular leaflet of Bandula's remarks.

Garrod sent back a nice note saying that he and his staff were glad to see the care and thought which went into the leaflets, and that the RAF would be happy to drop any we sent them.

We sometimes produced leaflets for special areas or for special types of people, but we concentrated mainly on *Lay Nat Tha*, a four-page miniature weekly newspaper printed on thin leaflet paper. The formula consisted of a page of war news, which always had a map and was always truthful. We reported reverses as well as successes. Then we had a cartoon, usually drawn by Kinch. (Later a patrol managed to bring out a well-known young Burmese artist whose cartoons were even more authentic.) Then we had a short leader with a general comment and message, and filled the remaining space with other news items and a few photos.

When we eventually returned to Burma after the war both Streenivasan and I went to great lengths to find out whether all this effort had been of any use. Our conclusion was that it had indeed had an effect. A great number of people knew about *Lay Nat Tha*. The Japanese ordered copies to be collected and burnt – but single copies were always kept back, and a network was formed which put the odd copies in hollow bamboos for passing to areas where there had not been a drop. Burmese read the paper first because they were starved of news. Then they came to believe it. And when the war turned against the Japanese its messages had real effect.

When Allied victories in the Western Desert released some experts for the South-East Asian theatres we were descended upon by high-powered publicists with Fleet Street training. In particular our output was criticized by a layout team from *Picture Post*, who thought *Lay Nat Tha* must be smartened up – better paper, better typeface, better drawn title design – and this team of specialists duly produced a mock-up which to Western eyes was certainly a more impressive product. Kinch and I fought them tooth and nail over it. We felt and argued passionately that we wanted *Lay Nat Tha* to be as Burmese as possible, so that its general appearance and style should be accepted in Burma as something familiar – there should be no unnecessary 'block' before Burmese readers took in the message. The paper and the typeface should accordingly be as close as possible to those of a Burmese newspaper; and it was much less important that the drawings and designs should be artistic by Western standards than that they should be essentially Burmese. The leaflets, we argued, were being designed to drop on Mandalay and not on Margate. We won most of our battles, and *Lay Nat Tha*, after an experiment with a new heading, was left alone.

Earlier we had received unexpected help in devising broadcasts and leaflets for Burma from two young Burmans who had escaped from the Japanese occupation. They reached India in August 1942. One of them was Thein Pe, a young Communist who was already a well-known journalist in Burma. His nickname, 'Tet-Pongyi', meant 'Modern Monk', and was the title of his courageous book attacking the parasitical corruption of many young Buddhist monks. This was indeed a target which needed attacking, but only a brave man would have taken up the cudgel. Thein Pe had done so and not only did he get away with it, but earned the respect of many of his countrymen.

If I remember right, Thein Pe was put in touch with me by the interrogating officers who examined him at the frontier. We soon established a mutual trust and confidence. He and his younger companion, Thakin Tin Shway, gave us just what we wanted, recent knowledge of actual conditions under Japanese occupation. Thein Pe told us, for example, how the villagers had found the Japanese mean in payment for labour and arrogant in their behaviour, quick to indulge in 'face-slapping'. A number of their habits had affronted Burmese susceptibilities, particularly the bathing of Japanese men and women naked in public, while the eating habits of their soldiery seemed barbaric – they mixed cane sugar and tea with their rice and had been seen, it was said, eating rice out of looted china chamber-pots. Moreover, they used bookcases from Burmese monasteries as firewood. The greatest shock derived from the fact that, in spite of the propaganda of 'Asiatic brotherhood', the Japanese seemed to consider the Burmese an inferior people. Japanese veterans of the Chinese and Korean wars instinctively regarded local populations with suspicion.

Thein Pe demurred as a 'politician' from accepting salaried employment from the British Government, but honour was satisfied and his independence respected through an arrangement by which we paid for his board and lodging and gave him a decent fee for each day he came to the office. Thein Pe, a slim, young-looking, round-faced man in spectacles, was a naïvely confident Communist and often talked to me happily of the inevitable economic collapse of the capitalist West, which he was convinced was imminent. I used to argue mildly with him, but my main concern was to harness his strong hostility towards the Japanese and to use his perception of his countrymen for the purpose of appealing appropriately to Burmese hearts and minds at that particular time.

He showed me a short first-hand account, written in not very good English, of the Japanese occupation of his country. Dr Spate, a professor of his from Rangoon University, now in India, had helped him, I believe, to prepare it. His little book was full of Marxist jargon and side-swipes against British imperialists and militarists. But the real bite of the booklet lay in its novelty and first-hand reportage, and in its deeply hostile references to the Japanese. We reckoned, for example, that the news that Japanese troops on entering a town swiped everyone's watches and fountain-pens would create at least as shocked a reaction in India as lurid tales of rape and slaughter. In contrast, the anti-British bits were such old hat in India that we thought they could do little extra harm, and would indeed add to the credibility of the story.

Since FEB had no mandate to operate within India to Indians, I went up to Simla to discuss the possible operation with Francis Watson, the historian, who was Director of the Government of India Counter-Propaganda Department. Francis approved, and promised his co-operation.

With Thein Pe's approval, I edited his text and even wrote in little bits myself (which I pride myself could not be distinguished in style from his), which he accepted. Marjorie Biddle designed an orange cover with a lurid design of red-and-yellow flames. I suggested the title, 'What Happened in Burma', and wrote the blurb on the back cover, on the lines of 'The frank revelations of a young revolutionary, etc. etc.'. Then we promised Thein Pe confidential funds, if required, towards publication and distribution, and told him to go off and find a left-wing Congress-orientated publisher.

He consulted Edgar Snow, the American recorder of Mao Tse-tung's 'Long March', who was in Delhi, and persuaded Kita Bistan, a Congress publisher in Allahabad, to take on the work. Editions were published in English, Hindi, Urdu and Gujerati. All went well. Some military intelligence people got hold of one of the first copies and suggested the book should be banned, and rumours of this helped the sales. Francis Watson, under the table, pushed distribution of sales all over India, and the sales, at a cheap price, achieved considerable momentum. Francis told me afterwards that he considered it one of the best bits of anti-Japanese propaganda done in India during the war.

Talking one evening to British Intelligence operators, I learnt that they were having difficulty in finding any agents willing to go into Burma. When I said I might be able to suggest someone to them, they leapt at this. I raised the matter cautiously with Thein Pe, who said at once that Tin Shway would be willing to go back.

Once the two Burmans had been put in touch with our clandestine organizations, they were gobbled up and sent to a carefully guarded training establishment at Meerut, supposed to be unknown to any outsider.

Thein Pe told me that some of the training his friend was receiving was a bit elementary, such as 'how to wait for a bus without looking self-conscious', which as a Burman he thought very funny.

But the operation was on. Tin Shway was landed by night in a rubber dinghy on the Japanese-occupied coast of Arakan. He eventually came out, with his girl-friend, and with more information than the intelligence organization had gathered from any previous source on the ground. I was excited at the prospect of debriefing him for propaganda purposes. But I was shouldered off. 'He is now our man,' I was informed coldly. 'You cannot see him.'

More important than the intelligence was the fact that this trip marked the opening of direct contact between certain Thakin nationalists, beginning to be restive with the Japanese, and our clandestine organizations. For good or ill this affected the whole political future of post-war Burma.

During the last stage of the war Thein Pe was diagnosed as suffering from serious tuberculosis of the spine. His new employers got him the best medical attention, but he had to stay in bed encased in plaster of Paris ('buried alive', he described it) for a full year, an imprisonment he bore with great fortitude. He was luckily able (with difficulty) to read and write. He even broadcast flat on his back from Calcutta studios on the reported success of anti-Japanese Burmese guerrillas in Arakan.

After the war he returned to Burma as General Secretary of the Burma Communist Party.

He was an honest man, and in his way a more influential person than any of us recognized at the time. By an odd coincidence, just when I was writing the first draft of these pages on Thein Pe (whom I had scarcely thought about in the time since I had last seen him, nearly forty years ago) the phone rang and the speaker identified himself as Dr Robert H. Taylor of the School of Oriental and African Studies in London. Dr Taylor said he was specializing in modern Burmese history. He had just translated a book on the wartime travels of a young Burmese Communist called Thein Pe, who had mentioned my name a couple of times in his book, and could I tell Dr Taylor anything I knew about him. An example of Jung's 'synchronicity' perhaps?

Dr Taylor's research and analysis continue to illuminate the history of this period. Under the Thirty Years' Rule the confidential official documents of those years are now available to historians, and from them Dr Taylor is able to form a much better overall view of the wood than most of us could when we were in the midst of the trees. I am grateful to him for perceptive insights into Burmese politics.

THE ANGLO-AMERICAN ALLIANCE

Working in Delhi in wartime, after seven years in the backwoods of Burma, made me realize that I was a bit of a provincial. The vast Indian Empire, run from Delhi, not only influenced the lives of hundreds of millions of people, it reached out into the Red Sea and the Persian Gulf in the west, and anxiously watched the Russians in the north. It was practically a world power on its own. Burma was just part of India's defensive glacis. The Government in India was government on a grand scale, burdened with the responsibilities of administering an enormous and immensely complicated and delicately balanced mixture of races and religions, and influenced by centuries of culture and tradition. The British had been nearly 300 years in India. Their roots were deep.

And in FEB I met for the first time a number of Foreign Office people with experience of many countries outside South-East Asia. Paul Butler had once been Consul-General in San Francisco, and he told me much about the United States, a country in which I was to serve for a total of seven years. But I was still pretty naïve about the complexities of international relations.

One day I met a fresh-faced young American airman, working in his Delhi headquarters. He told me that the Americans had a surplus of parachute silk and wondered if, as a propaganda gimmick, some of it could be dropped on the villages of Burma, known to be starved of cloth. I thought this a good idea. We had the silk cut up into suitable lengths, packed them into stout envelopes, described them as a joint present from the British and American Allies, and stamped the envelopes with crossed British and American flags.

The operation was suddenly cancelled from on high, by the American side. Anxious to find out the reason, I was finally ushered in to see a grey-haired senior American diplomat, representing President Roosevelt in Delhi. Ambassador William Phillips delicately indicated that the stumbling-block was the crossed British and American flags, and the implication of a joint operation.

'But why?' I asked in my innocence. 'Aren't we both on the same side?'

I was given to understand that, though we might be fighting the same enemy, we were not fighting for the same objectives, and that in propaganda to Burma the US Government would not wish to be too closely associated with the Imperialist Oppressor. It emerged that President Roosevelt was not much interested in the reconquest of Burma as such, or in 'recapturing the British Empire for the British'. His main interest was to get supplies through the Burma Road to his blue-eyed boy, Generalissimo Chiang Kai-shek, and the ineffable Madame. Sensitivity about not being associated with imperialist propaganda reached such proportions that objections were even raised to the use of records of American dance bands on our radio programmes.

At one stage Sir Evelyn Wrench, founder of the English-Speaking Union, turned up in Delhi with the laudable objective of encouraging friendly social relations between British and American officers. British officers grew to have a great respect for American energy, organizing ability and dash, both in flying supplies over The Hump to China, and in supplying and helping our troops. Their airmen were of legendary bravery. But at the start both nations looked on each other as rather freakish foreigners.

Sir Evelyn's series of joint lunches proved a flop. But at last someone realized the obvious: that the best ice-breaker was a special interest in common – and British and Americans often made lifelong friends in the playing of games together and sharing enthusiasms – for example, in philately, archaeology or religion.

Someone asked an American officer in our group what he thought was the most important thing British and Americans had in common. 'Golf,' he said.

9 India 2

Psychological Warfare Division (South-East Asia Command)

The year 1942 started badly, with the failure of the British offensive in the Arakan. The Japanese advanced in the other direction up a parallel valley, and – surprise, surprise – executed one of their famous hooks round our rear.

Denis Phelips, with a small staff, had accompanied the British forces as the first commissioned Civil Affairs officer. At one stage, dressed in his usual khaki shirt and shorts, he drove his jeep up into a front-line area. There he found a British officer parading a bunch of Burmese prisoners before a brigadier. 'Spies, sir,' said the captain. 'We found them up trees watching our movements. What shall we do with them?'

Denis had a word or two with the Burmese. 'These aren't spies,' he said. 'They are toddy tappers, carrying out their normal livelihood.'

'Who the hell are you?' said the brigadier. 'And what are you doing up in the fighting? I think I shall put you under arrest!'

'Wait a minute,' said Denis, fumbling in his pocket and bringing out a penknife, some string and some crumpled insignia. 'I forgot! I'm a brigadier too!'

On 1 August 1943 the Japanese declared the Independence of Burma – and this 'independent' Government was required by the Japanese to declare war on the Allies. We derided this mock independence (which it was, as Japanese 'advisers' at all levels ran the country) in our propaganda, but it may not have been without some psychological fillip to the Burmese.

Easiest to laugh at was the Japanese so-called 'South-East Asia Co-Prosperity Sphere' – a topic on which Kinch produced some brilliant cartoons of plump Japanese and hungry-looking, thin Burmese.

This was the year in which Mountbatten appeared in India as Supreme Commander of the South-East Asia Command (SEAC), Wavell became Viceroy, and Auchinleck succeeded Wavell as Commander-in-Chief, India. One consequence of this was that the Burmese and Japanese sections of FEB were absorbed into a new SEAC Psychological Warfare Division, a military unit, and moved to a forward base in Calcutta. At the same time the planning of the Civil Affairs Service, for the military administration of Burma on reoccupation, was stepped up. I was simultaneously made Head of the Information Division of the Civil Affairs Service (Burma) (CAS(B)), and, like many of my ICS colleagues, I emerged from all this as an officer in uniform. In my case I started (and ended) my 'military' career as 2nd Lt Glass, acting Lt-Colonel.

In Delhi we had been getting more involved with the military anyway. Peter Fleming was the GHQ deception expert. He and his friends are said to have invented a complete Armoured Division, for the arrival of which elaborate reception arrangements were made in various parts of India before 'new orders' apparently switched the new Division elsewhere. I was aked by a Chindit staff officer to do a Deception Plan for a Chindit operation. I prepared an elaborate plan; whether it was ever used, I doubt.

One day Peter Fleming came to ask my views on whether enormous inflated balloon figures of men, dropped from aircraft, would cause panic amongst the Burmese National Army then supporting the Japanese. It was possible, I suppose, that such unnatural ogres might 'spook' the remote tribesmen he had met in his travels in Mongolia. But I had to tell him that I doubted their effect on the relatively more sophisticated Burmese, officered often by Rangoon University students.

Wingate, with his 'brave captains', Mike Calvert and Bernard Fergusson in particular, excited us all by their daring forays behind the Japanese lines. It may be that Wingate's many military critics were right, and that the immediate military effect of these raids was not great, but after months of unrelieved defeat and gloom, the effect on everyone's morale of hearing of British troops on the offensive was of incalculable value.

Mike Calvert appeared in Delhi to collect the first of his

DSOs, and we were both invited by Robin Ridgeway, Auchinleck's personal secretary and a school-mate of ours, to dine quietly at Flagstaff House. He told us his chief would be out that night. Robin it emerged afterwards, had recently come from a secret assignment, running 'Section E', which dealt with 'escapers and evaders' in South-East Asia as MI9 did in Europe. When I arrived (Mike's personal celebrations had so diverted him that he did not appear at all), I found to my consternation that 'the Auk' was unexpectedly dining in, and that owing to some crisis there were also assembled the top commanders of the Indian Navy and Air Force, and a number of other generals. As a young and junior officer, I hastily said I would come another time, but Auchinleck insisted on my coming in, sat me on his right, and talked to me about my job for the whole meal. After dinner, before his conference resumed, we had a quick game of 'carom board', a sort of mini-billiards played on a little table with draughts flicked with one finger. I played with Admiral Somerville against 'the Auk' and his Indian ADC. 'The Auk' was a great and simple man, and it was no wonder that the Indians loved him.

Wavell I met only once. With his one eye and laconic, imperturbable manner he reminded me somewhat of a civilized version of Kutusov in *War and Peace*.

Mountbatten arrived among these weary veterans as a fresh young hero. He was determined to be served by his own planners, responsible only to him, and before long set up his Headquarters far away from Delhi in the luxuriant Peradiniya Botanical Gardens of Kandy in Ceylon.

The first idea was that FEB should be taken over by the South-East Asia equivalent of the Special Operations Executive, and I was summoned to meet one of their number 'by the third pillar from the window' in a café in Connaught Circus, a mysterious secrecy which defeated me – what were we keeping secret from whom? But in the end we came under the command in Kandy of Air Marshal Sir Philip Joubert de la Ferté, the Deputy Chief of Staff in charge of Psychological Warfare, Public Relations and Civil Affairs. In fact, his main job was to organize Mountbatten's public relations. He had done a good job for RAF PR in Britain. From now on he had the difficult task of coping with the experienced and resourceful American PR men, bent on getting maximum publicity for American efforts. Later he enlisted the professional help of Charles Eade, the young editor of the *Sunday Despatch*, who was given high military rank.

I went down to Ceylon in civilian clothes to talk to the Air Marshal. Joubert was an amiable, talkative man, who affected to believe that I was a war correspondent. He gave me a vivid description of serving in the Royal Flying Corps in the First World War, and was dissuaded from showing me the bullet-hole in his backside, received from a German rifle, only when again I protested that I was a junior officer about to come under his command. Below him on the Psychological Warfare side was Group Captain 'Josh' Bell, an Australian whose limited experience in this field lay in the actual dropping of leaflets in the Pacific, with a Scottish major as his main staff officer. None of this hierarchy knew much about psychological warfare, and mostly they left us alone, but helped us get the finance and equipment we needed.

Planning started for 'Psychological Warfare Field Units', and a regular lt-colonel came to discuss these with me. He proposed for each unit a major, so many captains and subalterns, so many warrant officers and other ranks, plus such-and-such amount of transport, and so on. I suggested that we might first decide what these units were for, and exactly what they would be designed to do. This was brushed aside. 'You don't understand, old boy. The first thing one does in the Army for a new formation is to get an Authorized War Establishment. Plenty of time afterwards to think up what they should do.'

CALCUTTA

I began to spend more time in Calcutta, with visits to Delhi and Kandy. Calcutta was a horrible place, smelly, humid and swarming hopelessly with poor and undernourished Indians, augmented by refugees from the countryside driven in by the recent Bengal famine. Yet, in spite of its deep underlying misery, the city had certain attractions. The old eighteenth-century Palladian buildings put up by the first Englishmen in India gave the city an atmosphere of its own. The business tycoons, in their well-appointed clubs, city and country, and their air-conditioned offices and houses, lived insulated and comfortable (if anxious and hard-working) lives, and were hospitable hosts. And there was an insidious sense of seductiveness in the centre of the city at night, with urchins playing 'Deep in the Heart of Texas' on tin whistles in the dark gutters of Chowringhee, and lights gleaming from cafés and night-spots – the whiff of sin in the anonymity of a big city.

CAS(B) HQ, where I spent part of my time, was with other Army HQs in Barrackpore, on the outskirts of Calcutta, housed in tin Nissen huts, where the sweat on one's hands and arms smeared the ink of whatever one wrote, and where the butter in the canteen was as liquid as tea. As I had my other offices in Calcutta I got permission to live in the central part of the city, and was let a room by my old Maymyo friend 'Beaver' Barton. The room, which had a small concrete cell with shower and loo attached, was simply furnished with a bed and someone's motor cycle under a dust-sheet.

By the time we had set up our 'psywar' base in Calcutta, our troops were at last taking Japanese prisoners, and Trevor Legatt was in virtual charge of a camp of prisoners up the Hooghly river. The same code of honour which led Japanese soldiers to commit suicide rather than face the shame of surrender meant that if they *did* surrender they had little resistance left. By their own code they were finished, so many of them co-operated with us without inhibitions. Their loyalty to their Emperor was unbreachable. But some of the more intelligent amongst them were openly critical of the militarist party which ruled Japan.

One Sunday Trevor asked me to lunch with him at his quarters at the camp. After lunch (which was the traditional Indian Sunday lunch of mulligatawny and a pudding called *goula malaka*, a tapioca with a sort of black treacle sauce and coconut milk) I settled down for a snooze.

'I think I would like to play judo for a bit,' said Trevor.

'OK,' I said, 'go ahead!'

'But you must play with me.'

'But Trevor! What nonsense! I can't possibly....'

In no time I was outside, clad simply like Trevor, in a pair of shorts. To make matters worse, we were out on a piece of grass on which lounged a number of Japanese prisoners. Making a desperate lunge at the Maestro I caught him round the body. Used as he was to wrestling with an opponent in a judo tunic, his fingers slipped momentarily on my sweating flesh, and there I was, like an all-in wrestler, holding him over my head. Abject terror overcame me. 'So sorry, Trevor! Don't know how it happened!' For the next ten minutes I was subjected to the widest possible variety of simple holds and throws, amply demonstrating that Trevor could, if he so wished, pulverize me on one leg with one hand behind his back. It took me days to recover.

At one stage I got involved in doing some leaflets for the Chin hills, and for a short while was loaned a Chin levy, brought out by a British officer. In our Calcutta office I took the Chin upstairs in the lift, not realizing that he might never have seen one before. As the 'small room' began to rise upwards he crouched in the alert and defiant posture of a frightened animal, the whites of his eyes showing. I reassured him and let him work the buttons, and for the next hour while I was busy, he spent a happy time going up and down, no doubt rehearsing in his mind the story he would tell his fellow-tribesmen in the hills. Primitive peoples adapt quickly to the marvels of modern science and very soon take them for granted. Magic is a normal part of their lives.

About this time for some reason or other I fell out professionally with some members of the clandestine organizations' staff and they planned to shift me. But they overdid it. Two complaints were received from Joubert's office in Kandy: in one it was asserted that I spent all my time in Delhi and was never in Calcutta; and in the other, that I spent all my time in Calcutta and was never in Delhi. I pinned them together and sent them direct to Joubert. My Calcutta chief was appalled. 'You did that to the Deputy Chief of Staff to the Supreme Commander?' he wailed. I heard no more about it, and was never moved. Jealousy between the clandestine organizations, of which there must have been about a dozen, was endemic.

CAS(B) planning was going forward under Freddy Pearce, a senior ICS colleague, looking a bit Gilbert and Sullivan in a major-general's uniform. Freddy had a conscience about taking officers away at this stage from genuine military duties and struggled for months with a small and somewhat inexperienced staff. Mountbatten was not satisfied with his progress, nor, I suspect, did he like dealing with an officer so closely linked with pre-war Burma, and there were growing policy differences. The great problem we were going to have to face was what to do about the thousands of young Burmese armed with modern weapons. Until some of these young men were enrolled in disciplined forces obedient to the Government, and the rest by persuasion, bribery, and force if necessary, completely disarmed, peaceful government would be exceedingly difficult. In the event we did not have the stomach for a ruthless general disarmament, and the governments of independent Burma have suffered for it since.

KANDY

In Kandy the atmosphere was somewhat unreal, with its show of smart white tropical uniforms and pretty Wren officers, and polite Sinhalese waiters in national garb with tortoise-shell combs in their hair. My main contact in the Military Administration HQ was Brigadier Gibbon, Joubert's senior staff officer, a colonial civil servant from Nigeria. Gibbon told me a lot about Nigeria. Little did I know that twenty-five years later my last overseas post would be as UK High Commissioner in that country. How 'Gibboon' would have laughed!

In the ICS we secretly prided ourselves on a somewhat higher intellectual standard than that of the British civil servants in Africa, but I have never met an official capable of quite the sustained ferocity of Gibbon in his attacks on masses of complicated papers, from which emerged lucid and sensible recommendations. We became good friends and, in spite of my lowly rank (in Kandy lt-colonels were mere bottle-washers), he used to smuggle me into the hotel by the lake, which was the brigadiers' mess. This was the lake across which a British officer swam in full uniform after a cheerful party given by the American staff in SEAC to welcome the US General Stilwell, who in Mountbatten's absence on short leave, contrary to expectation, agreed to come down as Acting Supreme Commander. Ostentatiously driving about in battle fatigues in an old jeep, he sent the Supremo's Rolls and chauffeur to the bazaar to buy vegetables. When he was told later of the British officer's swimming exploit he quipped sardonically, 'Maybe the idea will spread and we'll be able to get some of these people across the Chindwin this fall!'

American co-operation with the British was not helped by the personality of General Stilwell, 'Vinegar Joe', who was sent into Burma during the first campaign to command Chinese divisions. He had escaped from Burma over the mountains not far behind our party, with food and porters arranged by 'Boh' Case, the American missionary of Pyinmana. Stilwell, sixty years old, was a tough, brave, offensive-minded infantry soldier. 'All I ever wanted', he declared once, 'was to command American troops in the field.' He had long Chinese experience, but was uncompromising in his somewhat limited views of the world. The 'Limeys' he distrusted as 'unwilling to fight'; the Chinese he had to admit were corrupt, unreliable and keener to hoard arms for fighting the Communists than to face the Japanese. He believed that only true-blue Americans, inspired by pure motives, could save the day and, as he had only a handful of them under his command, he drove them practically to collapse. He was not at all the man for the diplomatic concessions needed when fighting in a coalition (a characteristic he shared with another great American general, Patton), and he could not come to terms with the fact that allies could legitimately have divergent national interests. Stilwell and his staff believed that the British held back from invading Burma because Churchill wanted to fight 'a cheap war' in terms of casualties, and was waiting for the Americans to beat the Japanese in the Pacific. A parody of 'Oh, What a Beautiful Morning' from the musical *Oklahoma!* called 'Oh, What a Beautiful Theatre' (the Americans described this Eastern one as the China-Burma-India theatre of war), circulating at one stage among the Americans in SEAC HQ in Ceylon, ran:

> The Limeys make policy, Yanks fight the Jap,
> And one gets the Empire, and one takes the rap.

After the war I was asked by the American journal *Pacific Affairs* to review a book written in this vein by Fred Eldridge, Stilwell's PRO. This book nowhere made the slightest reference to the fact that Great Britain, for some time alone, had been waging war by land, sea and air in the West and Near East since 1939. In my review I quoted the casualty figures of the Burma campaigns. The Ministry of Defence has kindly looked up again the figures for the two Burma campaigns during the period 1942–5 and they work out as follows:

	KILLED AND WOUNDED	MISSING AND POW
British and Imperial troops, all ranks	59,000	88,760
Chinese troops, all ranks	14,500	15,088
US troops, all ranks	2,100	2,119

It is perhaps the Chinese who have not had full recognition of their efforts in Burma.

Much of the fighting took place in wild, hilly and jungly country where 'the wind of death shook the grass and trees', and the Imperial War Graves Commission could not find many of the bodies. In fact, one British war memorial bears this inscription: *To the 27,000 men of the Commonwealth Forces who died in Assam and Burma in defence of freedom, to whom the fortunes of war denied the ordinary rites accorded to their comrades in death.*

I met several young and inexperienced American war correspondents who arrived with the axiomatic belief that every single Burman hated the British colonialists with an intense hatred, and that Burmese fifth-columnists had given the widest possible help behind our lines to the Japanese. These greenhorns saw India as a simple colonial situation with snooty white imperialists cracking their whips and sitting on the necks of suffering coloured men, like King Leopold's overseers in the Congo. This was in the happy far-off days of tremendous and uncomplicated self-confidence amongst Americans, who still had a robust belief in their own virtues and their own power. On the whole I am sorry that those days are gone.

I used to tease Americans a little about imperialism and ask them whether the Philippines, Puerto Rico, Texas and Hawaii had been brought into the American nursery by the stork, or found under gooseberry bushes, or whether there had been some old-fashioned imperialist fornication somewhere. But I recognized that their idealism on colonialism and imperialism, if sometimes purblind, was sincere and deep-rooted. Many years afterwards I met a senior journalist on the *New York Times* who remembered meeting me in the war, and told me that I had said to him, 'No need for you to get so righteous about India. After the war we will without a doubt have to get out of India. And when we do, the USA won't particularly like the long-term world consequences which will follow the end of the British Empire.'

Also in Kandy I met and worked with Frank Owen, once as Liberal MP for Herefordshire the youngest Member in the House of Commons, and in Kandy Editor of Mountbatten's racy newspaper for his troops – *SEAC*, which carried as a daily morale-booster the strip cartoon (strip is the *mot juste*) adventures of Jane from the *Daily Mirror*. After the war he was for a time Editor of the *Daily Mail*, when our paths were to cross again.

On the coast of Ceylon, which was nearer my vision of ideal tropic beaches than anything I had yet seen in Burma (I had not yet been down to Tenasserim), I found at the resort of Mount Lavinia the rest-camp of the operational officers of Force 136, who dropped in the jungle behind Japanese lines to gather intelligence and organize guerrilla bands among the hill tribes. Some were old Burma friends and others, incredibly brave, undertook these perilous trips without knowing the country or any of its languages. I had for some time done various jobs for Force 136 in Calcutta, and was made welcome in their mess. Some of them had been through indescribable hardships and dangers in the jungle. But their morale was terrific. A popular therapeutic routine amongst them was for an officer to set sail towards the tropic sunset in a catamaran, equipped with a bottle of brandy and a charming volunteer from the nearby WVS camp.

Amongst other officers I met the monocled Lt-Colonel 'Pop' Tulloch, a stocky and grizzled man of over fifty, who was reported to have been many years in Africa as a big-game hunter, and to have spied successfully in wartime Germany disguised as an Arab carpet-seller. He organized guerrilla warfare by the Karens, and carried out with them successful ambushes, road-blocks and demolition against the Japanese. I was to come across his trail after the war in embarrassing circumstances, during the post-Independence hostilities between the Burmese and the Karens, which I shall touch on later.

The HQ of the secret Special Operations Executive, which ran Force 136, was in a large closely guarded 'village' of buildings not far from the Supremo's offices. It was headed by the limping Colin Mackenzie, known to many of us as 'Moriarty'.

In the last (November 1980) instalment of his posthumously shown TV memoirs Lord Mountbatten spoke of his lifelong association from Cambridge days with his radical friend Peter Murphy. James Victor 'Peter' Murphy emerged in 1940 as a sort of personal staff officer to Mountbatten when the latter was Chief of Combined Operations. Later Murphy, on the SOE books, was brought over in the same rather vague capacity to Kandy. He was installed in a bungalow near to the Supremo's as his 'personal liaison with SOE', a position of considerable power. Mountbatten 'spoke with him every day', finding that his 'left-wing, progressive views' provided a different angle from the 'reactionary' views he received from most of his military and civil staff. Maybe an unconventional mind, outside the hierarchy and responsibilities of the Establishment, produced interesting and influential advice. But anyway this seems an aspect of the development of British policy in South-East Asia worthy of the attention of a professional historian.

Those far off in London and in Simla constitutionally responsible for future British policy in Burma did not, perhaps, realize what a highly political military commander was now installed in South-East Asia Command. In his own very different way he had perhaps a trace of MacArthur about him.

The role of SOE in the Second World War had controversial aspects. It was a two-edged weapon. Many of the best organized and bravest Resistance fighters in all theatres were Communists, who had long-term policies of their own, often inconsistent with those of Allied governments. De Gaulle was by no means a whole-hearted admirer of all French Resistance forces; and in Greece, Churchill blamed SOE for maintaining 'that brutal cockatrice' EAM-ELAS. In Malaya after the war we had to fight Chinese Communists originally armed and sustained by us. Incidentally, in 1944 when the Polish Nationalist Resistance forces rose against the Nazis in Warsaw, the Russians, who did not care for the long-term policies of the Resistance, had no compunction in standing off outside the city and letting the Nazis smash them. In that uprising 20,000 Poles were killed. The Russian attitude, if brutal, was logical. In a nutshell, this was that war is 'an extension of policy by other means', and that it is a gamble, only justified in case of desperate military need, to use a weapon which negates your long-term policy.

In Burma SOE's contacts with the Marxist-orientated Thakins, through Thakin Communists like Thein Pe, raised difficult and important points of high policy. The thirty young Burmese students led by Thakin Aung San, who had been trained and brought in by the invading Japanese, had gathered a snowball following of a mixed nature, which was known as the Burma Freedom Army, which attempted to take over administrative control of some areas of Burma. Their excesses and cruelties turned the local population against them, and the Japanese disbanded them, re-forming them later into a more disciplined force, also under 'General' Aung San, known as the Burma Defence Army and later as the Burma National Army (BNA). The patriots of this force were gradually induced to admit what the Burmese Communists had told them from the start: that Japan was a fascist and expanding imperialist power, and that Burma had simply been taken from the frying-pan and put into the fire. They could also see that the war was swinging against the Japanese, and that it would be prudent to reinsure with the probable victors if they could.

By the middle of 1944 an all-party secret resistance movement, called the Anti-Fascist Organization (AFO), was formed in Burma to back those in the Burma National Army ready to change sides against the Japanese. Leaders of both groups came from the Thakin Party, including its Communist element.

After a long period of expensive failure outside Europe, SOE were desperate for any sort of operational success. Anxious lest political objections might stymie his plans for co-operation with Aung San, Mackenzie kept this controversial project a tight secret for as long as he could from the Chief Civil Affairs Officer (Burma) and from the Governor who would successively have the responsibility of administering Burma after we reoccupied it, and of executing the policy laid down by HMG. In November 1944 Mackenzie promised large supplies of money and weapons to the Burmese resistance movement without consulting London. He afterwards expressed optimism that the young men would return their arms when the war was over. In the event, he gained the support of Mountbatten, who told the doubtful military that this was a political decision, reserved for the Supreme Commander.

In spite of SOE's enthusiasm, there was a good deal of hesitation before a deal was eventually made by the British with the AFO and BNA. To many in the British Government in London, in the Army, and in the Burma Government in Simla, it was clear that acceptance of BNA's assistance would run the danger of the AFO's claiming political control in return for their military co-operation. The Thakins in the last election before the war had gained only three out of the 132 seats in the House of Representatives, and it was at this stage at least doubtful whether they fairly represented the Burmese people.

Vernon Donnison, who covers the story objectively from the various angles (see reference, p. 12), has put concisely the hesitations of those whom Peter Murphy no doubt regarded as reactionary:

> To welcome with open arms an army which had fought against the British on the side of the Japanese for just so long as it had suited them, all of whose members were technically guilty of treason, was a poor way in which to reward and put heart into those Burmans who had remained loyal to the British connection, and who, without necessarily wanting the continuance of this connection nevertheless were opposed to the communistic and dictatorial attitude of the Thakins, and at least were prepared to achieve their emancipation along the gradualist lines to which the British were committed.

Militarily the BNA's assistance was unlikely to be of much value. But if rebuffed it might be enough of a nuisance to our forces to delay them in their drive to reach Rangoon before the monsoon. Perhaps, too, Mountbatten was more perceptive than many of us about the future, and the shortness of time left for British rule in India and Burma. The BNA's aid was finally accepted, and in March 1945 it switched sides, without getting any political promises about the future position of the AFO (or

Anti-Fascist People's Freedom League – AFPFL – as it came to be called).

Some post-war accounts suggest that Aung San thought of opposing the Japanese as far back as August 1942. It is conceivable that it did not take him and his comrades long to decide that the Japanese were not all they had expected. But for three years he gave the Japanese no reason to doubt his loyalty (indeed leading Thakins had a sort of comradely relationship with Colonel Minami Suzuki and General Sakurai, the chief advisers to the BNA), and no active resistance was taken, until the Allied offensive in 1945 which sent the Japanese Army streaming back in defeat. It has also been suggested that Thein Pe came out originally in 1942 as an emissary to the Allies from anti-Japanese Thakins. He and the handful of other Thakin Communists like Thakin Soe were doubtless anti-Japanese, but I think it more likely he came out to escape the Kempetai who were on his trail. Calcutta, where he had recently been a student and where he had first imbibed his communism, was an obvious place to make for. Most Thakins were at the time co-operating fully with the Japanese. The active Resistance in Burma came from the non-Burmese hill tribes in the horseshoe around the north, where guerrillas and levies fought bravely and stubbornly throughout the long years of the war. The Burmese Resistance, as Mountbatten himself recognized in using in communication with London the analogy of the Italian Army, was basically not a long, risky underground operation against the occupying power on the European pattern of, for example, sabotage, guerrilla warfare, operating escape routes, endurance of savage reprisals, and so on. On the contrary, it was a sudden switch of armed forces to the winning side. From August 1944, when the Burmese Resistance was formally organized, the secret was well kept until Aung San and the Burma National Army switched to support of the Allies in March 1945.

For the young Burmese nationalists the chance to play some active part in the victory over the Japanese was vital – not only so that they could sustain a claim that they had 'worked their passage' to acceptance as genuine allies, but to give themselves grounds for keeping their forces under arms.

As the war turned slowly in our favour, our 'psywar' campaign was getting much more tactical and specific. Our Japanese leaflets, backed sometimes by loud hailers from field units, were aimed at particular Japanese formations, and based on detailed information given to us by prisoners. We named, for example, particular officers as drunken and inefficient in looking after the welfare of their troops, and we commiserated with those troops on the lack of certain specific supplies. 'Safe passes' were dropped to encourage surrender, though for the Japanese 'I cease resistance' had to be substituted for 'I surrender'.

Our Burmese leaflets became more positive and detailed and authoritative. 'The era of face-slapping is over,' we declared, and some leaflets, on better paper, headed by the official Burma Government crest, gave instructions on how to contact Civil Affairs Service (Burma) (CAS(B)) officers who would be following our troops in order to organize the administration. And finally, when zero hour arrived, we did special leaflets aimed at the BNA, and calling on the Burmese to rise against the Japanese.

I am bound to say that we never dropped a message quite as succinct and dramatic as that recounted to me after the war by my friend John Proud, who was Director of Psychological Warfare for the Australian Pacific forces. This announced in pidgin to the natives of New Guinea the momentous news of the Japanese surrender thus: *Nau Pait I Pinis Japan I Bakarap Tru* (Now Fight He Finish Japan He Buggerup True).

In February 1944 the Japanese attacked in Arakan. British and Indian troops, when enveloped from the rear, stood their ground and received supplies from Allied aircraft. The Japanese were repulsed. But the main strategy of the Japanese was a pre-emptive attack on the British bases in India, Imphal and Kohima, by which means they cut all land communications. A tremendous air-supply operation, in which the US Air Force played a vital part, kept the 14th Army going, and in the battle the Japanese battered themselves to destruction. Indeed they suffered what was undoubtedly the greatest land defeat in their history, being thrown back across the Chindwin and suffering terribly in monsoon conditions. General Stilwell broke through to Myitkina in the north.

A first-hand account of the realities of fighting a tough and skilful enemy in the mazes of the jungle, and of the grim price paid by Allied troops in suffering and death, is given in *The Road from Mandalay* by John Masters, the Gurkha officer and Chindit who afterwards became a best-selling novelist.

In the 1944-5 offensive into Burma, General Slim wrecked Japanese defence and lines of communication by a clever stroke against Meiktila, 70 miles south of Mandalay, and began a drive to reach Rangoon before the monsoon broke. Finally, a great assault by land and sea was planned on Rangoon. One of our aircraft, flying a reconnaissance over a Rangoon prison where British prisoners of war were known to be kept, read a message spelled out on the roof of the building by its inmates: *Extract Digit. Japs Gone.*

10 Return to Burma

Civil Affairs Service (Burma)

'When elephants fight,' says the Burmese proverb, 'the grass is beaten down.' We returned to a Burma more damaged by the war than any other country in South-East Asia. Unlike Malaya, where the fighting had been short, Burma had twice had bitter campaigns fought over it, had been bombed by both Japanese and Allied aircraft, and had suffered the scorched earth policy of the British during the first campaign. Rangoon had been badly knocked about. In Mandalay the fort's great wall had been breached, and most of what remained within the old royal palace destroyed. The Irrawaddy Flotilla fleet (550 vessels) lay scuttled at the bottom of the river. The great Ava Bridge, the only bridge across the Irrawaddy (built in 1931) had been blown up by us in retreat and bombed regularly, if inaccurately, since.

And yet in a land which was almost entirely agricultural, damage was much less than it would have been in a modern industrial country. To anyone who knew the places referred to in Allied communiqués about bombing in Burma, the Western-style descriptions of the targets seemed to give a misleading impression. Bamboo and corrugated iron are no great loss, and easily resurrected. But there was a vital task of massive reconstruction work to do. Roads, bridges, docks, power, water, food supplies and basic consumer goods for the civilian population had to be built and organized. And law and order and an effective administration had to be restored.

Up-country, off the main path of our advancing armies, parties of the Burma National Army tried to set up an administration of their own. But the mere presence of a large, tough and victorious British-Indian Army gave the British Military Administration officers a sanction which enabled them to take over the country pretty quickly and thoroughly. Besides, most of the Burmese were genuinely glad to see us back. There were times in the up-country villages when it was difficult to realize how long we had been away. My bearer, Maung Shway Ba, was waiting for me in Rangoon. Like many other Burmese servants, he had buried and guarded a few household treasures of mine, and he proudly produced them again after years of safe keeping. Much of the old administration, which had always been run mainly by Burmans, had survived. Indeed Ba Maw had relied on the old civil servants to keep the country running. Many of the old Government officers had done more to help anti-Japanese resistance than the young Thakins would admit. I learnt afterwards that my old friend Dr Ba Than, inside left in our Pyinmana soccer team, had deciphered secret microfilm messages to the Resistance under the microscope in his laboratory in Rangoon General Hospital.

I cannot recall seeing many signs of the Japanese occupation, but in Rangoon some of the Burmese girls had learnt to use lipstick, and to loosen the tight bodices in which their breasts had traditionally been encased; rather a sad modernization.

I had had a set of large coloured posters printed in Calcutta for wide distribution on return. They were done by well-known Burmese artists. One showed a Burmese woman throwing a slipper, the ultimate insult, at a fleeing Japanese soldier. Another showed a British and a Burmese soldier arm in arm celebrating victory over the Japanese. Another showed a sort of magic castle in the sky – the 'New Burma' we were to build.

On the whole, this was a cheerful time. In Rangoon the senior CAS(B) officers, all with 'military' ranks, messed together under the aegis of Sandy Campbell, the old Director of Public Instruction, who in his spare time coached the mess cooks, as a result of which they produced very tolerable meals from Army rations. We were all enormously busy on useful tasks, repairing and reconstructing. All over the country Bailey bridges appeared like magic.

Hearing that an English civil servant, captured by the Japanese in their first drive into the country, was amongst the prisoners just released, I went to the hospital to see him. He looked a bit thin, but tanned and well, and seemed pleased to see me. After chatting for a bit I said to him, 'You'll be out of here soon, and will need some money. I've been to the Burma Government pay office and arranged for you to have three months of back pay at once, if you would sign here.' I offered him my pen. He began to tremble uncontrollably and his eyes filled with tears. He seemed too frightened to take the pen. 'Never mind,' I said hastily, 'I'll get you some money anyway.' Whether he had been under terrible pressure from the Japanese to sign some anti-British statement, or whether after years in mindless confinement the return of any personal responsibility for his actions terrified him, I don't know, but I looked at other released prisoners with a new sympathy.

On the floor below me in CAS(B) quarters lived the Rangoon Harbour-master, a ruddy-faced old mariner with clear, baby-blue eyes, and ears which could hear the clink of a bottle a mile off. One evening I was entertaining some Foreign Office officials en route for Singapore. The 'clink' soon produced the massive form of my friend, who lumbered in and sat drinking quietly in a corner of the room. I felt thoroughly upstaged by the visitors' reminiscences of the capitals and ambience of Europe, of which I knew little. When the talk turned to Venice, the old salt joined in. 'Venice?' he said. 'I've been there twenty-five times.' Game, set and match to our side, I thought delightedly. But he spoilt it. 'And never been ashore once!'

There was little time for recreation. The old Gymkhana Club was a burnt-out hulk, but the old Pegu Club was revived as an Officers' Club, and my elegant friend Major James Hartung, of the Royal Engineers, emerged by natural selection as Chairman of the NAAFI Wine Committee. There was still some shooting to be had within range of Rangoon, if one knew how to set about it.

Visiting Eire with my present wife in 1963, we attended a reception given by the British Ambassador just outside Dublin at the time of the Horse Show. 'I hardly knew anyone living in this part of the world,' I said to my wife, 'except that just after the war in Rangoon I met a Major Pakenham-Mahon who said he had an estate near Dublin.'

As I spoke, I saw a solitary figure down at the end of the buffet-table. There were the rugged country squire's features of Major P-M. 'Hullo,' he said, 'I've often cursed you.'

'Oh, why?'

'I so much enjoyed our jungle fowl shooting together that I imported some eggs after the war and hatched them out at my place. As soon as the wretched birds could fly, they disappeared into the tops of tall trees near my house. They utterly refuse to come out to be shot, and the cocks wake me up crowing at 5 a.m. every morning!'

Many of us who were not ex-servicemen felt rather awkward in military uniform, but a few enjoyed their unaccustomed badges of rank and playing soldiers. I was amused each morning at the daily CAS(B) conference of senior officers when the Deputy Chief (a policeman) crisply instructed us to synchronize our watches, as if we were all going 'over the top' instead of to our offices.

Slowly water and power returned, and the destruction was cleared away. On my side of the house the Army got going a small radio station for civilians, and we expanded *The Liberator*, a news-sheet in English started by Alington Kennard and by Streenivasan, the latter being sent ahead to Rangoon as the advance representative of our CAS(B) Information Department. This for a period was the only local newspaper available to the troops and population. In the early days, before electric power was restored, *The Liberator* was churned out by a number of Indian operators from the old *Rangoon Gazette* staff, pedalling away on treadle-machines.

To deal with transport in our Department the police lent us a Burman sub-inspector. He was energetic and cheerful, but trouble-prone. I had to bail him out for being drunk and firing off his pistol in an eating-house, and the sober and sensible Streenivasan used to shake his head and wonder if we might not be better off without him. But he became a devoted servant of the Department, the work of which he greatly enjoyed. For some personal reasons his great hate was the Burma Communist Party. Soon after Independence, when he had returned to his village, he was captured by Communist rebels. True to his nature, he spat in the rebel leader's eye and was shot dead. A reckless and likeable fellow.

When power returned, I removed my offices to the Government Printing Press, where we printed *The Liberator*, along with masses of forms as bureaucracy resumed its sway. I was visited there, the day after VE day, when the room was still decorated with Union Jacks, by Tom Driberg, who had come over to Rangoon in Mountbatten's train. He 'didn't think much of the décor', and in conversation supported immediate independence for the Burmese.

Amongst a number of young officers who steamed enthusiastically about, full of scepticism about the motives of 'old-time colonial officers', was Major Woodrow Wyatt, who soon left to become a young Labour MP. Woodrow was amongst the more balanced of the politically minded transients. In this year Nehru said to Woodrow that in many ways British rule had been good for India; but the time had now come for Indians to rule themselves. We 'old stagers' somewhat resented some of these young officers, full of rosy liberal, and some even of Communist, sentiments, and generous with 'simple' solutions to problems of which they little understood the complexity. Some Force 136 officers, flushed with success at their popularity with young Burmans, whom they would not have to try to control later, were sure that they knew much more about Burma than any old stager, and opposed the disarming of their young protégés. At one point, at a meeting of senior CAS(B) officers, early in the reinvasion campaign, Mountbatten, prompted by 136 HQ, appeared to give a stern warning to any CAS(B) officers who did not carry out his orders on how to accept the Burma Independence Army. A polite inquiry from a senior CAS(B) officer elicited from Mountbatten's staff that in fact the orders he referred to had not yet reached us. Looking round at the front row of grizzled heads, and gallantry medals of the First World War, the Supremo sensed that he was in the presence of highly disciplined officers well used to carrying out orders, whether they liked them or not. He did one of his polo pony turns and charmed and praised his audience. In due course, his orders were loyally carried out. Freddy Pearce, who had advised that AFPFL and its army should be declared illegal, was replaced as CCAO by a more amenable subordinate who had no previous Burma experience – Hubert Rance, a tall, amiable regular officer, promoted to Major-General for this post.

Early one morning in Rangoon in the grounds of Government House (an ugly Victorian pile) I came on Mountbatten personally pacing out the parade-ground to mark the exact area for various units for the next day's Victory Parade. This was the perfectionist who had written the standard manual for polo players and a naval handbook on wireless telegraphy. The parade included a somewhat untidy detachment from the Burma National Army. 'Very smart,' I heard the Supremo say firmly to General Aung San. Mountbatten's policy managed to absorb, on an individual and not a unit basis, nearly 5,000 of the Burma National Army into battalions of the regular Burma Army. But some thousands of armed young men were not absorbed and these, under cover of an 'ex-service welfare organization' called the People's Volunteer Organization (PVO), became a private army behind Aung San's political ambitions. The enjoyment of power from the possession of arms, and the perquisites of power and the style of life to be enjoyed by these young braves in the villages, were not easily to be given up. And in fact, when Aung San's controlling hand was removed, the PVO eventually went into rebellion against the newly independent Government of Burma.

Mountbatten was not in Rangoon for the earlier formal surrender of the Japanese generals, whose swords were accepted in a dramatic and old-fashioned ceremony (on which I enjoyed writing a colourful account in *The Liberator*) by General Browning. It was over; the Japanese were really and truly beaten.

During this period the Army and the CAS(B) under Major-General Hubert Rance worked like beavers to get Burma going again – money, supplies and equipment flowed in. We had a debt to repay. On the whole, a good deal of success had been achieved between the recapture of Rangoon on 3 May 1945 and 16 October of the same year, when Sir Reginald Dorman-Smith steamed into Rangoon harbour in brilliant weather for a ceremonial return, with all the ships in the harbour dressed to mark the occasion, and drove to a Thanksgiving Service in Rangoon Cathedral (which had, incidentally, been used by the Japanese as a brewery). I had written for that morning's *Liberator* an editorial welcoming the return of civil government, and praising the motives and personality of the Governor (who now had to face the really difficult political tasks). To my surprise, Hugh Rance looked cross when I saw him in his office. 'I didn't think much of that editorial,' he said morosely. I still don't know quite what had upset him. Maybe the old Army prejudice against Dorman-Smith was in his bones; maybe he didn't get on with him personally; maybe I had failed to include a sufficient tribute to Rance's own work. It seemed that I had once again suffered from the naïve belief that we were all on the same side. 'I suppose you must think of your own career,' he added in an untypical remark, for which I still find it hard to forgive him.

At the end of the CAS(B) period I went on leave. I was demobilized the day before I embarked in the troopship, the SS *Dilwara*, and on paper I was the only civilian aboard.

When I reached home I spent one night in London with my wife, and planned to go down to Tunbridge Wells the next day to see my parents, whom I had not seen for seven years. The next morning my father rang me to say that my mother had died in her sleep the previous night. I had known several cases of people who had struggled out of Burma, surviving terrible trials on the way, and who had died when safe in the clean sheets of a welcoming hospital. Their fierce determination to survive had wilted. I believe that my mother, worn out by chronic asthma, willed herself to live until I came home. When she knew I was safe and due to see her next morning, the will relaxed, and she slipped away.

Sir Reginald Dorman-Smith

One of my main CAS(B) jobs had been to set up, virtually from scratch, a new and expanded Information and Broadcasting Department for the Government of Burma. After leave I returned as what in London would be called the Permanent Secretary of this Department, responsible to a Shan Minister of the Executive Council. While on leave I had handed over the new Department to the Reverend George Appleton, later Archbishop of Jerusalem, and it then went to my old comrade-in-arms in Delhi, U Khin Zaw. Finally, after Burma's Independence, it went to a young Burmese schoolmaster and nationalist called U Thant. U Thant later became Private Secretary to U Nu, the Prime Minister, and then Burmese Ambassador to the United Nations, where I was to meet him again after many years, as Secretary-General.

The information job naturally brought me into close contact with the Governor. Reggie Dorman-Smith, as cheerful and debonair as ever, walked into a difficult situation.

In July 1945 a Labour Government under Clement Attlee, who had a somewhat different view of the British Empire from his defiant predecessor, had taken over in the United Kingdom. Nevertheless, the British Government's policy towards Burma, evolved during the wartime coalition Government, went ahead. Such time as could be spared for thinking about this part of the world was mainly directed at India, the pacemaker. Mountbatten, in increasingly oversimplified retrospect, was to repeat in more recent years the view that HMG made a bad psychological error in sending back to Burma after the war the old Governor, who stood in Burmese eyes for the old way of doing things. Had British policy in the immediate post-war period been to do things in a dramatically new way, and to hand over almost at once to the young guard of Japanese-sponsored, Marxist-orientated, basically anti-British politicians, this might be true. But we had, at heavy cost in blood, sweat, tears and treasure, just thrown the Japanese out, and were back in our old territory with a large and battle-hardened army. We were engaged sincerely in repair and reconstruction. HMG's policy still was, as in India, to hand over certainly but gradually to a responsible Burmese government. Disputes now were not to be about 'freedom', the early achievement of which was assumed, but about who should inherit 'power'. Handing over to Aung San was in many people's eyes on a par with handing over India to Subhas Chandra Bhose rather than to Nehru. There still had to be a lot of infighting before we were persuaded that it was the AFPFL who by now really had popular support in the country, and that a rapid and complete transfer of power to them was the best thing for the people of Burma (and for us!).

Looking back, with the benefit of hindsight, can one say that there was at any stage any real alternative to this course? We could hardly have refused the help of the BNA. Only perhaps a stern enforcement of total disarmament after the war of all men not enrolled in Government forces would have weakened Aung San's special advantages – and we had not the stomach for that. But even if this had enabled the British Government to hand over to a Burmese Government in which the old-established political parties and more experienced and realistic nationalists had been represented, the popular appeal of the Thakin Party and of the Burma Communist Party might have continued to grow and undermine a settlement. And as for the accelerated speed of our withdrawal, it was perhaps the French determination to hang on in Indo-China which gave Ho Chi Minh his chance to ensure that the Communist Party took over the major 'nationalist' role.

But all this was far from clear at the time. The Governor's announced programme sounded fair enough. He brought with him a message from the King that 'it is the purpose of my Government that Burma should at the earliest possible moment attain complete self-government as a member of the British Commonwealth'. 'Burma's right to freedom', he said, 'has been conceded, and all that remains to be done is to ensure that she attains that freedom literally as quickly as possible and in as orderly a way as possible.' An essential democratic step was the holding of elections of a House of Representatives with responsible Burmese ministers who could plan Burma's future constitution. The election, he urged, should be held as soon as physically possible, 'for otherwise no political party or combination of parties could confidently claim to represent the views of the electorate'. The Thakins had after all won only three seats in the last pre-war election. Meanwhile, an appointed Executive Council would run a temporary caretaker government.

This did not suit the AFPFL. They claimed the right to be accepted as the provisional government, to be translated as soon as possible into the recognized legal government of a free Burma. The AFPFL refused to join the Executive Council unless they had virtual full control, and went into full-scale opposition to the Government, with no holds barred. The difficulty was that Mountbatten's attitude to Aung San had half committed the British to a different course from the now declared official policy. The unfortunate Governor had to try to reconcile two different policies, which a clearer chain of political responsibility might have helped to bring about before he returned.

The struggle went on for nearly a year. Some of the rival politicians began to query Aung San's leadership; Thakin Tun

Oke (that curious anomaly, a right-wing Thakin) raised in the open the awkward fact that Aung San in 1942 had murdered a headman for helping the British, a fact that Aung San did not deny. The question arose of whether Aung San should be arrested. Dorman-Smith sent for me, told me in strict confidence that the operation was at least under consideration in Whitehall, and asked me to prepare a highly confidential provisional paper on how the event should be presented for world opinion, if in fact it came off.

Having written and submitted my memorandum I was horrified some days later to see the first page of it reproduced anonymously, but more or less accurately, in the Burmese press. I rushed to my office safe and could not find my copy. Ashen-faced, I tottered to the Governor and told him. I said I realized that revealing the paper at this stage could do great harm to him and the British Government. I could suggest only that he should state that I had prepared it on my own initiative, and register his disapproval by removing me from my post.

He sat me down, gave me a whisky and soda, told me not to worry, and said that we would cross bridges when we came to them. He seemed as calm and unruffled as ever.

I said that, as I was on good terms with a number of Thakins, I was prepared to go down to their headquarters to try to check on this leak. I received a friendly welcome there. When I tried to find out the channel for the leak, my contact not unnaturally laughed. When I said I had prepared the paper on my own initiative, and that if it were fully exposed I should get into deep trouble and probably be sent back to England, he smiled and said amiably, 'Ah, U Hman, we would not like you to get into trouble!'

The next week the AFPFL had one of their huge rallies at the Shwedagon, demonstrating that by now they did indeed have a lot of popular support behind them. The speeches as usual were violent and dramatic. I waited in apprehension for the subject of Aung San's threatened arrest to come up. No reference to it was made.

I still don't know why. Perhaps the AFPFL, who were well informed, knew by now that the idea of arresting Aung San had been shelved. Mountbatten, still the Supremo, was much opposed to the idea, and the police and military feared it would lead to an ugly clash, and to the sort of challenge which could be worthwhile only if we really intended to stay in Burma for a long time – which we did not. I believe that the Governor's first inclination had been to uphold the law and arrest Aung San, but soberer thoughts prevailed and he changed his mind. Evidence was accumulating that this slight, taciturn young student had in fact unusual qualities of leadership, and an increasing hold on the imagination and affection of the Burmese people. Nothing succeeds like success, and the respect paid him by Mountbatten helped build him up, but he was emerging as a charismatic personality and a strong character in his own right. Dorman-Smith is said to have advised London that, if Aung San were not to be arrested, the only other sensible course was to make him Prime Minister of Burma, but Whitehall at this stage found this sudden switch too much.

I then after all discovered my copy of the memorandum in a small safe in my bungalow, where I had forgotten I had put it, and went again to Government House to discuss how security had been broken. A senior official at Government House said, 'Well, it couldn't have been *our* copy. I always lock such documents in a steel cabinet, and after locking it I give it a sharp tug to see if it's really locked.' He demonstrated, and nearly fell over backwards. The lock was broken. It turned out that an Anglo-Burmese stenographer in the office kept the AFPFL abreast of affairs. We weren't very well trained in security in the old days in Burma. We had few secrets. Incidentally, it came out later that when Wavell was Viceroy, a stenographer in his office used to pass his secret memoranda to Nehru!

Although we were back, and with a large army on the spot, apparently in a position to call the tune, the fact was that British rule in Burma had really ended in 1942. The spell was broken. It was, perhaps, the Japanese who, by arming and organizing the Thakins, really dictated to whom political power would pass in post-war Burma. So we bowed before the storm. Early in 1946 Sir Reginald, who had done his best with ingenuity, good humour and courage to implement the Home Government's original and outdated policy (with which he by no means always agreed), sailed for home. He was thereafter a sad and ailing man. Unfairly blamed for his part in the military disaster of the Japanese invasion, he was later slated repeatedly by

Mountbatten for having failed to come to a quick agreement with Aung San and his radical comrades – a failure which, according to Mountbatten, 'lost Burma to the Commonwealth'. Complete independence of Burma outside the Commonwealth had been Thakin Party policy from the beginning, and, with the need to prevent the Communists outbidding them, Aung San and U Nu had little choice on this point. Dorman-Smith had genuine sympathy for the Burmese. He had indeed from the early days of his Governorship before the Japanese invasion been pressing London to give the Burmese a firm date for full Independence – advice not welcome to Churchill. He had understanding and friendship with, and understandably, some feeling of obligation towards, the powerful pre-Japanese-occupation nationalist leaders of Burma, to whom Aung San and his comrades were 'the boys'. And it is fair to bear in mind that his instructions on return to Burma had been laid down by HMG in London, not by Lord Mountbatten and Peter Murphy. Indeed, if immediately after his return and without fully exploring other options, he had proposed to hand the country over exclusively to Aung San and his young Marxist-minded friends forthwith, most of us (and a lot of people in England) would have thought him weak in the head. One can see that Mountbatten's instinct was probably right, and that our best policy was to cut our losses quickly, to settle with the more extreme nationalists and quit. But there had to be a period of testing the genuineness of popular support for the AFO. We could sensibly make a deal only with a body we believed could 'deliver'. Perhaps confidential papers recently released under the Thirty Years' Rule may enable the handling by Dorman-Smith of his difficult role during this testing period of trial and error to be reappraised more realistically and more sympathetically.*

The Prime Minister, Attlee, after looking round for a suitable successor, chose Hubert Rance, Mountbatten's man, to carry out Mountbatten's policy. Rance, a modest man, was as surprised as most of us that he had been selected.

Meanwhile, U Saw, old leader of the Myochit Party, was challenging the claim of the AFPFL genuinely to represent the

---

*The relevant official documents for 1944–8, edited by Professor Hugh Tinker, entitled *Burma: The Struggle for Independence*, have now been published in two volumes by HMSO.

people of Burma. His rival claims were not entirely idle. As Prime Minister in the period 1938-40 he had used the wide powers given to him under the 1937 Constitution to fight stoutly for many nationalist aims, against British and particularly against Indian vested interests. Although 'foreign affairs' was a reserved subject, he fought a successful battle against the British, Chinese and US governments for payment to Burma of transit dues for goods shipped along the China Road. His Myochit Party gained the powerful backing of the Burmese middle classes, and he impressed the masses with his growing private army, the Galone Tat. But for the war with the Japanese, the pressure from the Myochit Party on the British Government would no doubt have produced Independence within a comparatively few years – the timing no doubt influenced by the way things might have turned out in India. Nationalist Burma would never have tolerated being behind India in Independence. If he had retained power, U Saw knew enough about the arts of demagogy and the techniques of repression to have dealt effectively with Thakin and Communist opposition. But the four years of war, when he was detained in Uganda for flirting with the Japanese, undid him. In the years under the Japanese occupation the Thakins gained real power (and the guns to back it), which they were never to lose hold of, and, practising their Marxist-influenced philosophy, they steadily reduced the strength of such Western-orientated middle class as there was in Burma. After the war U Saw, though a formidable individual, had little chance of success. But his enemies still feared him. In September 1946 he was shot at in the street, lost the sight of one eye, and retreated, like a wounded and dangerous bison, into the elephant grass to await his chance for revenge.

Sir Hubert Rance

When Sir Hubert Rance arrived in August 1946 he ran into a violent and dangerous situation. But his brief was much easier than his predecessor's. He was virtually instructed to give Burma away to Aung San and no other as soon as he could. The mechanics of this required patience, tact and good administrative sense. It required above all a capacity to gain the confidence of the raw and suspicious young Burmese to whom we were handing over. Rance gained their confidence in good measure. Perhaps his very 'ordinariness' reassured them that he was unlikely to try to pull a fast one on them. Rance seemed to me an average, sensible man, conscientiously carrying out his instructions, rather than a man of special political judgement and imagination. Maybe because personally we didn't ever really get on, I underestimated him. He and his wife were generally liked by the European community. I have a vivid memory, in the later stages of his regime, of a dance at Government House and of his tall, stiff figure leading a conga procession in a self-conscious attempt at informal camaraderie.

Rance was greeted almost at once by a strike of the police force, inspired by the AFPFL. Strikes of other Government employees such as oil workers, and of railway workers, followed. The PVO claimed to have taken over the policing of Rangoon. The consensus, the general acceptance by the people of Burma of the Administration, on which British rule had been so long based, was breaking down.

The British Government rolled with the punch. The Governor virtually handed over the Executive Council and the government of the country to the AFPFL. Aung San, holding the portfolios of Defence and External Affairs, was Deputy Chairman. The 'lean and hungry' Thakin Kyaw Nyein held the vital portfolio of Home Affairs. After the formation of their new Council Than Tun, Aung San's attractive but fanatical brother-in-law, who preferred revolution to peaceful agreement, was expelled by the AFPFL with his White Flag Communists. Thakin Soe and his separate Red Flag Communist Army had been outlawed by the AFPFL earlier in the year. So, if a satisfactory agreement could be reached between the AFPFL and the British Government, the Communists would have lost all chance of getting control of the first government of independent Burma.

In January 1947 a delegation led by Aung San came to London. Under the Aung San–Attlee agreement the principle of Independence was conceded, elections to a constituent assembly were fixed for April 1947, and the Executive Council was accepted as the interim Government of Burma. Aung San is reported to have been impressed by the courteous and friendly treatment he received.

The most difficult problem remaining after the decision of the British to quit Burma was that of the hill tribes. The horseshoe of hills shutting off Burma in the north from its neighbours covered 43 per cent of the land area of the country. In this sparsely populated region lived 16 per cent of the population. With the exception of the Shans they had never been conquered by the Burmans. Throughout the war the men of these hill tribes fought bravely on our side against the Japanese. But we were going to have to abandon them, and the only sensible future for them was to become part of the new Republic of Burma. It required great diplomacy to persuade them, suspicious as they were of the Burmans, to accept this course – which the British, to salve their consciences, said must be effected with the 'free consent' of the hill areas. Since the whole precarious agreement on the peaceful handover of Burma to the Burmans depended on this arrangement, the British brought heavy pressure to bear on the frontier areas, and in the end their inclusion in the Republic was bulldozed through, at the Panglong Conference in February 1947. This would, however, have been hardly possible if Aung San, who was growing in stature with responsibility, had not promised them, amongst other things, full autonomy and the right of secession: in fact, the first President of independent Burma was a Shan Sawbwa.

Meanwhile the old administrative system was maintained. I was promoted to Bernard Binns's old job as Commissioner for Settlements and Land Records. U Maung Maung Gyi, the senior Burman Superintendent who had taken on as Commissioner during the Japanese occupation and kept the Department in being through all those dark days, was due for retirement. Since it was clear that the days of the British were numbered, I felt somewhat awkward taking over. There was little I could do except see that the Department ticked over reasonably well. But the job had one great advantage: I was entitled to visit any part of Burma I wanted to on tours of inspection. So I planned immediately, before it was too late, to tour those parts of the country I had never visited before.

To start with, I plunged into the muddy swamps of the Irrawaddy delta, which G.E. Harvey has called in his *History of*

Burma 'an unending plain of wet rice-fields larger than Wales'. During the monsoon months over 100 inches of rain fell each year in the delta. We traversed the winding waterways, startling the white paddy-birds (egrets) into lazy flight with our smelly old Government launch. On the whole in the mud of the delta I understood better why Eric Blair had disliked Burma. Here in its most acute form was the worst problem which flowed from the British occupation of Burma. Two-thirds of the rice-lands were held by non-resident landowners (mostly Indian money-lenders). The peasants had light-heartedly taken large loans in expanding times, and lost their lands in bad times, particularly in the slump of the early 1930s. It was one of the failures of nineteenth-century *laissez-faire*. While the Indian chettyars, or money-lenders, are often described as the villains of the piece, and although the Government should have had the sense and courage to control them, the chettyars did in fact fulfil the role of providers of agricultural credit and played an important part in the dramatic development of the delta. When they were finally expelled, the Burmese Government found that not only was the provision of wholesale agricultural credit by the state a very large task, but that often the villagers preferred dealing with the chettyars, who knew them and their circumstances personally, to the cold bureaucracy of a State Agricultural Credit Bank. More sinister were the kabulis, huge, baggy-trousered North Indian figures, armed with long staves, to be met with in many parts of Burma. They asked for no receipt for their loans; they merely announced the interest and due date of repayment, and noted them in their registers. On the dread day they would reappear like fate, and the debtor feared whacks from the great staves. Should the debtor have died without paying, the kabulis visited his grave and gave it symbolic whacks of chilling power.

I was interested to find Burmans in remote districts, where there were no longer any European officers, still, after the years of Japanese occupation, keeping up a ghostly Club life. The tables still bore ancient copies of British periodicals, with an occasional more up-to-date, yellow-covered copy of the weekly overseas edition of the *Daily Mirror*. Bridge and billiards were still recreations, and local Burmese officials changed into whites to play tennis, and had their drinks brought by decrepit Indian butlers.

Then I took a driver and one clerk, and drove in a Ford station-wagon all the way through the Shan States up to Bhamo. To be able to travel light, I took no cook, and we ate mainly at wayside Chinese kaukswe stalls in between our major stops. I was entranced by the charms of the Shan States and their peoples. Near Bhamo I spent an idyllic day swimming and fishing by a series of small waterfalls.

Up near Myitkyina, in the wildest country, I found a young British major commanding a Frontier Force detachment. The only European for many miles, he lived rough in a primitive bamboo hut. He was burnt brick-red by the sun, and off duty he wore native clothes. His eyes shone with excitement as he talked to me. 'I was fighting up here in the war,' he told me. 'I loved the country, and I spotted the most wonderful mahseer fishing hidden away here. I determined to get back after the war, and even dropped a rank to wangle this job. Now every spare moment I go after mahseer. There is no fishing like it. Your spoon tumbles down the fast water past the rocks, where there may be God knows what lurking in the shadows, and then comes – WHAM! – a pounce like a tiger (you have to watch out lest the rod is pulled out of your hand), and the fight is on.' Mahseer, called the Indian salmon although it is virtually inedible, is a powerful silver fish with large scales and not unusually weighs some 30 pounds in those parts, and sometimes more than 100 pounds. Even the smaller ones fight, as my friend said, like tigers. He was living the fulfilment of a dream and I never saw a happier man. No one can have enjoyed more the last days of the Raj.

Wherever I went, the peasants seemed to be going about their lives as they had always done, and many seemed hardly to know what had been happening over their heads. The old rural Burma seemed much the same. I took no weapons or escort, and did not find myself in danger at any time. In the more distant Upper Burma districts there seemed a general relief that the old Asoya was back.

Down in Pyinmana I found things sadder. Much of the town had been burnt. My old Bench clerk, the jolly and ebullient Ba Aye, had lost members of his family in the bombing, and been reduced to a shadow by a severe bout of typhoid. He seemed suddenly to have become an old man, and clutched a Buddhist rosary as he talked to me in a high, thin, almost unrecognizable voice. Some of my old friends entertained me to a Burmese meal, but this was a place which had suffered in the war and the old spirit was gone.

By the time I finally left Burma I had visited, at one time or another in my career, every one of the thirty-six districts except the Arakan, from the mountains of Myitkyina down to the white sands and palm trees of the beaches of the Tenasserim archipelago, 'where the South Seas begin', the background of Maurice Collis's book, *Siamese White*.

In April 1947 the AFPFL won a big majority in the elections for the Constituent Assembly, which was to prepare the constitution for independent Burma. In June 1947 I went back to the UK to be interviewed for possible new employment when the ICS packed up. While I was away there were dark and dramatic developments.

On 19 July 1947 two men in jungle green with tommy-guns burst into a session of the Executive Council and opened fire. A couple of councillors fell under the table and survived. Bogyoke (Commander-in-Chief) Aung San, aged thirty-three, and seven other councillors were killed. This political 'St Valentine's Day' style killing was the work of the Tharrawaddy U Saw, hoping that in the vacuum he would emerge as the obvious leader of the country. The wounded bison had charged.

Once again the Time of the Changing of Kings was proving full of danger and trouble.

The Governor appealed to U Nu, the oldest and wisest and nicest of the Thakin student group, who, with great courage, formed a new Council at once and government could continue. This was a moment of the greatest danger, when a false step could have led to anarchy. Much credit was due to Sir Hubert Rance and to U Nu that such a step was avoided. I suspect that some credit was due also to Bernard Binns, who in an interregnum between chief secretaries, was as Financial Commissioner, the Governor's senior civil service adviser. I remembered, when the Japanese plane had dived at us on the Chindwin river, Bernard's firm and steadying hand on the shoulder of the syrang at the helm. U Saw, who, but for the Japanese invasion could very well have emerged top of the heap, carried Burma through to Independence, and run the country afterwards with a ruthless and unscrupulous hand, was arrested, tried (the evidence was collected by a young British policeman) and hanged.

Captain Vivian, a corrupt British Ordnance Officer, who had sold U Saw arms, was sentenced to imprisonment in Insein gaol, whence he was released by Karen rebels in their advance on Rangoon in 1949. From then on he was a desperate fugitive in a strange land, and it may have been a relief to him when early one morning in the Salween Valley he was surprised by a Government patrol and shot dead.

U Nu, a dedicated Buddhist (and a great believer in meditation), who later said 'Buddhism and Marxism are incompatible', brought a character of singular sweetness and a sort of charming naïveté into the Government of Burma.

11 British Embassy, Rangoon

Earlier in 1947 some of us were flown home to be interviewed for possible other employment when the Indian Civil Service came to an end. We travelled in one of the splendid old Imperial Airways flying-boats, equipped with a lounge with drinks and up-to-date periodicals, which landed each evening so that passengers could have dinner and sleep in a comfortable hotel. We took off from the Hooghly river at Calcutta, landed for nights at Karachi, Basra, on the Nile at Cairo, and in Sicily (where for the first time I discovered that Chianti could be white as well as red), and finally settled gracefully down on the waters of the Solent at Southampton. I have seldom had such an agreeable journey.

After some personal interviews, we were summoned to Burlington Gardens, where we had once spent tense and anxious hours doing our original Civil Service examinations years before, to appear before the Civil Service Selection Board of some eight to ten people of varying backgrounds. To my neverending surprise, I found myself at the Foreign Office, learning my new trade in the Eastern Department, which dealt with the Middle East. Time and chance, which play such a great part in people's lives, had worked kindly for me.

ICS officers coming into the FO, usually from some fairly senior and responsible post in their old service, went through a short period rather like 'fagging' at a British public school, and equally as good for deflating any personal pomposities. I unlocked the telegram cylinders which whizzed round the office like change around old-fashioned drapers' shops, and distributed the contents to the proper desks. I passed round tea. I struggled without much advice or aid with the FO filing system, which was of devilish complexity, and altogether and quite properly felt rather a fool. But pretty soon one learnt the ropes, and picked up the tempo, which in a political department was fast and furious. In the Indian Civil Service I had learnt thoroughness, accuracy, and to speak my mind. In the FO above all I learnt speed.

Walking to the FO through the winter mist of St James's Park one morning, I heard geese flying overhead towards the lake. As an instinctive reaction I raised my umbrella and, following through correctly, let them have both barrels. 'Bang! Bang!' I cried. My 'gun' grazed a black Anthony Eden hat on a small man with a grey moustache, who ducked hurriedly. I glanced back to see how he had taken it, and saw him peering over his shoulder suspiciously at me. That was my first meeting with Sir William Strang (later Lord Strang), Permanent Under-Secretary of State in the Foreign Office. We met again soon afterwards at an official lunch, where he gave me a puzzled stare.

One day I was wrestling with some abstruse problem to do with Arabian railways when I was summoned to visit my old Delhi host, Sir Gilbert Laithwaite, now Deputy Under-Secretary of State for Burma. 'How would you like to go back to Burma?' he said. 'We are going to set up a Commonwealth Relations Mission there as soon as possible, to be fully functioning by the time of Independence, when it will become our Embassy.' He said he understood that some of us who had served in Burma were too disheartened by the last few years to want to return so soon. I was, on the contrary, delighted at the prospect of dealing with something I actually knew about; and in no time George Crombie of the Commonwealth Relations Office, the prospective Counsellor in Rangoon, and myself, the prospective 'Oriental Secretary', were sitting at Gilbert's feet as plans were formed. Gilbert had the most lucid and speedy mind I had yet encountered. As each problem came up, he studied the views of all concerned, and then in his precise voice he would dictate, without hesitation or correction, a minute, a letter or a telegram which summed up the position and called for the appropriate action.

Before long George and I were out in Rangoon with a skeleton staff. We found everyone still subdued from the shock of the massacre of the Executive Council. The AFPFL, no doubt with the example of Lenin in mind, had embalmed their martyred heroes (not too successfully at first shot), and one of our first official duties was to pay formal homage to the dead. I still have a photograph of George, in a thick black morning coat, standing with bowed head beside Aung San's bier, in the stiflingly hot and rather ripe atmosphere of the old Queen Victoria Jubilee Hall.

From then on, as the Burma 'expert' and the only officer in the Mission who could speak the language, I had a busy and fascinating time, helping choose offices and bungalows for the Ministry of Works to buy or rent; taking on servants and local staff; setting up liaison with the Burma External Relations Department. As chief official of this Department (under the Foreign Minister, U Kyaw Nyein) I found James Barrington, an Anglo-Burmese colleague of mine from ICS days. I had known James as Assistant Settlement Officer to 'Orphan' Thomas, and had been a guest at his wedding in Mandalay. Many of the Anglo-Burmans who had thrown in their lot with the Burmese had adopted Burmese names, but James, as always, was a man of courage and independence, and not willing to give up the family name he had inherited from his Scots father. The Burmese respected this, and James later became Burmese Ambassador at the United Nations.

In fact, Burmese ministers and officials, from U Nu and U Kyaw Nyein down, all seemed glad to see me. After the war a number of well-meaning radical politicians in Britain tried to argue that no 'ex-colonial' officers should be sent back in diplomatic posts to their old territories. Their argument (not unnatural when based on an erroneous and dogmatic belief that British imperialism had everywhere been hated and oppressive) was that such men would be automatically disliked and distrusted. In fact, this theory was wrong. Ex-colonial peoples had little against British officials personally, and indeed often got on well with them. After Independence, friendships were easier still. All through my diplomatic career I had only to mention that I had been in the ICS, and Indian and Pakistani ambassadors all over the world opened their houses to one they knew understood something of their countries and their problems. One met few Burmese diplomats, but their delight in finding someone who could after a fashion speak their language, both linguistically and figuratively, was obvious. In a wider context the comparatively small number of officers from the ICS and the Indian Political Service had considerable success in their new service, and in due course filled many ambassadorial and High Commissioners' posts (our brightest star was, of course, Humphrey Trevelyan, later Lord Trevelyan, KG). It could be that this arose not only from the high standards of their previous service, but from their experience of the grass roots, their first-hand knowledge, gained through many sweaty years, of the problems of the vast, 'non-affluent' majority of mankind. When Catherine the Great was sent an elaborate programme of proposed reforms by French Encyclopaedists, she replied to the effect that it was all very well for learned gentlemen who wrote on parchment to propose such measures, but she had to write on human skin. In our apprenticeship we had at least learnt something of the sensitivity of writing on human skin.

The Chancery offices of the new British Embassy, Rangoon, were sited on the Strand, by Rangoon river, and close to the Strand Hotel, Rangoon's only decent hotel, now run by my old friend Pete Arratoon, late of the Silver Grill. As first choice for the Embassy Residence George and I selected a large but somewhat dilapidated house by the cool breezes of the lake outside the city, but the new Ambassador's wife wanted to be in the middle of things and near her husband's office. Luckily we were able to buy, lock, stock and barrel, the old Irrawaddy Flotilla Company's 10-acre compound in Signal Pagoda Road, which included a number of bungalows, and this was soon transformed into a convenient Embassy enclave.

Jim Bowker himself, my first Ambassador, was the epitome of what an ambassador should traditionally look like – at once tall, slim and elegant. With only a certain amount of exaggeration it could be said that his comments on the whole range of human experience were confined to variations in tone on two epithets: 'agreeable' and 'tiresome'. He was never put out, and never in a hurry.

Years later I was giving lunch in the Metropolitan Club in Washington (I believe we risked terrapin stew, the house speciality) to Hugh Foot (later Lord Caradon), who had just given up being Governor of Cyprus. I had first met him when he came to take over Cyprus, as I was then on the staff of his predecessor, Field-Marshal Sir John Harding. Hugh was wondering whether to accept an appointment under the Foreign Office with the United Kingdom delegation to the United Nations. 'I am not sure I'd like to work for the FO,' he said. 'They always seem so bored and casual about things.'

'Don't be misled,' I said. 'I had the same impression when I first came into the Service after the war, but I soon learnt that this was a deliberate and professional show of unconcern, just as policemen are trained to walk and not run towards troubles in the street. They are really very concerned indeed.'

Certainly the only outward sign of emotion I ever noticed in Jim Bowker, when passing over to him dramatic and alarming news, was when he occasionally cracked his finger knuckles in an abstracted way.

Elsa, his recently married wife, was a new experience for Rangoon. She was and is a vivid, dynamic, outgoing personality. The Middle East was her home, and her background was Beirut, Alexandria, Cairo, Vienna and of course Paris. Wives of Burmese officials and politicians who could speak no English had often sat in bored silence at English parties in the past. Elsa swept the Burmese wives upstairs, threw open her cupboards, and let them try on her clothes and jewellery, to their great delight and entertainment. I remember one dinner party at the Embassy for U Nu, the Burmese Prime Minister, after some days of frustrating and disappointing negotiations. Half-way through dinner Elsa turned on her distinguished guest. 'Oonoo!' she exclaimed. 'Why are you being so difficult? You are worrying Jim so much, and I don't like it!' U Nu was charmed by this direct assault, and gave her one of his sweet, enigmatic smiles. I really believe he was more reasonable the next day.

Jim Bowker's main task was to get the Burmese to trust him, and to believe that the British had really left Burma, and were not plotting some insidious interference to maintain control. He accomplished this with great success, though there were some awkward moments.

For a short period to start with, while Rance was still Governor and the King's representative, Jim Bowker was called High Commissioner, but on 4 January 1948 Burma became an independent Republic, in one of those moving ceremonies of which we have seen so many since the war. India had had its independence in July 1947, and Ceylon became independent a month later. As the Jack came slowly down I saw sadness on several Burmese faces. I don't think it was just emotion on their moment of freedom. I believe that to many of the older educated Burmese, who had been brought up on Burke and Shakespeare and J.S. Mill, the Union Jack had special significance. They had in their way served the flag with loyalty. It had stood for many good and civilized values they were going to miss. But when the Burmese national flag crept up the flagpole, joy was unconfined and all looked forward to a golden future for Shwe Pyi Daw – the Royal and Golden Land.

In the background, escorted by U Thant, was J.S. Furnivall, an old, tortoise-like, retired ICS officer, who had once been a great master of the art of Settlement. He was in the tradition of the ICS officer Alan Octavian Hume, who in 1885 had founded the India National Congress 'to interest the natives in current affairs'. Furnivall had established the Burma Book Club, near the University, and founded the Burma Education Extension Association, and the Burma Research Society. His Fabian conscience had turned him against colonialism, and his learned researches and books on South-East Asia had won him liberal renown. He was revered by the young Burmese nationalists as a hsaya, a teacher, and had been invited to give the new Government advice on the fashionable subject of National Planning (to no great avail). Nearby too was Kingsley Martin. He and Dorothy Woodman had always been good to Burmese students in London, and he had always spoken up for Burmese nationalism in the *New Statesman*. He seemed to be under an odd delusion that he personally rather than 'the wheels of fate', the inexorable march of events, had attained freedom for Burma. It may be that his influence played some part in assuring that for the AFPFL, socialism became their guiding principle, but there were many other powerful factors which led this way. The most obvious was that most of the rich men in Burma were foreigners, so that nationalization was doubly tempting.

Not all the older generation of Burmese approved of the new regime blessed by the British. 'Does the new Governor really know what he is doing?' I was asked anxiously by an old and experienced Burmese ex-'mayor' of Rangoon. And in conversation with Kingsley Martin on a plane returning to England, Daw Khin Khin Gyi, the most successful (and handsome) of Burmese businesswomen was heard to say of Lord Mountbatten, 'Is he not rather a "drawing-room" sort of person, Mr Martin? And why are you handing over our country to a bunch of schoolboys, who call me Aunty?'

These anxieties were justified. The Burmese middle class, such as it was, was about to be nudged rudely off the stage. But the die was cast. Perhaps indeed it had been cast some time ago, when Colonel Suzuki Minami and General Sakurai armed 'the schoolboys'.

After the presentation of credentials to the new President of Burma, the Ambassador had drinks for the staff who had accompanied him. 'A nice uniform,' he said politely of the white tunic with gilt buttons, slim trousers, the ceremonial sword and white helmet with a gold spike, which had arrived for me from England just in time for the ceremony. 'But what is it? It doesn't happen to be the Foreign Office uniform.' I'm still not sure what it was. In any case, throughout my service I never had to wear uniform again, though the sword and helmet have since been utilized in many games of charades.

On the whole the British, in a difficult political situation in post-war Burma, had 'got out from under' in an atmosphere of reasonable good humour and goodwill. Indeed, with Mountbatten's touch we had even got out with a certain amount of style. Governor Rance received a genuinely warm and friendly welcome from independent Burma when he returned on a visit in 1956. In the same year the Burmese Government gave Lord Mountbatten their highest honour, Agga Maha Thiri Thudhamma ('Summit of Excellence'), to add to his more exotic decorations – such as the Special Grand Cordon of the Cloud and Banner (China), the Order of the White Elephant of Siam, and the Grand Cross of the Order of the Seal of Solomon (Ethiopia). But there were testing times ahead for the new independent Government.

Edgar Snow, a sympathetic commentator, headed a contemporary article in the *Saturday Evening Post*, 'The Rover Boys Rule Burma'. The new leaders were patriotic, honest, eager young men, but they perhaps approached the immense problems of governing Burma with the same sort of confidence as my new lugale when he said to me, 'Thakin *anyone* can drive a car!'

Soon the new Burmese Government began to suffer from the fact that the country was still full of arms and unresolved disputes. Already the Red Flag Communists, under Thakin Soe, and Mujahids, the Muslims of North Arakan, were in revolt. And the differences between the Burmese and the hill tribes had only been patched over. In the end it did not make much difference to the more remote hill areas, as Burmans rarely ventured up there. But the minority most affected and most anxious were the Karens, many of whom had settled in the plains, mixed up in Burmese areas. The Burmese kings had always treated the Karens as an inferior race. The fact that many Karens were converted to Christianity and served the British loyally, especially in the Burma Rebellion, did not make them any more popular. And amongst the misdeeds of the original Burma Independence Army, which grew up in the wake of the invading Japanese (and which the Japanese later were forced to disband) were many atrocities against the Karens. Burmese-Karen mutual suspicion soon came to the point of savage violence. The defection in 1948 of the Karen National Defence Organization put not only intense Karen national feeling, but a lot of trained regular soldiers, against the Government. The Karens were to remain under arms for many years; they were still fighting in 1984.

Jim Bowker did his best to effect a reconciliation between the Burmese and the Karens. But things had gone too far. Later Great Britain and other Western aid donors tried to bring pressure to bear on the Burmese by suggesting that peace with the Karens should be one of the preconditions for aid. U Nu, exasperated and frustrated by the failure of his own efforts to this end, which had earned him the nickname of 'Karen Nu' from his hard-liners, blew his top and brought the negotiations temporarily to a halt. So hard were the hard-liners that Gordon Seagrave, the justly famous American missionary doctor who had for years the hill people of northern Burma in his hospital at Namkham, was in 1950 convicted to five years' imprisonment for treason, for having given medical attention to some wounded Karen and Kachin rebels. (He was released eventually and worked at his post until he died many years later.) Thakin Nu used to assuage his conscience about fighting the Karens by equating himself to Abraham Lincoln fighting to save the Union. Twenty years or so later I was to find General Gowon in Nigeria with a life of Abraham Lincoln at his bedside as he fought, so he believed, a similar battle against secessionist Biafra.

One evening an Anglo-Burman friend of mine came up to me and whispered, 'Do you know that there is a British Colonel Tulloch in the hills helping to arm the Karens?' It was indeed 'Pop' Tulloch, of Force 136 who, in command of Operation Walrus, had led one of SOE's most successful military operations in Burma, during the vital race for Toungoo in April 1945. 'Pop' was now incensed that the hillmen who had for three years fought (and died) so bravely under his command against the Japanese, were getting what he thought was a raw deal. Like so many of his adventurous breed, he was a romantic rather than a realist.

I told Jim Bowker at once, and we agreed that the only way to maintain the credibility of the British Government was to inform the Burmese immediately. Jim did this expertly, in a flat and factual manner, adding that the British Government was totally opposed to any such enterprises.

Some time later a journalist called Campbell, representing the *Daily Mail*, was reported as talking darkly of mysterious secrets in the bar of the Strand Hotel and arousing the suspicions of the Burmese police. He was rumoured to have been a jockey at the Calcutta Turf, and to have had a dashing war record in SOE. It seems that Frank Owen, now Editor of the *Daily Mail*, was, with his SEAC background, interested in a possible story, no doubt ignorant of his correspondent's double role. The next step in the story was that Campbell approached a steward of the BOAC and entrusted to him a package of papers for safe delivery to Colonel Tulloch, then in Calcutta. He paid the steward a suitable fee, but added several times that the papers were Very Secret and Very Important. The steward, intrigued by this, opened the parcel and read evidence of gun-running to the Karens. These papers he sold for a handsome sum to the Burmese Ambassador in Karachi. When the evidence reached Rangoon, there was an immediate meeting of the Burmese Cabinet. Passions rose high, and angry allegations were raised of

Churchillian plots to dismember independent Burma. U Kyaw Nyein, the Foreign Minister, then intervened to tell his colleagues that the British Ambassador had personally passed him the first information about Colonel Tulloch some time ago, and had formally dissociated the British Government from anything to do with him. U Kyaw Min, the senior Burmese official present, told us that the temperature instantly and dramatically dropped and that trust was restored.

When I told this story later in London to Verney Lovatt-Campbell, my friend from Pyinmana days, who had himself won an MC with SOE in the Kachin hills, he looked distressed. 'If you ratted to the Burmese about Pop,' he said, 'I don't know that I should be seen talking to you!'

I can understand how such officers felt. One of the more sorry aspects of the surrender of Empire is the surrender of any power to help the minorities who had often relied on our presence and protection. The ending of 'colonialism' is often neither neat nor just for many innocent people.

Within six months there were so many insurrections against the new Government that I roneoed an elaborate chart for visiting journalists, showing the main groups in rebellion. I suppose there is still a copy somewhere in the FO archives. First there were the two Communist factions: the Red Flag Communists (Russian orientated); and under Aung San's brother-in-law Thakin Than Tun, the White Flag Communists (Chinese orientated). Then there were the minority groups: the Karen National Defence Organization, the Mon National Defence Organization, the Arakanese Muslims, and some Kachins. Finally, there were mutineers from the PBF and PVO units of the Military Police and Army, and then the PVO itself. The PVO and PBF, whom Aung San alone might have been able to control, were armed youths unwilling to surrender power, a common occurrence in the aftermath of war.

In September 1948 a Burmese friend came into my office. 'U Tin Tut has just been "pineappled",' he said. He meant that Tin Tut, of the ICS, the ablest of all Burmese officials, and then an invaluable national leader, had just been killed by a grenade popped into the open window of his car – probably by some disgruntled member of the PVO.

By the spring of 1949 practically the whole of Burma was in

the hands of some rebel group or other. There was fighting on the very outskirts of Rangoon – bloody clashes between the Burmese and the Karens. But there was still a particularly Burmese and insouciant air about the whole disastrous business. Busloads of civilians drove up from Rangoon to the fighting at nearby Insein, where they paid one rupee to fire off a rifle, and two or three rupees to fire off a mortar or machine-gun, just for the fun of the thing. General Bourne, the one-armed and dynamic Head of the first British Military Mission, lent to the Burmese to help organize and train the new army, had been succeeded by a mild-mannered 'supply' general whose personality the Burmese found less overawing. The story went the rounds that during the crucial battle for Rangoon he wrote something on these lines to General Ne Win: 'Dear General, You have a battery sited just near my bungalow and tennis-court. Every time they fire I serve a double fault. There is an even better site for a battery on —— Hill, a little farther away. I wonder if the battery could be moved?' The reply was reported to have been: 'But of course, General.'

Even in the worst days we somehow never felt that Rangoon was seriously threatened. The food supply, the money, the trained regular battalions of the Army, and the legitimate Government of the country recognized by the world, were still all in Rangoon. Opposing them the Rebels had no common organization or purpose, and often opposed each other. By the end of 1949 the Government's counter-attack began to succeed, and from then on slowly regained a measure of control.

The lower half of the country was still in turmoil, however, when Harold Caccia (now Lord Caccia), the Chief Clerk (the traditional Foreign Office title for the Head of the Administration Departments) and another inspector came out from the Foreign Office to look at the new Embassy and consider the advisability of an outpost in Maymyo. So we had to fly over the lower area in the Air Attaché's ancient aeroplane. When we landed to refuel for the hop over the hills to Maymyo, the clouds suddenly descended on the Shan plateau, and the Air Attaché declined to risk a flight through them to a rudimentary airfield with few, if any, landing aids.

Harold Caccia was keen to press on to Maymyo, so he and I left the rest of the party on the airfield. I borrowed an old car from a Burmese friend and we set off by road. Very soon I informed the Chief Clerk that the car seemed to have no brakes. 'Press on!' he cried. Bowling along a bund with a steep drop into the rice-fields each side, I saw ahead a stationary bus blocking most of the road. With the inevitability of a dream in slow motion we sailed into the back of the bus, the cries of the passengers mingling with the cackle of hens and the hiss of steam from our radiator. Harold, standing by the roadside in a pin-striped suit and a trilby hat, looked an unlikely figure to be stranded in the middle of Upper Burma. With great good humour he endured two bus rides, along with livestock, a spell in another ancient car, and finally a jeep. Thinking he would like to see the real Burma, I got beds for the night in the large, gloomy bungalow of the Burmese Commissioner of Mandalay. Harold toyed apprehensively with the curry dinner, to which I gave full justice.

The next morning he was a little fractious. 'You snored all night,' he complained. 'And early in the morning an old Burmese lady came and peered at me for a long time through my mosquito-net.' This was the Commissioner's aged and somewhat senile mother, intrigued by an unusual guest.

Later in the morning, dusty, hot and weary, we arrived in Maymyo, to find the rest of our party lolling on a veranda and eating strawberries and cream. Half an hour after we had left them the clouds had lifted, and the aircraft had hopped over the hills in no time.

Some of the villas in Maymyo still looked neat and bright, with nasturtiums and sweet-peas left from the days when English wives tried to re-create for themselves an illusion of Home. Red poinsettias still bloomed round the little lake. But on the outskirts were more isolated dwellings that the jungle had claimed, choked with the voracious verbena-scented weed lantana, which someone had imported into Burma as innocently as someone else had introduced rabbits into Australia. It was sobering to see how easily and quickly the signs of man's presence could be obliterated. The Maymyo Club, scene of many of my bachelor frolics, was a burnt-out ruin. As I stood among the blackened timbers I could in my mind hear the saxophones of the regimental dance bands wailing out their dated old tunes against a background of chatter and laughter.

Nous n'irons plus au bois, I thought, as I drove slowly back to join the Chief Clerk and the rest of the party.

As a newcomer to the FO I did not at the time realize what an august personage the Chief Clerk is – in many ways second only to the Permanent Under-Secretary. Harold Caccia was the youngest man ever to hold that post, which perhaps misled me. But I don't think he held that uncomfortable trip against me. Later I served under him for four years when he was Ambassador in Washington, and for three years in London when he was Permanent Under-Secretary.

In spite of anarchy throughout the country Rangoon life went on without much disturbance. There were, however, reminders that these were troubled times. One day the wife of the General Manager of the Burma Oil Company, sitting on her lawn by the lake in Rangoon and sipping tea, slid quietly off her chair to the ground, killed by a stray bullet from a careless Burmese soldier on the other side of the lake. A shooting party of Europeans just outside Rangoon, expecting jungle fowl to burst from the trees, were startled to see a line of PVO emerge with rifles cocked. The sportsmen had their shotguns and watches removed. 'Red' Parker, from the Bombaing, who had earned a DSO and MC in the gruelling war against the Japanese in the Chin hills, was escorting teak rafts to Rangoon in January 1949 when a young Burman on the bank shot dead his friend and comrade, a Burmese assistant, U Hla Aung. Our bungalow was burgled twice. The amiable Burmese policeman, in whose manor we were, advised me to take a night-watchman from the 'criminal' village nearby. We were soon provided with the granddad of one of the villains, a small, ancient, toothless and cheerful figure. He carried out few if any duties, he pinched the neighbours' chickens, and he was regularly and beatifically drunk – on more than one occasion I had to drag him off our drive into a comfortable nook in the bushes before the arrival of guests for dinner. But we had no more burglaries.

It was fun having our two small children Julia and Nicholas with us in the bungalow by the lake. When the first torrential monsoon rains came down, I remembered an intensely pleasurable experience from my far-off childhood. I suggested that the children should strip off their clothes and run around 'Nunga-Punga' in the garden. I still have a happy memory of those excited and cavorting imps, laughing and splashing. I have another vivid memory of Julia, then aged four. Turning aside for a moment to fasten a punt on the lakeside, I left Julia by herself on the jetty and told her not to move. When I turned round she was gone. A few bubbles came from the green water, and reaching down I seized her hair and yanked her back on to the jetty. Purple in the face, and weeping with rage and fright, she instinctively applied the maxim that the best form of defence is attack. 'Dad-day,' she bawled, 'why didn't you look after me bettah?'

Coming out of the Chancery early one morning after a spell as night-duty officer, I found all the wheels of my car gone. Very cross, I called in the young Burman in charge of the city's main parking lot. After the war there had been a great many unemployed vagabonds roaming the city, often blackmailing car-owners to pay for them to guard their cars against damage. Some friends had joined with me in calling a bunch of these vagabonds together. We gave them shirts with official badges, paid them a modest monthly wage and enrolled them as 'official car-watchers'. The change was remarkable, and they did a good job.

'Who arranged your job?' I asked my young protégé. 'Who gives you the best tips?'

'Very sorry, Thakin, there must have been a mistake. Leave your car outside tonight.'

The next day my car was on four good wheels again. Looking closely I discovered that they were not *my* wheels, but I decided not to pursue the matter.

However, on the whole Rangoon was peaceful and orderly enough, and the Burmese friendly.

Late one night I was eating chicken curry and drinking beer in Rangoon's Chinatown with an Irish policeman, who had been temporarily kept on by the Burmese Government. We munched away in silence for a while, and then my friend got up wearily and walked over to an old telephone on the wall. Giving the machine a couple of violent cranks he asked the operator for the British Embassy office, where he demanded the duty officer. I then heard him, in a very passable imitation of a Burmese policeman, say, 'Sir, good evening, sir. I am Latter Street police-station officer. We have here Mr X of British Embassy, not able to proceed. No, sir, do not send Embassy car. I will arrange police jeep to take Mr X to bungalow. Thank you, sir. Don't mention.'

'Why did you do that?' I asked curiously.

'Bored, my boy, dead bored,' he sighed.

Mr X, a fairly senior officer in the Embassy and a popular man, had a well-known Plimsoll line. Four whiskies he could manage. A fifth took him at once to dangerous depths.

The next morning the Head of Chancery, who had by chance been the duty officer, felt that the previous night's episode had been a little too much. Latter Street was in an unsalubrious quarter of the city, and it seemed a bit over the odds to have a senior embassy officer carted home from there by the police. So he did his duty and tackled X with the story of the night before. '*Did* he?' said X with a gratified smile. 'How very kind of him!' And he sat down to write a gracious note of thanks, enclosing a suitable present, to the presumably mystified police-station officer. It seems that, the evening before, X had had his fifth and subsequent whiskies while seated alone in the garden outside his bungalow. When he had gently subsided, his servants had moved him indoors, and he had awoken next morning without any clear memory of the night before.

I thought I'd better leave well alone. Sometimes Thurber-type situations are too complicated and irrational to explain.

I soon learnt the important part entertainment plays in diplomatic life. Entertaining people at home, in one's own house, relaxes relationships and tends to make guests more understanding and receptive if business has to be done with them subsequently. Almost every one of the Ambassador's parties had a special objective, the faculty of the University, the administration of the city of Rangoon, as well as national political leaders. Elsa Bowker happily agreed that the guest list for the King's Birthday Party should be expanded to include a sprinkling of top Burmese actors and actresses, jockeys, boxers, footballers, writers and artists. The other guests were delighted to see and talk to these popular figures. Only Po Sein senior, the most famous of the actor-dancers of the pwes, got a bit tiddly. As he was a very funny man anyway, his performance was uproarious.

The most fascinating job I was given in Chancery was to

prepare the Rangoon Embassy's first confidential 'Personalities' File, for which I prepared potted biographies and character sketches of over fifty Burmese who I thought would have influence in Burma in the future. When I saw an up-to-date copy ten years later, most of my selection had been dropped!

An early visitor was Sir Ralph Stevenson, our Ambassador in China. Suave, dark and handsome, he again had the style of a traditional diplomat, the sort who has an astrakhan collar to his overcoat and smokes Balkan Sobranies. He briefed us on the situation in China. Calmly and objectively he set out why nothing could now stop the complete domination of the whole of China by the Communists. My heart fell. Surely if the Chinese and Russian Communists really got together, the West was in peril. And as for Burma, with Than Tun and the White Flags to help, the Chinese could easily convert it into a Communist satellite. Neither of these things in fact happened; though I believe much of Burma's apparently rather eccentric foreign policy in the last thirty years has been dictated by fear of offending the Chinese. It may be that the slight easing and opening up recently reported in Burma is a reflection of China's current tentative *rapprochement* with the West.

I next saw Ralph Stevenson when he was Ambassador in Cairo in the 1950s, during which time he impressed the Egyptians almost as much with his delicate violet shirts and black-and-white shoes as with the sang-froid he demonstrated by playing his customary round of golf while mobs raged in the city.

Another distinguished guest from outside was Earl Mountbatten of Burma, now briefly Governor-General of independent India. During a large dinner party given in his honour by the Ambassador, the flames of a pressure lamp out of control could suddenly be seen in the background. 'Go and see to that!' ordered the Governor-General peremptorily to a naval officer on his staff, who leapt off at once.

After the dinner I found the Ambassador none too pleased. The incident had not quite matched his standards of etiquette. 'It was my house,' he said, 'and a guest should have ignored any little trouble of that sort, and let me and my staff deal with it.'

I could see his point – but his main guest happened to be a

compulsive man of action at the height of his powers.

Nearly twenty years later in New York I went to collect Lord Mountbatten from the house of his American hostess, to take him to call on the Secretary-General of the United Nations. As we waited for Mountbatten to appear, his hostess confided gently to me, 'We are proud to have Dickie to stay. But he *is* a very difficult house guest!'

An odd incident seemed to link me again with India. Playing in a men's doubles on the tennis-courts of the Pegu Club, I checked in the middle of serving. 'A much-loved world figure has just died,' I announced flatly. I then completed my serve. After the game when other friends joined us, my fellow-players reported my remark as yet more evidence that I was slightly unbalanced.

The next morning at breakfast my telephone rang. It was the Head of Chancery, one of the tennis four. 'Well,' he said, 'you might have given us a few more details.'

'What do you mean?'

'Haven't you seen the morning papers? Gandhi was assassinated yesterday.'

I still don't understand it. I have had no other notable psychic or telepathic experiences, and I felt no particular emotion or sensation at the time – the bare fact just came into my head. Had I tapped by chance a radio wave generated by the emotionality spread from Delhi as the Indian masses learnt of the death of their Mahatma?

Other visitors to Rangoon soon after Independence included many of the better-known foreign correspondents of British papers – Patrick O'Donovan and Christopher Buckley among others. Years later, when snowed up at the Cedars of Lebanon, I found an old English paperback without a cover. As I read it, the hero seemed strangely familiar – the lean, serious figure, the Shan bag always over his shoulder, even his favourite quotations. Through the last clue I came to realize to my astonishment that this must be a real-life love story of Ian Morrison of *The Times*. I had become a good friend of Ian's in Rangoon and was shocked when he and Christopher Buckley were killed by a land-mine in Korea not long after he left. Since then the book, *A Many-Splendoured Thing* by his lover, Han Suyin, has, of course, been made into a film.

One of the most perceptive journalists to visit us was *The Observer*'s Patrick O'Donovan, still sensitive about the facial surgery (which was in fact extremely successful) he had undergone after a bad wound as an officer in the Irish Guards. He had a real empathy with the bewildered villagers of South-East Asia. The next time I saw him was in Washington, DC, about ten years later. This was an era when it was fashionable at Washington parties, as elsewhere, to sit around on the floor after dinner singing folk-songs to the accompaniment of a guitar. I am not very musical, and anyway I have a limited tolerance of folk-songs. Seizing a glass of whisky at one party I crept out on to the snow-covered veranda for a respite. In the shadows I found a tall figure, also with a glass in his hand. 'What are you doing here, Patrick?' I asked. 'Dodging another verse of "Hang Down Your Head, Tom Dooley",' he said lugubriously. Our friendship was sealed.

If Rangoon were not dramatically changed, up-country things were running down. The oil companies did not find it possible to reopen the pipeline from the fields to the Rangoon refineries; it was holed like a colander, and there were too many locals waiting to tap it again. Denis Phelips, who had planned to retire, with his Burmese wife Susie, in the surroundings where he had been so happy, temporarily accepted the post of British Vice-Consul at Yenangyaung and helped the oil companies in their withdrawal. But before long he realized that conditions were too dangerous and the atmosphere too prickly for any chance of a peaceful retirement. 'Staying on' did not work out. He lives now with Susie at Exmouth, where he spends much of his time studying yoga, and can sometimes be seen standing on his head in his garage.

His great friend, Colonel Ronnie MacRobert of the Indian Medical Service, for some time after Independence ran a private nursing home in the house by the Rangoon lakes rejected as the Embassy Residence. He also decided enough was enough, and that he would go home. Surrounded by friends reluctantly seeing him off at the airport, he stepped backwards, stumbled over some baggage, hit his head on the angle of a concrete culvert, and died almost at once.

Those Anglo-Indians and Anglo-Burmese who did not feel that they could whole-heartedly become Burmese left for

England, Australia and Singapore. In June 1948 the Burmese Government nationalized the great and historic Irrawaddy Flotilla Company, founded in 1865. It became the Burmese Inland Water Transport Board, and the Scots managers, along with the skippers and engineers of the few remaining vessels, left the sunshine and went home to their mists and heather. In March 1949 Karen troops attacked Maymyo, and the last Bombaing staff operating in Upper Burma, trapped with their families between opposing forces, had to be rescued by RAF aircraft organized by the British Military Mission. All the BBTC forests were nationalized, some modest compensation being paid in logs. In 1952 the last log belonging to the Corporation was shipped from Rangoon, and the company's eighty-six years' connection with Burma came to an end.

One of the AFPFL's objections to Britain's immediate post-war policy for the reconstruction of Burma was that it seemed to involve the reintroduction of the big British timber, rice and mining companies. In the event, the AFPFL successfully resisted the reintroduction of the 'extraction capitalism' which their new ideology abhorred. But even during the post-war era of generous aid from overseas, especially from the United States, they did not succeed in establishing successful industries of their own, and their rice exports, which before the war reached $3\frac{1}{2}$ million tons, diminished to a small fraction of that.

Some would say that the failure to produce industries was a blessing. There has been a lot of critical writing about how capitalism has blighted the happy lives of primitive rural societies, but it has usually been industrialization, the almost unstoppable world-wide results of the industrial and technological revolution which, while bestowing certain compensating blessings, has done the damage. Indeed, one of the great objectives of anti-capitalist communism is that every self-respecting country should have its own steel foundry and count its strength by the smoke belching from the chimneys of heavy industry. Perhaps in the long run Burma, a comparatively poor rural society, but fertile and not overpopulated, is better off as it is.

After Pamela and the children had preceded me home I took a short break with an English lawyer friend, Peter Beecheno, down on the beach at Maungmagan in the peninsula of

Tenasserim. Close by was a village whence the fishermen regularly disappeared in a straggling fleet for islands beyond the horizon, to gather birds' nests (allegedly aphrodisiac) for Chinese soup. At night, with fireflies winking in the dark outside, we slept, lulled by the breeze in the casuarina trees, in a bungalow with its back legs on earth and its front legs in the white sand of the beach. Each morning we waded chest-deep into the warm and sparkling sea with small baskets round our necks, and, fishing not far in front of us with slim wands and shrimp bait, we caught our basketfuls of little fish for breakfast. After half a papaya with a squeeze of lime, these fried 'sardines' were delicious. It was Christmas time, and in the evening the two of us, and our host, a solitary old mining engineer, sat on the beach after dinner and drank whisky before a roaring fire. The usual bunch of village children squatted half in shadow at the edge of the firelight, and watched us in silence. The three of us sang at the top of our voices 'The Holly and the Ivy' and other incongruous carols. 'I remember', said our friend, 'when there were fifty or sixty of us on this beach at the Christmas bonfire – miners, planters, and their wives.'

Farther down this story-book tropic coast an old miner with a handsome and eccentric Austrian wife had had, before the war, a house on a beach to which I always wish I had been invited. Guests did not have to assemble for regular meals, everyone did his or her own thing, reading, writing or resting. If anyone was thirsty or hungry, a drink or a tray of food would be brought by a servant at any hour of the day or night to any part of the house, garden or beach. If anyone felt like swimming, the lazy waves were but a few yards over the sand. Hardly anyone bothered with a bathing-dress. After the war I got to know the lady of the house. But it was too late. The Garden of Eden was gone.

Maurice Collis, who became such an elegant writer on the East after retiring from the ICS, had as his last post the Deputy Commissionership of Mergui, down this enchanted archipelago. His daughter records that in 1934, as he stood on the wharf for the last time, saying goodbye to his private paradise, 'he burst into tears, to the consternation of his immediate subordinate, the Superintendent of Police'.

I had the unique experience in Burma of going straight through from being part of the Administration, in a country governed for many years by the British, to being a member of a foreign embassy in the same territory, and I have sometimes been asked if I found it to be a traumatic one. The answer is No. Ever since 1937 we had handed most of the government of the country over to the Burmese. The new Burmese Constitution in that year, the year of the separation of Burma from India, had given elected Burmese ministers more power than their counterparts in any Indian province, since they had taken on many of the powers which in India went to the Central Government in Delhi. Life for a British administrator under a Burmese Ministry and Burmese Parliament was getting increasingly difficult. The Japanese occupation accustomed us all to drastic changes in our lives and habits, and the Independence of Burma was anyway a long-expected and natural historical development. Many of us felt relief that the British were no longer responsible for events which we could not control, and that we were finished with the dangers and strains of a rearguard action. It was a relief to look on troubled situations without feeling that one ought to step in at once in order to do something about them personally. It was a relief not to be fussed by divided loyalties. After years of offices in which I had often been the only English face, it was agreeable and comforting to be surrounded by my countrymen and countrywomen, and to dictate to British secretaries.

Like other British administrators, I had been educated in Britain, spent my long leaves in Britain, planned to educate my own children in Britain, and planned to retire in Britain. So when the time came to leave India and Burma, few of us were inextricably involved. This detachment had helped us give these countries a just and impartial administration; though it had not helped us evolve radical or long-term policies. Naturally most of us developed a deep affection for, and loyalty to, the peoples amongst whom we had worked at such close quarters, and a nostalgia for the exciting days of our youth. So on my posting back to the Foreign Office it was a sad moment when, from the aeroplane, I saw for the last time the sun glint on the golden flanks of the Shwedagon. But moving on seemed natural enough to me. I had much to look forward to, and a lot to learn, even a bit of growing up still to do.

Epilogue

Since I left Burma in 1949 I have never been back. I did not lose touch at once, as I worked in the South-East Asian Department of the Foreign Office under 'Rob' Scott until I was posted to Hungary. At the next desk sat Bernard Ledwidge, afterwards HM Ambassador to Israel, who had been Secretary to the Panglong Conference on the Excluded Areas of Burma.

When U Nu, the Burmese Premier, came to London, I prepared an exhaustive brief on important subjects about which Ernest Bevin, our Foreign Secretary, was expected to tackle him. Bevin was a great man, beloved by all of us, except, of course, by the the scruffy and ebullient Guy Burgess, whose room was two doors away down our corridor, and who never missed a chance to make a snide remark about Ernie. To take the record I sat in on Mr Bevin's interview with U Nu. The meeting, in fact, went something like this:

'Good morning, Prime Minister.'

'Good morning, Mr Foreign Secretary. How are you?'

'Well – since you ask, not too good. It's me piles bothering me again.'

U Nu's face lit up at so intimate and uncontroversial a topic.

'Ah! I understand – I understand well! There is an excellent Burmese remedy – made of opium and medicinal leaves. I will send a cable for some to Rangoon this very day!'

'Very good of you, Mr Prime Minister, very good indeed. Mr Attlee suggested we went to lunch a little early, so why don't we toddle over to No. 10 now?'

They went off chatting happily, already firm friends. I was left to draft a dispatch on the interview to our Ambassador in

Rangoon. I was reduced to the formula, 'The conversation was mainly of a personal nature.'

From then on I had little to do with Burma or the Burmans until 1967, when I was posted from being Ambassador in Romania to be Deputy UK Permanent Representative at the UN, New York, under the Minister of State, Hugh Caradon. The Secretary-General of the UN at that time was none other than U Thant, who in 1948 had taken over the job in Burma which I had held shortly before Independence, that of Secretary of the Department of Information and Broadcasting. He received me cordially. 'Ha! U Hman!' he said, and offered me a Burma cheroot from the embossed silver cheroot-box on his table.

Occasionally I sat in his office on the famous 38th floor, looking down at the East River, and chatted in English and Burmese. I am sure the Russians thought of my knowledge of Burmese as a British secret weapon, though when we talked thus informally we never talked shop, but rather of old times in Burma. He had been one of Furnivall's protégés. However, links with the past certainly made things easier for me on the rare occasions when I had to approach U Thant officially.

He did not seem personally to harbour much anti-colonial resentment. Indeed, as Burmese delegate to the UN Fourth (Colonial) Committee in October 1952, he had expressed 'heartfelt thanks to the United Kingdom for their foresight and magnanimity in granting independence – really genuine independence – without bloodshed, without resentment, without ill-feeling'.

After Dag Hammarskjöld, the Russians had been determined never again to allow the appointment of a Secretary-General with a powerful intellect and strong character, and they believed that they had done their homework before agreeing to the choice of U Thant as his successor. He must have proved something of a disappointment to them. He was a modest, honest and decent man, strengthened by his deeply held Buddhist principles, and not without courage when faced with a challenge.

As his *chef de cabinet* U Thant had an Indian former member of the ICS, C.V. Narasimhan. We became friends, and it was 'C.V.' who organized a farewell dinner for me in the UN building when I left.

Also in New York I met another link with the past, General Aung San's posthumous daughter, Ma Su Kyi. It says something about the nature of the relationship between Britain and Burma that this girl, daughter of Burma's acclaimed Independence hero, was married in London from the house of Paul Gore-Booth (British Ambassador to Burma from 1953 to 1956), whose ward she was. When I chatted to Ma Su Kyi at a New York party, at last she said to me hesitantly, 'Did you know my father?'

'Yes.'

'What was he like?'

I cast my mind back, and remembered the short stature, the shaven head, the still, enigmatic, Mongolian features, and above all the feeling of somewhat menacing energy, held in check. Aung San had a short, slight figure, and moved rather awkwardly, but his presence and voice had genuine authority.

'Do you go to the movies?' I asked.

'Yes.'

'Well, to my mind he was rather like Yul Brynner.'

A pleased smile spread slowly across her pretty face. 'Why,' she said, 'that's exactly what my mother says!'

I have no first-hand knowledge of what Burma is like now. It has been governed for the last twenty years by an isolationist military dictatorship guided by doctrinaire 'socialist' principles, which has succeeded in taking Burma back into the bullock-cart age, and generally lowered the standard of living, yet which has kept the country out of all foreign entanglements or even connections. By modern industrial standards it sounds a ramshackle and dilapidated country, and by democratic political standards it gives the impression of a police state. It may be that the average Burman was in a number of ways better off in 'colonial' days. But national independence, the satisfaction amongst Burmans of doing their own thing their own way, no doubt makes up for it all. And in Central Burma, away from the main roads, villagers must carry on their lives in a way not very different from that before the British came, in what Michael Edwardes has called 'a cheerful and violent arcady'.

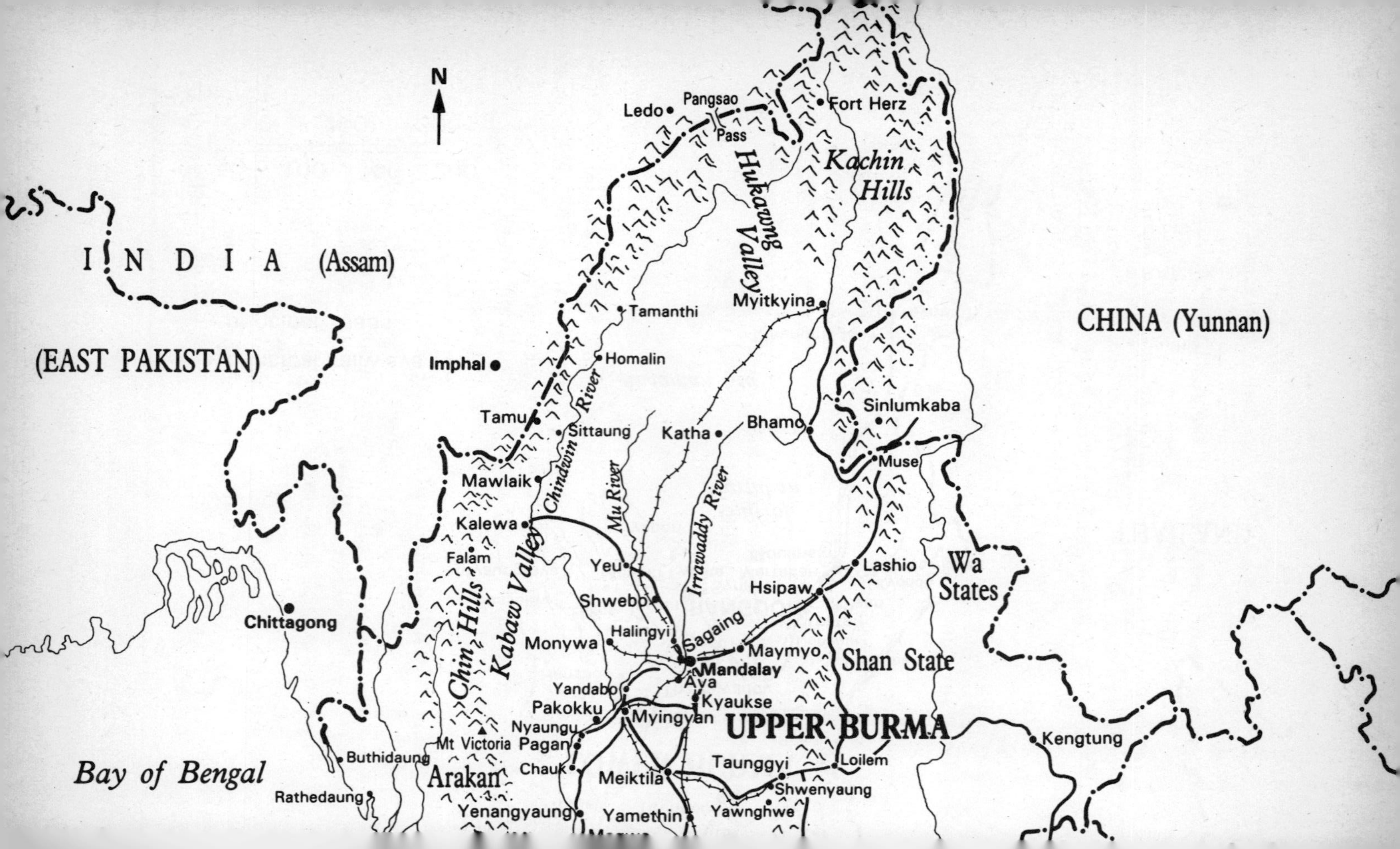
N
Ledo
Pangsao
Pass
Fort Herz
Kachin
Hills
Hukawng
Valley
INDIA (Assam)
(EAST PAKISTAN)
CHINA (Yunnan)
Myitkyina
Tamanthi
Homalin
Imphal
Tamu
Sittaung
Chindwin River
Mu River
Irrawaddy River
Katha
Bhamo
Sinlumkaba
Muse
Mawlaik
Kalewa
Falam
Kabaw Valley
Chin Hills
Yeu
Shwebo
Halingyi
Sagaing
Monywa
Mandalay
Maymyo
Aya
Kyaukse
Lashio
Hsipaw
Wa
States
Shan State
UPPER BURMA
Kengtung
Chittagong
Yandabo
Pakokku
Myingyan
Nyaungu
Pagan
Mt Victoria
Buthidaung
Bay of Bengal
Arakan
Chauk
Meiktila
Taunggyi
Loilem
Shwenyaung
Rathedaung
Yenangyaung
Yamethin
Yawnghwe

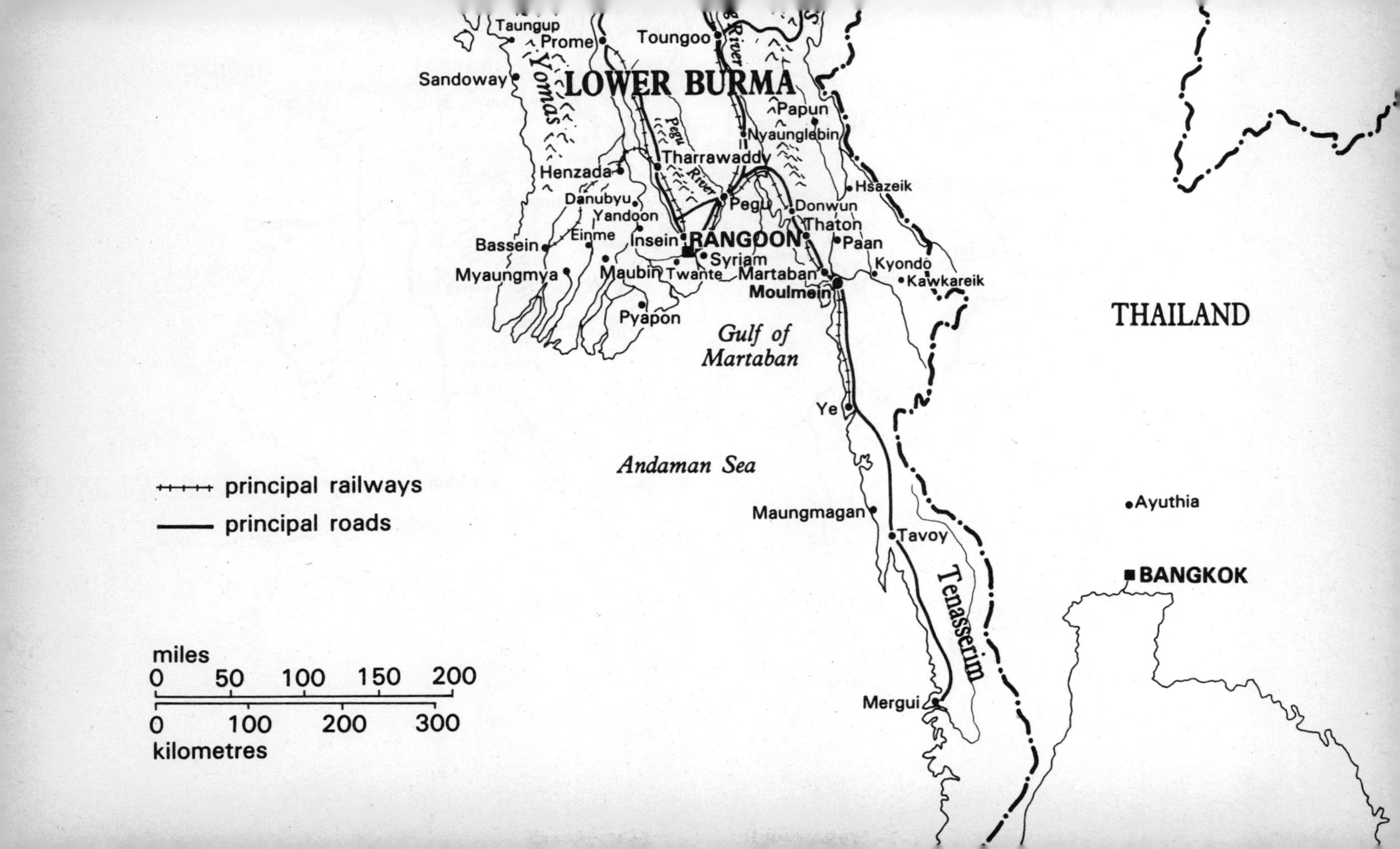

Taungup
Prome
Toungoo
River
Sandoway
Yomas
LOWER BURMA
Papun
Nyaunglebin
Pegu
Tharrawaddy
Henzada
River
Hsazeik
Danubyu
Pegu
Donwun
Yandoon
Thaton
Einme
Insein
RANGOON
Paan
Bassein
Syriam
Kyondo
Myaungmya
Maubin
Twante
Martaban
Kawkareik
Moulmein
Pyapon
Gulf of Martaban
THAILAND
Ye
Andaman Sea
principal railways
principal roads
Maungmagan
Ayuthia
Tavoy
BANGKOK
Tenasserim
miles
0 50 100 150 200
0 100 200 300
kilometres
Mergui

Index

Adams, Alec, 159
Air Volunteer Group (AVG) (The Flying Tigers), 136, 142
Akers, 'Blacky', 84
Alaungpaya, King, 79
Alexander, General Sir Harold, 139
All-India Radio, 160, 166
Anti-Fascist Organization (AFO), 186
Anti-Fascist People's Freedom League (AFPFL), 188, 195, 198, 199, 200, 202-3, 204, 208, 212, 215, 228
Apedaile, Gordon (ICS), 136, 155-6
Appleton, Revd George, 197
Arakan, 172, 175, 189, 217
Armstrong, Willy, 83
Arnold, Eric (ICS), 155
Arratoon, Pete, 122, 213
Aspinall (BBTC), 62
Atkinson, Tom (ICS), 91, 156
Attlee, Clement, 198, 202, 204, 231
Auchinleck, General Claude, 176, 177
Aung Gyaw, Ko, 130
Aung San, General (Bogyoke), 186, 188, 196, 199-201, 208, 233
Aung Thein, Maung, 160, 202

Ba Aye, Maung, 160, 207-8
Bailey, Edward, 29, 30, 32
Ba Maw, Dr, 57-8, 93, 132, 163, 164, 165, 192
Bandula, General Maha, 166, 168
Banks, Peter 156
Ba Pe, U, 131
Barrington, James (ICS), 212
Barton, 'Beaver', 117-18, 179
Barton, Philip, 52
Ba Saw, Maung, 160
Ba Than, Dr, 53, 192
Bathgate, Gordon, 75

Batten, Colonel, 53, 67-8
Baxter, Walter, 201
Beadon, Roger, 144
Beecheno, Peter, 228-9
Bell, Group Captain 'Josh', 178
Bestall, Frankie, 87-8, 92
Bevin, Ernest, 231
Bhamo, 40-1, 207
Bhose, Subhas Chandra, 198
Biddle, Marjorie, 159-60, 163
Binns, Bernard (ICS), 32-3, 102-3, 114, 120, 121, 144, 145, 205, 208
Blair, Eric (George Orwell), 35-6, 38, 206
Bodawpaya, King, 110
Bombay Burma Trading Corporation (BBTC, Bombaing), 24, 26-30, 33, 228
Bonvillein, M., 80
Booth-Gravely, Sir Walter (ICS), 31
Bourne, Major-General Geoffrey, 220
Bowers, 'Bonzo', 77
Bowker, Elsa, 214, 224
Bowker, Sir James, 213, 214, 217, 218
Bracken, Brendan, 161
Bradfield College, 5
Bradshaw, Eric, 84
Braham, Harold, 159
Braund, Harold, 156
British Burma Petroleum Company, 94
Brooke, Anthony ('Peter', Raj Kumar of Sarawak), 126
Browning, Lt-General Sir Frederick, 196
Brownrigg, John, 14
Brynner, Yul, 233
Buckley, Christopher, 226
Buddhism, 18, 19, 38, 47, 118
Burgess, Guy, 231
Burma Communist Party, 172, 199
Burma National Army (BNA), 163, 176, 187, 191, 196, 198

237

INDEX

Burma Oil Company, 83, 94, 222
Burma Rifles, 74, 98, 123, 151, 156
Butler, Sir Harcourt (ICS), 119
Butler, Sir Paul, 159, 162, 173

Caccia, Sir Harold, 220-1
Calcutta, 96, 178-9 and *passim*
Caldecott, Revd, 33-4
Calogreedy, Mattie ('Fanny'), 80
Calvert, Brigadier Michael, 141, 176-7
Campbell, Sir A. (Sandy), 192
Caradon, Lord *see* Foot, Sir Hugh
Case, 'Boh', 65, 182
Catherine the Great, 213
Chapman Andrews, Sir Edwin, 141-2
Chennault, Colonel, 136
Cheyne, George, 69
China/Chinese, 8, 41, 43, 45, 51, 123-4, 140, 182, 183 and *passim*
Chindits, 18, 29, 141, 176
Chindwin river, 15, 19, 33, 146, 181, 208
Chins, 42, 47, 77, 156, 180
Chit Hlaing, U, 131
Chü-i, Po, 53-4
Churchill, Winston S., 185, 202, 219
Civil Affairs Service (Burma) (CAS(B)), 176, 189, 191, 192, 193, 194, 195, 196, 197
Clemenceau, Georges, 157
Cochrane, Sir Archibald, 125, 136
Collis, Maurice (ICS), 90, 208, 229
Cooper, C.R.P. (ICS), 38
Crombie, George, 211-12
Curzon, Lord, 72

Davis, Dr (SOS), 100, 101
Defence, Ministry of, 182-3
De Gaulle, General Charles, 185
De Graaf Hunter, Dickie, 135
Delhi, 101, 114, 156, 157, 173, 176-7 and *passim*
Desai, Dr, 130
Donnison, F.SV. (Vernon) (ICS), 12, 187
Dorman-Smith, Sir Reginald, 135, 136-7, 196, 197, 198, 200, 201-2
Driberg, Tom, 195
Drucquer, Seth (ICS), 10, 16
Drysdale, John, 139
Duke of Wellington's Regiment, 148-9
Durrell, Lawrence, 106-7

Eade, Charles, 178
Ebden (Accountant-General), 13, 14, 63

Edgerley, Leo, 55
Edward VIII, King, 56
Edwardes, Michael, 233
Edwards, Seabury, 80-2
Eldridge, Fred, 182

Fann, John, 144
Far Eastern Bureau (FEB), 154, 156, 159-61, 163
Fergusson, Brigadier Bernard, 176
Fielding Hall, John (ICS), 139
Fleming, Peter, 176
Foot, Sir Hugh, 213-14, 232
Force 136, 184, 185
Foreign Office, 210, 211, 219, 220, 230-1
Fort Herz, 43
Foster (demolition expert), 140
14th Army, 30, 138, 147, 189
Fraser, 'Cam', 116
Furnivall, J.S. (ICS), 215
Furse, Major, 8

Gage, Pamela *see* Glass, Pamela
Galone, Tat, 131
Galvin, John, 159, 161, 162
Gandhi, Mahatma, 11, 128, 226
Garhwal Rifles, 98
Garrod, Air Chief Marshal Sir Guy, 168
General Council of Buddhist Associations (GCBA), 131
George V, King, 55-6
George, Frank (ICS), 76, 108, 109
Gibbon, Brigadier, 181
Girling, Captain, 152
Glass, Julia, 157-8, 162, 222-3
Glass, Kathleen, 4, 5, 88, 121, 128, 154, 155
Glass, Nicholas, 222-3
Glass, Pamela (née Gage), 155, 157, 161, 168, 228
Gledhill, Alan (ICS), 116-17, 118, 119, 144
Gloucestershire Regiment, 123
Goldberg, Norman, 150
Gore-Booth, Sir Paul, 8, 233
Gowon, General Yakubu, 218
Grant, C.F. (ICS), 38
Graves, 'Whitey', 84
Grigson, Aubrey, 152
Groves, 'Gentleman Joe', 84

Haile Selassie, Emperor, 16, 65, 142
Hainworth, Henry, 159
Hall, Raymond, 152

INDEX

Hammarskjöld, Dag, 232
Hampshire Regiment, 79
Harding, Field-Marshal Sir John, 106, 214
Hartung, James, 101, 193
Harvey, G.E. (ICS), 205-6
Haswell, Jack, 77
Healey, Tim (ICS) and Mrs, 62
Hedley, John, 28
Hla Aung, U, 222
Ho Chi Minh, 199
Htoon Aung Gyaw, Sir, 129, 155
Hughes, Lt-Commander, 57
Hume, Alan Octavian (ICS), 215
Hurst, Captain Leslie, 77

Iida, General, 163
Imperial War Graves Commission, 183
Indian Civil Service (ICS), 1, 8, 24, 25, 51, 54, 59, 103, 208, 210, 211, 212, 213 and *passim*
Indian Political Service, 213
Indo-Burma Petroleum Company, 94
Innes, Sir Charles (ICS), 119
Irrawaddy Flotilla Company, 15, 40, 80, 144, 145, 147, 148, 150, 191, 213, 228

Japanese, 135 ff., 156, 159-60, 163 ff., 175, 176, 179, 182, 184, 186 ff., 196, 198, 201-2, 203, 205, 208
Jesse, Tennyson, 79
Jones, Jonah, 28
Joubert de la Ferté, Air Chief Marshal Sir Philip, 177,178, 180

Kabulis, 206
Kachins, 40 ff., 219
Kai-shek, Chiang, Generalissimo and Madame, 174
Kandy, 177-8, 180, 181
Karen National Defence Organization, 217, 219
Karens, 42, 47, 73, 156, 184, 209, 217-18, 219, 220, 228
Kashmir, 161-2
Kelly, Norman, 52
Kemp, Lt-Colonel Dick, 88, 121, 138, 154
Kennard, E. Alington, 159, 163, 194
Kewley, Revd H., 4
Khanti, U, 79
Khin Khin Gyi, Daw, 216
Khin, Maung, 160

Khin Zaw, U, 160, 166, 197
Kiernander, 'Bull', 55
Kinch, E.G.N., 48, 168, 175
King's Own Yorkshire Light Infantry (KOYLI), 123, 134, 140-1, 148-9
Kipling, Rudyard, 5, 23, 65, 166
Kita Bistan, 171
Knight, Peter (ICS), 10, 100, 101, 112
Kublai Khan, 88
Kya Ayebaing, 119
Kyaw Khine, Oo (ICS), 32
Kyaw Min, U (ICS), 121, 155, 219
Kyaw Nyein, Thakin, 204, 212, 219

Laithwaite, Sir Gilbert, 157, 211
Lay Nat Tha (The Spirit of the Wind), 166-9
Learmond, 'Tarzan', 77
Le Bailly, Bill (ICS), 157, 158
Ledwidge, Bernard, 231
Legatt, Trevor, 159, 164, 179-80
Leyden, John, 52
Liberator, The, 194-5, 196
Lindop, Janet (later Humble), 57, 149-50
Lindop, Jim (ICS), 57, 109, 150
Linlithgow, Lord, 157
Li Po, 134
Lloyd, Sir Idwal (ICS) and Lady, 13-14
Lo, General, 140
Logan, Dudley, 100
Lovatt-Campbell, Verney, 62, 219
Lutyens, Edwin, 157
Lyall, Alfred, 112

Mabel, Mahadevi of Mongmit, 114
MacArthur, General Douglas, 185
Macaulay, Lord, 26
McCallum, Dugald (ICS), 10, 139, 140
Macgregor's, 27, 29, 156
Mcguire, Robin (ICS), 41, 45-6, 140
Mackenzie, Colin, 185, 186
Maclean, Angus, 65
MacRobert, Colonel Ronnie, 227
Makarios, Archbishop, 19
Mandalay, 15, 20, 21, 78-82, 113-19, 142, 143
Marakhan (bearer), 3
Margary, Augustus, 41
Martin, Kingsley, 11, 215, 216
Mason, Philip (ICS), 104
Masters, John, 190
Maugham, Somerset, 36-7
Maungmagan, 228-9

240 INDEX

Maung Maung Gyi, U, 205
Maymyo, 27, 74-5, 220-1
Mindon, King, 115
Mitchell (Veterinary Service), 65
Mo, U, 16, 42
Monk, Gemma, 152
Mon National Defence Organization, 219
Monywa, 15, 23, 141, 143-5
Morris, David, 160
Morrison, Ian, 226
Morton, John, 148
Mountbatten, Lord Louis, 176, 180, 181, 184, 185, 187, 188, 195-6, 198, 199, 200, 201, 202, 216, 225, 226
Mount Lavinia, 184
Mujahids, 217
Munro, H.H. ('Saki'), 37, 38
Murphy, Jack (ICS), 152
Murphy, James Victor (Peter), 185, 187, 202
Mya Sein, Daw, 135, 160
Myint Thein, U, 129
Myitkyina, 41, 207, 403
Myochit Party, 131, 202, 203

Nagas, 42, 151
Nanda, U, 95
Narasimhan, C.V. (ICS), 232
Nehru, Pandit Jawaharlal, 198, 201
Ne Win, General, 128, 130, 220
Nishiwaki, 160
Nu, U, 197, 208, 209, 214, 217, 218, 231

O'Donovan, Patrick, 226, 227
Orwell, George *see* Eric Blair
Owen, Frank, 184, 217

Pagan, Mount, 88
Pakenham-Mahon, Major, 193-4
Panglong Conference, 205, 231
Parker, 'Red', 28, 222
Paw Tun, Sin, 129, 155
Pay Tun, U, 56
Pearce, Freddy (ICS), 133, 180, 186, 195
Pearl Harbor, 134
Pearn, Professor B.R., 150
Pe Khin, U, 64
Pe Maung, U, 16-17, 18
People's Volunteer Organization (PVO), 196, 204, 219, 222
Pfaff (Veterinary Service), 65
Phelips, Denis (ICS), 83, 84-6, 135, 175, 227

Phelips, Susie, 227
Phillips, Ambassador William, 173
Po Kyin, Oo, 35
Political Warfare Executive (PWE), 156
Popa, Mount, 88, 116
Po Sein, U, 224
Prendergast, Major-General Sir Harry, 80
Prescott (Commissioner of Police, Rangoon), 122
Proud, Commander John, 159, 189
Psychological Warfare Division, SEAC, 176, 177, 178
Psychological Warfare Executive, 156
Puckle, Sir Frederick (ICS), 160-1
Pyinmana, 53 ff., 207

Rakosi, Comrade, 22
Rance, Major-General Sir Hubert, 195, 196, 202, 203-4, 208, 214, 216
Rangoon, *passim*
Rangoon, University of, 128-31, 170
Rawlings, 159
Red Flag Communists, 204, 217, 219
Redman, Vere, 160
Richards, C.J. (Dick) (ICS), 32, 110-11
Richards, Cynthia, 111
Ridgeway, Major Robin, 177
Robertson, Eric, 159
Roosevelt, President Franklin D., 173, 174
Roughton, Brigadier, 151, 152
Russell, Sir John, 65

'Saki' *see* Munro, H.H.
Sakurai, General, 188, 216
Sao Hkunhkio, Sawbwa of Mongmit, 114
Saw, U ('Galone'), 58, 93, 202-3, 208, 209
Sawbwas, 42, 114, 205
Saya San, 109-10
Sayers, Ted, 159, 162
School of Oriental Studies (SOS), 100, 172
Scott, Rob, 159, 231
Seagrave, Dr Gordon, 217
Seagrim, 'Stooky', 156
Settlement Department, 104-8, 132-3
Shackleton, Sir Ernest, 108
Shan States, 139, 207
Shan-Tayokes, 42, 50
Shway Ba, Maung, 54, 105, 115, 128, 192
Shwedagon Pagoda, 14, 127, 128, 230
Simla, 2, 154, 155
Singapore, 134, 136, 228
Sinlumkaba, 40 ff.

INDEX

Sinyetha Party, 131
Slim, General Sir William, 190
Snow, Edgar, 171, 216
Soe, Thakin, 188, 204, 217
Spate, Dr, 170
Special Operations Executive (SOE), 177, 185, 218, 219
Stanford, J.K. (ICS), 41
Steel Brothers, 27, 29, 62, 94, 152
Steer, George, 142
Stephenson, Sir Hugh (ICS), 13
Stevenson, Noel, 51-2, 137
Stevenson, Sir Ralph, 225
Stewart, Colonel and Mrs, 4
Stewart, Dr (ICS), 9, 15
Stewart, Robin, 28-9
Stilwell, General Joseph, 181, 182, 187, 189
Strang, Sir William, 211
Streenivasan, 160, 194
Su Kyi Ma, 233
Suyin, Han, 226
Suppayalat, Queen, 79, 126
Suzuki, Colonel 'Minami', 31, 188, 216
Swithinbank, Bernard (ICS), 38, 119, 139

Taylor, B.L., 52
Taylor, Dr Robert H., 172-3
Tenasserim, 14, 184, 208, 228-9
Thakin Party, 93, 131, 132
Thant, U, 197, 232
Than Tun, Thakin, 204, 219, 225
Tharrawaddy District, 108 ff.
Thein Pe, Thakin ('Tet-Pongyi'), 169-70, 171, 172, 180, 188
Thibaw, King, 21, 79-80
Thomas, Geoffrey (ICS), 116-19, 135, 144
Tilman, Harold, 109
Tin Shway, Thakin, 169, 171, 172
Tin Tut, U (ICS), 219

Tin U, Maung, 160
Trevelyan, Sir Humphrey (ICS), 213
Trinity College, Oxford, 56, 96
Tse-tung, Mao, 90, 171
Tulloch, Lt-Colonel 'Pop', 184, 218, 219
Tun Hla Oung, Captain, 66
Tun Oke, Thakin, 199-200

Wadi Maroo (servant), 42, 44-5
Waley, Arthur, 53
Wallace, Major Jim, 151
Wallace, W.I.J. (Ian) (ICS), 144, 151
Wallace, William (BBTC), 27
Ward, Kingdon, 43
Was, Wild and Tame, 51
Washington, 1, 222, 227
Waterhouse-Brown, Bill, 77
Watkins, Gino, 108
Watson, Francis, 171
Wavell, Field-Marshal Lord, 171, 176, 201
West, George (Bishop of Rangoon), 13, 127
White, 'Chindwin', 147
White Flag Communists, 204, 219
Whiting, Noel, 152
Williams, J.H. ('Elephant Bill'), 29, 30, 147
Williamson (ICS), 119
Willingdon, Lord, 6
Wingate, Colonel Orde, 137, 141, 142, 176
Women's Auxiliary Service (Burma) (WAS(B)), 145
Woodman, Dorothy, 215
Wrench, Sir Evelyn, 174
Wyatt, Major Woodrow, 195

Xavier, Mr, 63-4

Yenangyaung, 83-5, 91